YOUR NEW HOUSE

The alert consumer's guide to buying and building a quality home.

Alan and Denise Fields

The Deadly Serious Copyright Page

Framing of Spelling Errors by Alan Fields
Nailing of Punctuation Mistakes by Denise Fields

Produced by Alan and Denise Fields
Engineered by Mr. Mac N. Tosh
Remixed by Mike Crow Softword and Quark X. Press

Congas, cuica, stand-up bass and tambourine by Denise Fields
Fluegelhorn, bassoon, steel guitar and drums by Alan Fields
Backing vocals on "Real Estate Agents" by Ric Ocasek
Keyboard solo on "The Builder" by Randy Newman
Additional guitar and harmony vocals on "The Paper Trail" by John Hiatt

Special thanks to the Bare Naked Ladies for their "Gordon" CD, Las Palomas in Austin, TX, for their molé enchiladas, and the entire mail-order catalog industry.

More special thanks to our panel of expert editors, whose insight and comments were invaluable: Heidi Richardson, Michael Malinowski, Keith Gumbiner, Anita Holec, Jim Parker, T.C., and, of course, Patti Fields.

Extra special thanks to Michael O'Connor of Cary, North Carolina, for his expert analysis of this book.

Denise Fields appears courtesy of Helen and Max Coopwood.
Alan Fields appears courtesy of Patti and Howard Fields.

To order this book, call 1-800-888-0385 or write to
Windsor Peak Press
1223 Peakview, Suite 9000, Boulder, Colorado 80132
Quantity discounts are available.

If you have a question or comments on this book,
feel free to contact the authors at (303) 442-8792.
Or write to them at the above address.

Library of Congress Cataloging-in-Publication Data

LIC 93-93751

Fields, Alan 1965–
Fields, Denise 1964–
   Your New House: The Alert Consumer's Guide to Buying and Building a Quality Home/Alan and Denise Fields

   Includes index.
   1. Homes—United States—Construction. 2. Consumer education—United States. 3. Shopping—United States.

                                         93-93751 LIC

ISBN 0-9626556-2-7
Distributed to bookstores by Publishers Group West, 1-800-788-3123

Table of Contents

Introduction

Chapter 7
Bring on the Builder...122

Chapter 8
The Paper Trail: Protecting Your Rights
with a Good Contract 146

Part II
Go! Building the Home and
Other Traumatic Experiences 173

Chapter 9
Key Inspection Points, Part 1: The Skeleton House 175

Icons

 Biggest Myths

 Eco-Friendly Alternative

 Getting Started: How Far in Advance

 Key Inspection Points

 Money Bombs: Scams to Avoid

 Questions to Ask

 Reality Check

 Sources

 Step-by-Step Strategies

 What Are You Buying?

Power Home Buying: Getting Ready, Getting Set...

1

Reality check: Bob Vila Is NOT Building Your Home

L et's say right here and now that building or buying a new house is an insane experience. In fact, a recent survey of "people who should be slapped silly" ranked "folks building a house" third... right before "bungee-cord jumpers" and just after "people who get on the freeway doing 25 mph."

And trust us, we know what we're talking out. We built a home... and lived to talk about it.

Actually, to be more accurate, we didn't build anything. A builder and a crew of misfits, ex-felons and drunkards labored on alternate Tuesdays to build our house. We just stood by in horror with our mouths wide open. In the end, we signed a piece of paper saying that we would pay for this thing. Until the year 2023.

Fasten your seatbelts—you are about to embark on this same journey. Like the Wizard of Oz, we should advise you that you are not in Kansas anymore. As you follow the yellow brick road paved with good intentions, you're going to need a lot more than courage—you need a tour guide. And that's where we come in. We're your Good House Witches, here to guide you around the bends, twists and turns in your new-house journey. Just click your heels three times and repeat after us. . . "There's no place like a new home."

So, Who Are You Guys, Anyway?

You might be wondering why we're writing this book. We aren't builders, developers or real estate agents. We think the toaster is a complex power tool. We couldn't tell a router from a band-saw if it snuck up and bit us on the fanny.

Nope, we're just average, ordinary home buyers—like you. When we decided to buy (and build) a new house, we immediately trotted down to the bookstore to find wise advice on the topic. Blame it on an occupational hazard—as writers, we always think the answer is in a book.

We made a beeline to the "House & Home" section and searched for wisdom from the all-knowing and all-seeing God of Home Improvement.

Yes, we're talking Bob Vila.

Surely, Bob would dispense reassuring words of wisdom that would guide us on this new home journey. Surely, Bob would tell us everything we needed to know.

After sifting through piles of books on fixing toilets and how to make a million dollars in real estate, we found what we thought was the answer: a Bob book entitled *Bob Vila's Guide to Buying Your Dream House.*

Since we're cheap, we first read some sample passages in the bookstore before deciding to buy the book. Try it before you buy it is our motto. Smugly, we pored over the book, secure in the knowledge that we had found the ANSWER TO OUR PRAYERS. Suddenly, our excitement turned to gloom as we read Bob's advice on new homes, in a chapter titled "To Build or Not To Build." After going on at some length about why building a house is so difficult, Bob writes:

> Building a new home can also be a brilliant solution. You may have a special shot at a choice piece of land. You may be living in a region where builders are desperate for work. You may be in a position in which financial factors are not constraining. If so, good luck and God speed.

That's it. No chapters of endless advice. No words of wisdom. Just "Good luck and God speed." Thanks, Bob.

Bob then goes on for the remaining 280 pages to talk incessantly about how wonderful *old* homes are. Bob apparently has not seen old homes in our area. We have, and report to you three good reasons why you should not buy an old home. Let's put that in bold caps.

Three Good Reasons Not to Buy an Old House

1 **Revenge of the 1970s Decor.** Was everyone who built a home in the 70s out of their mind? What else could explain the "Harvest Gold" bathrooms, "Chocolate Brown" kitchen cabinets or "Mustard Surprise" wallpaper? The time, effort and money to rip out cabinets and redo bathrooms is on top of the steep prices most "old" homes command.

2 **June Cleaver Kitchens.** Perhaps even worse than mustard yellow decor is the incredibly poor design of most older homes. While you can replace ugly wallpaper, it's hard to fix a dinky kitchen or tiny master bedroom closet. Did folks in the 50s or 60s not own any clothes? Those tiny hallway kitchens may have worked for June Cleaver, but they don't for us.

3 *Mechanical Systems Dying for the Day You Move in.* When we toured older homes, we could almost hear the furnace, air conditioner and major appliances snickering behind our backs. They all seemed to be plotting to work perfectly. . . until the day we moved in. In one massive show of solidarity, all of these mechanical systems will die at that moment--at least that's our fear. And frankly, buying an old home is like purchasing a used car. Everything from the roof to the refrigerator is, well, used.

We had one additional reason to pass by older homes—we needed a home office. Now, when most builders think of a home office, they assume you're going to cram all that computer equipment, the fax, the files and the desk into a closet that's euphemistically referred to as a "spare bedroom" or "study." The only nice-size space in many homes is a dark and dingy basement—climate controlled to be freezing in the winter and clammy in the summer.

So, we embarked on the task of building a new home. And we decided to write this book. But you get more than just our experience—we also interviewed home buyers across the country. From North Carolina to California, we talked to new home buyers whose experiences ranged from "traumatic" to "disastrous." We also met with scores of builders, architects and other "real estate professionals" to get the inside story on why these things happen. In this process, we've uncovered the following truths about buying a new home.

Four Truths About Buying a New Home No One Tells You.

1 *Bob Vila is not building your home.* You've seen Bob's TV show "This Old House," where careful craftsmen lovingly restore a home. Bob and the workers ruminate endlessly about the correct way to install this door or that siding. Many home buyers think they are getting this level of care when they build or buy a new home. And why not? It's not like builders are giving away these homes.

Sorry, folks, this type of skilled building is seen only on television. Real life means building crews who are more like Larry, Curly, and Moe—bumbling idiots who couldn't tell their butt from a two-by-four. The only thing these guys ruminate on endlessly is which bar they'll hit at quitting time.

One home buyer we interviewed said she was shocked at the level of workmanship on her $140,000 semi-custom home. Sloppy carpentry, lousy cabinet installation, incompetent roofers—the buyer got the full treatment. "You think you're getting quality craftsmen," she told us. "What you really get is Larry, Daryl and Daryl, from the old Bob Newhart TV show."

This is the ultimate reality check on building a new home: Bob

Vila is not your builder. As a result, you need to protect yourself. That's the goal of this book: we'll tell you exactly how you can do this and get the best deal for the dollar.

2 *You get to pay for all those wonderful advancements of science.* Building a home in the 1990s is a quick lesson in environmental "correctness." Water-saving toilets, extra insulation, super-efficient furnaces—who do you think pays for all this? You, in the form of higher home prices. Sure, some of this stuff may pay dividends down the line (in lower utility bills), but you still have to pay for all these expensive toys today.

Tighter building standards to meet environmental laws filter their way down to your wallet. as well. The builders' lobby estimated that the spotted owl related reduction of logging in the Pacific Northwest has raised prices by $3000 per house. Even more insidious are "impact fees," which are taxes on new home buyers to fund parks and schools in many communities.

Hence that home built today may be more "environmentally correct" than one built in 1969—but you get to pay for the privilege.

3 *It always takes more time, money and patience than the original estimate.* So, your builder says he can build you a $165,000 home in just four months? Six months later, you're pulling your hair out because that home is now $180,000 and isn't even finished yet?

The percentage of homes finished on time and on budget must be infinitesimally small. Nearly every home buyer we've interviewed across the country recounts a similar story—it cost more and took longer than they anticipated. Recognizing this at the outset is the best course. In the following chapters, we'll give you specific suggestions for minimizing the pain.

4 *"New construction" does not mean "soundly constructed." High price does not mean high quality.* In the bizarre world of new homes, "new" doesn't have the same meaning as say, a new car. A new home means only that no one has lived there yet—and that's a plus and a minus.

"New" does not mean the house was soundly constructed. A quickly slapped-up tract house with the cheapest of cheap materials may be "new," but it could cause years of headaches.

At the same time, just because you're spending a lot of money does not mean you're getting commensurate quality. A $300,000 house may be loaded with cheap windows, a lousy paint job and poor roofing—if you don't pay attention, you might get a house that's really worth much less than you're paying . . . especially if you're stuck with repair bills and costly maintenance.

Who Should NOT Buy or Build a New Home

Frankly, not everyone should be building or buying a new home.

Real estate agents like to pitch new homes to anyone with a pulse—but some of these folks could sell ice to Eskimos. What you won't read in those slick new home magazines are the types of buyers who should NOT buy new homes. If you're in one of these groups, we advise you to think twice:

1 *New-to-towners.* Just moved to a new area? Think you already know where the good neighborhoods and schools are? Think again. It takes more than a few weeks or months in a new town to really get the lay of the land. Asking a real estate agent for advice is dangerous. Most work for the seller (or builder, in this case)—hence, they'll promise you it's a great neighborhood just to get that commission. Never mind the toxic waste dump or lousy schools . . . you probably won't notice them until after you've closed on the home. Not all real estate agents are liars, but if you run into a con artist, you could lose your shirt.

Another subtle reason that "new-to-towners" should not build: most are unfamiliar with local construction methods and practices. If you move from a dry climate to a wet one, you might not realize that builders are supposed to do special types of waterproofing. Assuming builders use the same or similar practices as those in your hometown is a major mistake. For example, many Californians who recently moved to Colorado were the victims of a variety of new home rip-offs. They didn't realize that at a higher altitude, windows must be treated to cut down intense UV radiation. Builders sold untreated windows to unsuspecting buyers, who later discovered that their furniture and carpet faded in the intense sunlight.

The best solution would be to rent a home for a year or so—that way you really know which locations are best and what places are the dregs. By taking your time, you can talk with previous home buyers, builders, architects and others about local construction and what you really should get in your new home. If renting is not an option, consider buying an existing home that's been thoroughly checked out by a private inspector.

2 *Long-distance buyers.* So, you're being transferred to a new location? It seems like the perfect time to buy a new home. Perhaps there's a partially built home in the "right neighborhood" that will be finished when you move to town. Sounds great, huh?

Ah, there's nothing that makes shoddy builders happier than snaring a long-distance buyer. If you're hundreds (or thousands) of miles away, there's nothing to keep them from taking you for a ride. Doing sloppy work, switching to cheap materials, "forgetting" to add expensive features—when the buyer's away, the scum will play. Any unsupervised builder could be a one-way ticket to housing hell.

Retirees often fall into this trap. Building a dream vacation or retirement home may be a life-long goal—but doing it long distance is too great a risk. "Back home" most of the builders are reputable, you say. Don't assume that's the case in your retirement destination. Areas with the most defective housing (North Carolina and Florida, for example) also just happen to be hot retirement markets. Coincidence? Don't bet on it.

3 | *Cash-strapped buyers.* If you've scraped and saved for years to come up with that 20% down payment, you may think you have enough money to build a home. But remember one truism of new home buying: it always costs more than you originally think.

A million things can push up the final price. Cost overruns caused by weather delays are common. "Hidden expenses" such as the low-ball allowance game (which we'll describe later) can zap you for hundreds if not thousands of dollars. Throughout this book you'll notice "money bombs"—these pitfalls unexpectedly can cost you money.

As a result, we strongly recommend that you have a cash buffer of at least 5% of the home's price. Ten percent is even safer. That means if you're building or buying a $200,000 home, you should have another $10,000 to $20,000 stashed away to deal with emergencies. (An alternative would be to increase your mortgage by that amount—assuming you are willing and able to handle the bigger mortgage payments.)

If you don't have this cash buffer, consider alternatives: scale back the house to provide a buffer zone. Instead of that $200,000 home, perhaps you should aim for $180,000 or $170,000. Or delay your purchase until you can save the extra money or earn the extra income to cover higher payments.

4 | *Couples with shaky marriages.* Building or buying a new home exacts a huge emotional toll. From the anxiety of committing yourself to that scary mortgage to the stress of making a trillion decisions, this is not for the faint of heart. Adding the stress of building a home to career and family responsibilities is a precarious undertaking.

Some couples try to fix a failing marriage by building a home—big mistake. They might think that since such a massive project requires a "team effort," it will bring them back together. The reality is that the stress usually does these people in. While we are not psychologists, it's our opinion that anyone with marriage difficulties should think twice about such a huge undertaking.

Does this mean that every couple who fights over the right color for the faucets will end up in divorce? Of course not. Thousands of couples successfully navigate the emotional land mines of the new home process every year. But don't say we didn't warn you. Fasten your seat-belts—this will be a bumpy ride.

The Key Ingredients of a Quality New Home

Building a home is much like baking a cake—forget one key ingredient and you might as well chuck it. You might use the finest chocolate in the world, but if you forget the flour or sugar, the cake will not be a taste treat.

Similarly, the recipe for a quality new home is composed of several "key" ingredients:

Paper The basis of a quality home starts before one brick is laid: the "paper" that makes up your agreement with the builder. As you'll note in chapters 6 and 8, this is much more than a boilerplate contract. The paper must protect you as a consumer. To do this, you need:

- Detailed plans for the house and foundation drawn by a qualified professional. The safest course is an experienced, residential architect and structural engineer. A soils test should be done to ensure that the proper type of foundation is used.
- A thorough contract that specifies all the "standards and materials" to be used—down to the brand of skylights, shingles, faucets and more. Installation of the materials should be clearly spelled out.
- A clear warranty that doesn't limit your consumer rights. Some builders try to sneak in clauses that restrict "implied warranties" or methods of compensation if things go wrong.

Scissors The "scissors" is a tool you use to "poke" the builder to make sure he or she lives up to the paper. The scissors is actually a team of watchdogs who work for you, not the builder:

- An experienced structural engineer to inspect the foundation and other critical structural construction points.
- A retired contractor/private inspector/engineer as a home inspector who can flag other problems. In chapters 9 and 10, you'll learn about the key inspection points an inspector should be looking at.
- An architect to make sure the builder conforms to the design/materials as drawn on the blueprints.
- A real estate attorney to make sure the contract gives you maximum legal protection in line with your state's laws.

Note that the "scissors team" does not include municipal housing inspectors. Nor does it include the real estate agent—most work for the builder and know zip about new construction.

Rock The "rock" in the new home building process is gold—the money (your money) that builds the house. Always keep in mind the Golden Rule of House Building: *He who holds the gold makes the rules.* If you control the money, you stand a better chance of getting a quality home. Here's how you do it:

- Finance the construction by taking out the construction loan in your name. Someone must finance the construction process—we argue it should be the homeowner, not the builder or developer. In Chapter 2, we'll tell you how to do this.
- Control the bills: any money disbursed from the construction loan should be done only after the work is completed to your

satisfaction. You sign off on all the checks and see all the bills for the home.

- The money goes directly to the subcontractors or material suppliers.
- The builder gets the profit only after the home is completed to your satisfaction. This is done at the closing. While draws are allowed to reimburse direct expenses (permits, approval fees, etc.), the big profit check isn't written until the end. By holding the gold until the end, you give the builder a powerful incentive to do it right.

Of course, there is a downside to this control. You may have to purchase the land or building site outright—this early down payment may be months before you move in. Also, the paperwork can be a hassle.

Jargon Check

Before we launch headlong into this process, let's pause for a second to make sure we're all on the same planet. Real estate folks love jargon—they've never met an acronym they didn't like. Here are a few terms you'll encounter and our interpretation of their meanings.

The Five Types of New Houses

A   *Tract or production homes.* A production house is mass-produced by a builder or developer in a tract-style development. Drive into a subdivision in Anytown, USA, and you'll notice cookie-cutter homes that are cloned from one or two basic styles. Production builders are interested in just that—quantity, not quality. They want to slap up as many houses as possible. As a result, you must choose from one of a small number of predetermined styles. You can't change anything, except for the color of the carpet or paint. Some builders do offer "upgrades" such as nicer carpeting or better appliances, but the basic house (the rooms, windows, etc.) stays the same.

Of course, the advantage to production homes is their price. All those "economies of scale" and "builder's special" materials drive the prices of production homes below those of fancy custom homes.

B   *Semi-custom homes.* These homes exist in a gray area between production and true custom homes. While the builder once again provides a series of floor plans and styles, the buyer can "customize" the home by changing several interior aspects. Want the master bedroom closet to be larger or the dining room to be smaller? Most semi-custom builders can adjust the walls to fit your needs. (The only things that can't be moved are "load-bearing" walls, which are walls that hold the weight of the home. Any move of a load-bearing wall would require the home to be re-engineered.)

We've discovered several builders that have deceptively marketed their homes as "semi-custom." A builder that offers to "customize" the home by changing the color of the kitchen tile or exterior paint is not a true semi-custom builder. Many production builders like to pretend that they are doing semi-custom homes to dupe buyers into thinking they're more than just a tracthome builder. True semi-custom builders can change (for a price) any element of the home, except for the exterior shell or load-bearing walls.

| C | ***Custom homes.*** Only 20% of all homes built in this country are custom-built for buyers. The home is designed from scratch to meet the buyer's needs and wants, by a professional architect who is working for the buyer (not the builder). Typically, the lot or building site is owned by the home buyer—this can be a roadblock if land is scarce or expensive. Also, the land may need to be purchased outright; coming up with this cash early in the process can be a challenge as well.

Production and semi-custom builders would like you to think that all custom homes cost $500,000 or more. The truth is custom homes are more affordable than you think. You can build a custom house in the price range of many production and semi-custom homes. How? First, you don't have to pay the 6% to 7% real estate agent commission that's built into the production-home price. This savings usually covers the cost of hiring an architect or design professional. Most important, you control the quality of the materials that go into your home.

Why do custom homes always seem to cost so much money? It has more to do with custom-home buyers than the homes themselves. Many "custom" buyers are interested in high-end features such as huge gourmet kitchens, whirlpool baths, fancy cabinets and so on. Load up any home with these expensive features and the price will soar. But you don't have to desire a 5000-square-foot home with gilded faucets to build a custom home. Many custom builders we've interviewed are willing to build in the "affordable" price ranges—they just don't advertise it. Hence, in most areas, you can get a custom $150,000 house built just as easily as you can build a $300,000 or $400,000 custom home. Granted, the lower price home will be smaller and will have fewer features than the more expensive homes, but the house will be built to your exact needs.

And that's the best advantage to building a custom home: You get a house that fits you, not some pre-fab "Average Family." If you need a home office with a fax line, you get it. If you want a kitchen with an island rangetop, it's yours. In a sense, a custom home is a finely tailored suit or dress that exactly fits your body. In contrast, a production or semi-custom home might fit right in one place but be too small here or too large there.

| D | ***Spec homes.*** These homes are built on "speculation"; that is, the builder is taking a risk by starting construction without a buyer. Hopefully, one will come along at some point and buy the home. If the buyer shows up at the midpoint of construction, some minor alterations (colors, styles) may be done to the home. However, the basic floor plan is usually literally set in concrete. In hot markets, some production and semi-custom builders may gamble on building a

few spec houses, since the likelihood of finding a buyer is good.

As you'll read later, the advantage to buying a spec house is that it may be ready in a short period of time. You don't have to wait until another home is built from scratch. Unfortunately, when you buy a spec home, you're also vulnerable to several scams. Since you weren't there at the beginning, several critical construction stages may have come and gone without your supervision. The pouring of the foundation and/or footings is a good example. It's hard to tell whether the footings were done correctly when they're now buried under four feet of dirt. If you buy a spec home with a defective foundation, you may only find out later when the home collapses.

E *Presold homes.* As the name implies, the home is "presold" to a buyer before construction begins. All types of builders (production, semi-custom and custom) will gladly sell you a home before one shovel of dirt is moved. Of course, just because the home is presold does not mean the builder gets all (or any) of his profit before the home is completed. It's just a commitment by you to buy the home—if it's built in accordance with your contract, design plans and specifications.

The biggest advantage of going "pre-sold" is that you monitor the construction from day one. Your team of watchdogs (architect, inspector, etc.) can catch any problem before it's set in stone. On the other hand, this takes time—you may have to wait three to six months until the home is completed.

Getting Organized

There are only one to two trillion details involved with building or buying a new home. As a result, it pays to try to organize this mess.

We recommend a three-ring binder with pockets. We put a spiral notebook in the binder—we used the notebook to jot down details during meetings, trips to plumbing supply centers, etc. Another useful organizing tool is an accordion file—you'll use this to hold brochures and other material you'll gather during this process. Each section can be labeled with categories such as kitchen cabinets, lighting, plumbing fixtures, design ideas, etc.

Also, consider videotaping and/or photographing the progress of your house. Not only does this make a great keepsake, but also if anything goes wrong with the house, you will have some evidence of the building process.

Introducing the Money Bombs.
As you read this book, you may come across this symbol. These are "money bombs," special scams and rip-offs that can trip up new home buyers. A money bomb might be anything from cheap materials "hidden" behind the walls of your new home to defective installation of products such as skylights, mechanical systems, etc.

We call these pitfalls "money bombs" because they tend to

explode and cost you money—sometimes lots of money. The "bomb" may go off just a few weeks after you move in or it could take years. A leaking skylight will be apparent after the first hard rain; however, a lousy paint job without any primer may not be apparent for a year or more—that's when you notice the paint is fading and cracking.

There isn't a product that some person hasn't found a way to make cheaper or of lower quality. And too many builders operate under the philosophy that the cheaper, the better. The rush for profit can be at your expense—leading to higher utility bills, repair expenses, maintenance costs and more.

In building a house, there is often a right way to do something and a shortcut that will suffice if the buyer doesn't notice. Sadly, the shortcuts become tempting to shoddy builders, who are trying to meet a deadline or make up for a delay. Some "penny wise and pound foolish" builders may take dangerous steps to make an extra buck—for example, forgoing the hiring of a structural engineer to design a proper foundation. This shortcut could save the builder $1000 to $2000. However, if the resulting house is defective and sinks to China, the repair bills could top $20,000 or more. Scam artists may decide it's easier to declare bankruptcy and move to another state than pay that repair bill.

How widespread is defective construction? Home inspectors we've interviewed say that one out of every three new homes they inspect has serious flaws or code violations. Determining the exact extent of defective construction is difficult since many defects don't show up for months or years.

Theoretically, if you could peek under the roofs of all new homes, you could tell whether the home was soundly constructed. Well, that's exactly what happened in Florida when Hurricane Andrew blew through in August 1992. The roofs of 100,000+ homes were blown away, along with much of the rest of the house as well. According to an investigation by structural engineers, much of the damage was due to defective construction: seriously flawed roofs and homes were no match for any strong wind. Was the problem with the housing codes? Nope, Dade County has some of the strictest building codes in the country. Despite these tough laws, defective homes were put up by the thousands. One observer noted that if defective construction was this widespread in strict Dade County, you can only imagine the situation in areas with less stringent housing codes.

As a result, carefully read about each money bomb. Hopefully, your new home will be free of any of these traps. However, if you're aware of what can go wrong, you can only be better off in the end.

A Revolutionary New Approach to Home Buying

Buying or building a new home will be your biggest life investment. And it is an investment—a well-designed and built home in a good neighborhood will appreciate in value much faster than a quickly-built production home.

How do most Americans buy new homes today? They walk into

the model of a production builder and buy a "brain dead" home. It's brain dead because the builder already owns the land, has prepared the design and will finance the project. Except for a small deposit, the balance is paid at closing. There are no checks on the construction, except for a brief walk-through prior to closing to check for any cosmetic problems.

Instead, we think you as a consumer should be actively involved in the new home process—from financing, to design, to construction, to closing. At the same time, this book is not a "do-it-yourself" book where you pound the nails. Instead of "how-to," this is a "how-NOT-to" book. We hope to show you how not to get ripped off, spend too much money or get an inferior home. The only way to accomplish this is to hire a team of professionals, who are screened for their reliability and monitored for quality during the job. Through savvy consumer maneuvering, you can get a quality new home at a price you can live with.

We think of this book as a two-way street—we encourage you to write or call us with your experiences. If you discover a problem we haven't discussed or a great tip that you think would help other home buyers, please contact us. You can call us at the number listed on page ii at the front of the book. Our address is on the same page, so feel free to drop us a note.

Are All Builders Con Artists?
Is Every New Home a Construction Nightmare?

Of course not. This is one of the big dilemmas in writing any consumer guide—we want to tell you about all the scams and rip-offs, but not spook you into thinking every builder is a con artist.

The fact is that we've met many builders who are honest, competent and talented. They truly care about their customers. This doesn't mean they don't have an occasional disagreement with a home buyer—however, it's usually handled in a professional and fair manner.

And that is what often separates the "good guys" from the scum: the way they handle problems and complaints. Less-than-professional builders forget that the customer is king. They cut corners and, when caught, try to lie their way out of the situation.

Now, we could tell you that the majority of builders are good and that the bad builders are few and far between. Then, we'd be lying. In our research, we found that the top-quality, professional builders are few and far between. The same goes for architects, real estate agents and lenders.

At the same time, the con artists are also relatively small in number. Like nomads, they move from town to town, looking for new victims. Other scammers are big corporate builders who talk quality but deliver crap. These guys operate by surrounding themselves with high-priced lawyers who successfully intimidate unhappy buyers into submission.

So what about the rest of the builders out there? They fall somewhere in the middle. Some are incompetent, while others are just

Why You Should NOT Build a House Yourself

"If you completely absorb the information we provide here, you should be able to build your own house."
— *From a "do-it-yourself" book on home building published in 1990*

Visit any bookstore and you'll discover dozens of "do-it-yourself" house books. These books passionately try to convince you that building a house yourself will be the most rewarding, least expensive method of getting a new home. Pound the nails yourself and you could save that fat 15% profit the builder is charging.

Add to this the large number of "do-it-yourself" home centers that have sprung up across the country and the "home-building" shows on TV—the mantra of "do it yourself" building is mind-numbing.

However, there are many aspects of doing it yourself that get scant attention from do-it-yourself books. Slick salespeople and TV hosts don't always reveal potential problems for the do-it-yourselfer.

For example, you can't build most houses in this country without a building permit, obtained from a local building department. Many building departments will only issue permits to *licensed* contractors. Do-it-yourselfers don't count.

Lenders also are often unwilling to lend money to an unlicensed contractor. One aspiring do-it-yourselfer wrote to syndicated columnist Robert Bruss about this problem. "I can't find a bank which will make a construction loan to a do-it-yourself contractor such as myself," the home buyer said, adding that the bank gave as its reason that "virtually their only foreclosures on construction loans have involved do-it-yourselfers." And, can you blame the lenders? Would you lend $100,000 or $200,000 to someone who's never built a home before?

Along with the technical and financial difficulties of building your own home, there is another big roadblock: time. Do you know how much time it takes to build a home, to get bids from subcontractors or to schedule workers and deliveries of materials? Building a home is a full-time job and the average house can take anywhere from three to six months to construct. If you have another full-time job and expect to work on the home on the weekends, your home-building project could last a year or more.

Among the biggest risks of doing it yourself is Murphy's Law of Home Building: Whatever can go wrong will go wrong. You're on the hook if a problem with the home's construction occurs. By contrast, if you hire a professional builder to construct your house and an unforeseen problem occurs, it is the builder's responsibility to solve the problem. With few exceptions (soil problems, to name one), the cost will be absorbed by the builder. Any increase in materials costs also will be paid by the builder (if they are working on a fixed-price basis). And builders get contractor's discounts that the do-it-yourselfer may not be able to qualify for.

Finally, the best subcontractors like to work for professional builders, not do-it-yourselfers. The prospect for repeat work motivates the subs to do the best job possible. When you're building a home by yourself, the electrician, plumber and roofer all know they will probably never see you again.

As book authors, we may be blasphemers to say this, but we believe no book can teach you how to be an expert plumber or electrician. It takes years of experience to be a good builder—you can't just substitute a 250 page book or a 2-hour videotape for this level of expertise. While building a home may not look that complicated, you also have to navigate a minefield of regulation, building-code requirements and other laws. The bottom line: Leave the work to the professionals.

inexperienced. A few try hard but don't have the financial or managerial skills to run a successful business. Some big corporate builders get tripped up by the rush for profits or bureaucratic snafus. Take any 10 builders, and 6 or 7 will fall into this middle category. Only one or two builders will be top-notch professionals. Two more will be scam artists pretending to be builders, who should be put in jail.

How bad is the problem of defective construction? New home inspectors tell us that, on average in the U.S., one out of three new homes they inspect has problems. Some homes have minor problems such as sloppy workmanship, while others have serious code violations that threaten the home's structural stability. Now, you can look at this as "the glass is half full," as the builders do. They'd argue that an only one out of three chance of being ripped off is pretty low. That means that two out of three homes are fine.

Call us cynics, but we find those odds to be very unappealing for what is your biggest life investment. The odds of getting ripped off, in our opinion, are way too high. So, if you want a puff piece on building or buying a new home, then read any of the builder-sponsored publications (from newspaper articles to books) that say how wonderful this experience is. However, if you want to know what can and actually has gone wrong with new homes, read on. Consumers who arm themselves with the knowledge of scams and rip-offs can only be wiser for it.

 If you have any questions or comments on this chapter, please feel free to call the authors. See the "How to Reach Us" page at the back of this book!

2

How Much New Home Can You Really Afford?

O ne of the truly horrifying moments in building a house is having to come face to face with the American banking system. That's because bankers have the special ability to find 157 reasons why they ABSOLUTELY CANNOT HELP YOU BUILD YOUR HOUSE. No wonder a recent survey of "Things Most Likely to Be Slimy" ranked bankers just above real estate agents and right below pond scum.

Of course, if you have a spare million dollars sitting in the bank, financing your new house is a moot point. Bankers will fawn all over you, gladly approving loans the size of Peru's GNP to build shopping centers in Arizona.

Unfortunately, most of us fall in the category of "Just Short of a Million Dollars in the Bank." For you, a typical conversation with a banker might be like the following:

Consumer: Hi, I'd like to talk to you about...
Banker: NO! WE CAN'T DO THAT! IT'S TOO MUCH MONEY!
Consumer: But, I just wanted to see if...
Banker: FORGET IT! ARE YOU CRAZY? DO YOU WANT ME
TO LOSE MY JOB? WHAT DO YOU THINK WE DO HERE—
LOAN MONEY OR SOMETHING?

Adding a new dimension to this drama is the so-called credit crunch, a phrase invented by the same economists who said the recession of 1990-1992 would be "short and painless." With the new "credit crunch," banks are not just refusing to loan money to consumers and builders to build new houses. No, now they've installed radar dishes on their roofs that can detect anyone within a 1000 feet who is even remotely thinking about a home loan. A special team of bankers is then dispatched to intercept the consumer and beat him to a pulp with Hewlett-Packard financial calculators.

On a more serious note, a recent report in *Builder* magazine quoted a builder in New Hampshire who said that new home buyers are being turned down for mortgages—despite the fact that they are willing to make 50% down payments. While a regional collapse in banking in the Northeast has certainly made getting a mortgage there more difficult, the reality is that new home buyers across the U.S. have found that getting a mortgage ranges from "challenging" to "not on your life."

Given this exciting new climate, home buyers must arm themselves with weapons to do battle with bankers: inside know how on what it takes to get financing on a new home. So, next we'll calculate fun stuff such as your net worth, down payment and. . . the mortgage.

What Does It Matter Anyway?

This chapter is at the front of this book for one reason: You can't hire the players (the builder and others), buy the dirt, or plan the design without knowing the answer to the Money Question: How much can you spend on your new home?

Knowing the answer is important because:

| 1 | *Everyone is going to ask you.* Builders will ask you a "price range" in order to show you what that money can buy in your area. If you are designing from scratch, a good residential architect will need to know your price range to match your needs to reality.

| 2 | *It prevents "false starts" that cost you money and hassle.* Not knowing exactly what you can afford will not only cost you time, but also it could very well cost you money. Assume you hire an architect and tell her to design a $200,000 home. Later, you discover you can only afford $165,000. Forget that fancy kitchen, that extra bathroom, the three-car garage—all of these changes may cost you extra money to have the plans altered.

| 3 | *The Ultimate Reality Check.* It's fun to look at fancy houses with marble floors and giant master bedrooms. The problem is that marble is intoxicating—you can forget what planet you (and your bank account) are on.

"Showing-All-Your-Cards" Fear.

One natural fear of discussing what you can really afford with builders and other sundry real estate types is that they will take you for a ride. Tipping your hand and revealing all your cards is like saying, "Take all my money, please." Or is it?

The reality is that the chance of being taken for a ride is slim—*if* you do your homework. The next few chapters will show you how to build protections into this process. Putting in checks and balances— such as hiring a private inspector to look over your home at critical points to make sure the appropriate materials are being used—helps prevent rip-offs. If you are building a custom house, bidding the project out on an "apples to apples" basis to two or three builders will provide a good price comparison.

That doesn't mean there aren't rip-offs out there. If you aren't careful, you could get cheap, inferior materials. That $150,000 house you thought was such a good value might have cheap windows more common on an $80,000 tract house. Worse yet is shoddy workmanship (faulty foundations, bad wiring, and more) that could cost thousands of dollars to correct.

The bottom line: Bidding your home out to several competent builders or (even better) using an experienced residential architect who knows a good value for the dollar will protect you more than trying to hide the true amount you are able to spend.

The goal is to get a "pre-approved" letter from a mortgage company that says, in essence, they've checked you out and are willing to loan you up to X amount of dollars on a new home. You can take this to the architect and builder to show that you are serious about a home in that price range. A legitimate fear of these professionals is the expenditure of significant time, money and effort on designing and bidding out a house that the client can't afford in the end.

 ### Reality Check
As a home buyer, you have two basic options when buying or building a new home.

Straight purchase. You give the builder a small deposit and the balance of the money at closing. The builder finances the actual construction. This is most common with tract houses, where the builder/ developer owns the land and you have very little ability to "customize" the house beyond the color of the carpet, paint and a few other cosmetic details.

Now this sounds simple, but it's a major trap. You don't have any of the hassle dealing with a construction loan, but you also lose all financial control over your new home's construction. That control is crucial to getting a quality home. This book is full of sad stories from home buyers who lost control of their new homes and ended up with nightmares. Many of these disasters were straight purchases.

Consumer-active construction financing. The best route for buying a new home is to take an active role in construction financing. By taking out a construction loan in your name, *you* control how the money is spent on your house. You see all the bills and can confirm that your house contains those items. The builder is kept on a short leash. This option is most common with custom or semi-custom homes where you (not the builder) own the lot or building site.

What if the builder owns the lot and refuses to let you control the construction loan? What if you can't get a construction loan? A possible solution may be to let the builder finance the project, BUT stipulate that you have to approve each and every "draw" (or disbursement) of the construction loan. You still see every bill and can balk at paying a subcontractor who has done substandard work. As a side note, an architect (or even a private inspector) can help look over the loan draws and point out any problems—a valuable service to consider.

The Golden Rule of New Home Buying or Building

"He who holds the gold makes the rules." Sounds a little harsh, doesn't it? But that's the reality of real estate today—by simply taking control of the "gold," you dramatically stack the odds in favor of getting a quality house. Lose control and the chances of getting a "lemon" are higher.

What is the "gold"? Quite simply, it's the money used to build your new house. That money pays for the bricks, windows, shingles, paint, light switches and everything else in and on the house. And, oh yes, part of the money goes to the builder as her profit for her time and effort.

Where does the gold come from? You, of course. Whether you pay for the house from your own pocket or get a loan from a bank, you're the person on the hook. Ultimately, you'll be paying monthly installments on this house for 30 years. In 1992, consumers shelled out $150 BILLION to buy new houses—and that doesn't include the interest to be paid over the next 30 years.

That's a lot of money. But would it shock you to learn that most consumers voluntarily give up control on the majority of all new homes bought today? Builders and developers control the "gold" in a whopping 85% of all new houses sold.

How do builders control what is really your money? By getting the construction loan in their name, they essentially finance the construction. The builder controls your money, doling it out to subcontractors and suppliers as they perform the work on your house. At the end of the construction, your "permanent mortgage" pays off the builder's construction loan—anything left over is their profit.

Savvy builders realize that controlling your money gives them a free hand in building your house—and maximizing their profit. The temptation to substitute cheaper materials is easier since you never see the bills. Maybe you'll notice the cheaper brand of windows or less expensive siding—and maybe you won't.

Perhaps most dangerous is the builder's ability to pull his profit out of your house even before one shovel of dirt is moved. That's right, the builder can "draw" large chunks of profit from the construction loan long before you move in. Scam artists can siphon huge sums of money from construction loans and leave you with a half-finished house—and guess who's on the hook to pay back this money. Hint: It's not the builder.

The best strategy is for you to hold the gold. You can do this by insisting that the construction loan is in your name and that no money is disbursed on your new home without your signature. Construction loans are typically set up like your average checking account. Each check must be signed by both you *and* the banker. The builder can't spend any of your money without your approval.

What about the builder's profit? We believe the builder should not get one dime of profit until the house is completely finished to your total satisfaction. The money (your money) is the builder's biggest incentive to make sure the house is right.

Of course, holding the profit until the end doesn't mean you're holding all the money back. It is fair for the builder to expect you to pay all the other expenses associated with building your house. Building materials and supplies are one major category, as is subcontractors' labor. As you'll note later, we recommend paying the subcontractors and other suppliers directly, as opposed to giving the money to the builder and hoping he pays these folks.

Reimbursing the builder for his actual out-of-pocket expenses during construction is also kosher. For example, the builder may have to pay $1000 to get a building permit for your house—you should reimburse the builder for this.

A gray area to be negotiated are items such as "overhead": This could include the builder's office expenses, salaries for a foreman or superintendent, etc. But how much of the builder's office rent, telephone expenses, and other "soft expenses" are due to your house? How about the other house(s) the builder is doing at the same time? While the lumber delivered to your house is truly your expense, "overhead" expenses are harder to classify.

The best rule of thumb is to pay any expenses the builder incurs that are directly related to your house. Any indirect expense (office rent, phone, advertising, donuts) will not be paid out of your construction loan—but instead from the lump-sum profit payment made at the end of your house's construction.

You might dismiss this process as being too much work. The builder may also look very trustworthy. But don't kid yourself—most builders are fixated on the prize, which is the profit on your house. Giving them control over that prize before they deliver your new house is dangerous.

Getting Started: How Far in Advance?

You should leave at least 60 days for the "loan application process." That's officially defined as the length of time between application and when the bank rejects you—just kidding! Most home buyers are surprised at this length of time, but bankers need this period to check your employment status, income level and whether you've robbed any convenience stores in El Salvador.

And what about shopping time? We recommend another 30 days for shopping for a mortgage, to compare fees and rates. Hence, if you are building and want to break ground June 1, you'll need to start shopping in early March to make application by April 1. If you are buying a house already under construction, you'll need to leave at least 90 days before closing/completion to do mortgage shopping. Honestly, the best strategy is to shop and qualify for a mortgage first, before you hire a builder and/or architect.

Sources for Mortgage/Construction Loans

The process of getting a mortgage or construction loan was relatively easy a few years ago—that was before the entire savings and loan industry crashed and burned in a sea of greed and corruption. The fallout was twofold.

1 S&Ls were the primary mortgage lenders for most Americans—the closure of many institutions helped dry up the pool of avail-able funds.

2 The federal government, saddled with foreclosed real estate (like 97% of the state of Texas), decided the only way to fix this was to make it tougher for average Americans to get mortgages. This would prevent them from going out and building shopping centers in the Arizona desert. With lightning quickness, the feds tightened mortgage requirements, requiring more income, bigger down payments, and, whenever appropriate, six pints of blood.

Of course, there are still a few sources for mortgages and construction loans. Here are a few of the options.

A *Commercial banks.* Not the world's most consumer friendly institutions, but banks still do a good amount of mortgage business.

B *Credit unions.* Really the last bastion of sane banking in America, credit unions typically offer very competitive rates. The only problem: You have to be a member (usually an employee of the government or some large company). Fewer than 50% of all credit unions make mortgage loans.

C *Mortgage companies.* These guys have picked up the S&L slack and have been increasing their share of the mortgage market. A majority of VA and FHA loans are made by mortgage companies.

D *Savings and loan associations.* Yes, a few do still exist out there. Most do "conventional" mortgages (as opposed to VA and FHA loans).

E   ***Mortgage brokers.*** These folks don't actually make loans, but shop other mortgage sources for the best rates and terms. The fees and "points" can sometimes be higher when you go through a broker. As the other lenders have withdrawn from the mortgage market, the nation's 15,000 mortgage brokers have increased their business. Now up to 48% of all new mortgages are originated by such brokers. Contact the National Association of Mortgage Brokers in Phoenix (602-992-6181) for a local referral.

F   ***Government agencies—public housing agencies.*** Did you realize that state and local housing agencies occasionally make below-market-rate mortgages available to first-time buyers and others who meet low or moderate income requirements? Most loans are administered by financial institutions. Check the "Blue Pages" of your phone book for a local/state agency for more information.

Sources to Find the Best Rates

1 *Newspapers.* Check the real estate section of your local paper and you'll probably find a chart of the latest rates from area lenders. This provides a nice overview of who's out there. Note that the rates are typically quoted as the interest rate plus points such as "10+1." That's a 10% loan plus 1 point. More on points later.

2 *Reporting agencies.* Another source for mortgage rate information is title companies, which compile the rates as a customer service. If you contact a real estate broker (as a buyer's broker, of course), he or she usually can provide you with a copy of these weekly rate sheets. There are also several national (or multistate) rate reporting services that can provide rate information—they are profiled in the box on the following page.

Stuff to Know

Points. A point is a prepaid interest charge that lenders use to dupe you into thinking you're getting a lower rate than realy are. One point is equal to 1% of the loan. If your loan is $150,000 and the lender is charging you one point as an "origination fee," you pay $1500. So, in essence, you are only receiving $148,500 in loan proceeds—but you must pay back $150,000 and interest. Great deal, right? Perhaps the best thing you can say about points is that they are tax deductible (as of this writing).

Obviously, it pays to shop for the lender with the lowest points, as well as the lowest application/processing fees. In down markets, some builders may offer to pay points as an incentive—shop around to see whether this is truly a good deal or merely a gimmick.

Private mortgage insurance (PMI). PMI is required by lenders on homes that have low down payments. If your loan is more than 80%

The Rate Chase

L ooking for a mortgage rate? If you can't find a local source, check out these mortgage rate reporting services.

HSH Associates
(800) 873-2837 or (201) 838-3330

HSH is a loan rate-tracking company that offers what we think is the best deal for new home buyers: The Homebuyer's Mortgage Kit ($20). In addition to getting a survey of lenders your local area, you also get a 44 page booklet that details the mortgage process from top to bottom. The process is clearly laid out, including help on estimating how much you can afford and a table that compares different rates and points. In business since 1979, HSH surveys over 2000 lenders in 36 cities, including most of the largest metro areas in the country. If you have an IBM PC-compatible computer, HSH even has a software version of the kit. This interactive program asks you for your income level and then determines the size mortgage you can qualify for. You also get the latest rates on disk. If you need additional surveys, the cost is $18 for two weekly issues.

National Mortgage Weekly
(800) 669-0133 (for Ohio and Michigan)
(216) 273-6605

National Mortgage Weekly tracks mortgage rates in the industrial Midwest. The cities covered include Cleveland and Columbus in Ohio, as well as Detroit, Michigan. Over 80 lenders are surveyed in each market. Cost is a reasonable $4 per issue—or you can get a 13 week subscription for $32.

Gary Meyers & Associates
(800) 472-6463 or (312) 642-9000

This company tracks mortgage rates in 60 different cities. Their report for Chicago is the most detailed—they include mortgage rates from 150 lenders. Other cities have information on 10 to 80 lenders per market. The cost for one city is $22 per issue. For those interested in moving to Chicago, the company publishes a magazine called "Living in Greater Chicago." With profiles of 320 communities in the Chicago area, the book provides information on home values, taxes and schools. Available directly from Meyers & Associates or in bookstores, the cost is $5.95 plus $2 shipping—or you can get a copy free from the Chicago Chamber of Commerce. The book is updated annually in March. The company is considering publishing editions for other cities in the near future.

---

of the sales price, the lender may require you to pay monthly premiums on a PMI policy. If you default on the loan, the PMI covers some of the lender's costs in foreclosing on you. Notice, we said *the lender*. This insurance is not for you, but, of course, you're the one who pays for it. Some consumers mistakenly think PMI covers them if they default on the loan. The short answer: it doesn't.

One money-saving tip: ask the lender whether you can stop paying the PMI after a certain number of years. By that time, your loan balance may have dropped below 80% of the home's value.

Locks. Mortgage rates fluctuate daily. Some lenders offer you the ability to "lock" in a rate before closing. When interest rates are expected to rise, buyers like to lock in a low rate. Locks vary from 7 to 30 days. We've even heard of 60-, 90- and 150-day locks. (Any lock for more than 30 or 45 days will probably require some kind of fee, either in points or a higher interest rate.) A 30-day lock means you must close on the home within 30 days to get that rate. If the home isn't ready, the lock expires and you may have to re-lock.

As a side note, if you lock and the rates rise, you win and the banker loses. Conversely, if rates drop, you're the one who loses. Most lenders will not negotiate on this point. Furthermore, the rates for longer locks tend to be higher, since the lender is assuming the risk that rates may rise in the future.

Questions to Ask
We've divided this section into two parts: the first concerns construction loans and the second focuses on "permanent" mortgages.

Construction Loans

1 **What are your procedures for construction loans?** This gives you an idea of what requirements must be met and the steps to get there.

2 **Can you give me a written estimate of all fees?** These would include origination fees, application fees, credit-check charges, closing fees and so on.

3 **Do you need a permanent mortgage commitment letter?** This is a critical area—most lenders will require that you have a permanent mortgage commitment before they're willing to approve a construction loan. Some lenders will limit their construction loan to the size of the permanent mortgage.

4 **Do you offer construction to permanent loans? Are there any savings in fees if I give you all my business?** Some lenders offer "savings" if you get both loans from them. For example, the construction loan lender may require a credit report. If you go to another bank for your permanent mortgage, you may have to pay for this twice.

5 **Will I have to deposit money into the construction account?** You may have to cough up some money at the outset. If the construction is estimated at $200,000, but the permanent mortgage will only be $175,000, the lender may require you to deposit another $25,000 into the construction account. If you own the lot, you may be able to pledge it as collateral—this could lower the initial deposit.

6 *What's the procedure for payment of "draws"? Is my signature required on every check?* It better be—the worst case is when the builder has the power to draw money out of this account without your permission. Some banks pay draws based on bona fide bills that are presented to the home buyer. Another method is described in the next question.

7 *If you authorize draws based on a loan officer's inspection of the house, what experience and training does this employee have?* Some banks pay the builder based on the percentage of completion for certain elements. For example, if 50% of the roof is completed, the builder (or subcontractor) gets 50% of the estimated roof cost. Is that smart? We don't think so—we think the builder should finish the roof to your (or your inspector's) complete satisfaction before getting any money. Later in the "money-bomb" section of this chapter, we'll describe a real-life story of how this method scammed a home owner out of thousands of dollars.

If the lender insists on this draw method, demand "veto" power over draws for work that is not totally completed. Check the experience level of the lending officer who is signing off on these inspections.

8 *What protection do you offer from liens?* A good construction lender should have a special lien waver that they stamp on the back of every draw check. When a subcontractor or material supplier endorses and deposits the check, he agrees that (in essence) the bill has been paid in full and that a lien won't be filed against the property. (Technically, a lien—or more properly a mechanic's lien—is a claim placed against your house by unpaid workers or material suppliers.)

An age-old scam in real estate is builders who take money from homeowners and then "forget" to pay their subcontractors. The subs then file liens against the house, forcing the homeowner to, in essence, pay twice for his or her house. A good tip to avoid this: some title insurance companies offer "extended coverage" policies that give protection against mechanic liens. The cost is usually less than $100—ask the builder whether they are willing to pay for this.

9 *What tests on the lot are required?* Examples could be a soils test to determine what type of foundation is necessary. Other possible tests/reports may include a survey of the lot and/or appraisal of the plans. If a septic system is required, a "percolation" test may be called for by the lender before the construction loan is approved.

The "Permanent" Mortgage

1 *Please provide me with a written estimate of all fees and charges.* These could include application fees, credit reports, origination fees, appraisals, and all closing and recording fees. Mortgage insurance premiums also may be required for homes with down payments less than 20% of the sales price.

2 *What is the annual percentage rate (APR) for your current loans?* Truth-in-lending laws require all lenders to disclose this to you— the APR is the real rate you pay after you factor in all those special charges and fees. Generally speaking, every "point" you pay adds 1/8% to the loan rate. Hence, a 9% mortgage with two points is equivalent to a 9.25% APR.

3 *How long will it take for approval?* As mentioned earlier, the average length is 30 to 60 days. The exception is when low interest rates have flooded the market with buyers—causing approval delays of up to 90 days.

4 *What proof of income is required?* Many lenders require a copy of your tax return to verify your income. If you're self-employed, that may be just the beginning. Later in this chapter, we'll look at the "special treatment" lenders give self-employed individuals.

5 *What "lock-in" options are available?* Are there any lock fees? Most lenders will let you lock-in rates 30, 45 or 60 days in advance of closing. That way you can guarantee yourself a certain interest rate (if you think rates will rise). Some lenders have "lock fees" or may require you to pay a deposit. Longer locks are available, but at a price. In our area, lenders offer 90 day locks if you're willing to pay a one-half percent higher rate.

6 *Do you offer "no-doc" loans?* No-doc means "no documenta- tion"—these are loans that require no documentation of income, employment and so on. As you might have guessed, such loans are available to buyers who make hefty down payments (over 25% to 30%, for example) and have an impeccable credit history. Tight federal lending requirements have restricted many "no-doc" loans—now lenders are offering "low-doc" loans. A low-documentation loan is one with expedited approval—providing you put down 30% or more of the purchase price.

7 *Given the house we're considering, what loan product is best suited for us?* The lender should give you a range of options.

8 *Can I pay my own property taxes and insurance?* Some lenders require that they collect property taxes and insurance for you, since you're so darned irresponsible that you may forget to pay them. These "impounds" (great word, huh?) are zapped into your payment every month; the lender then takes this money and pays the insurance company and county tax department once a year. The big rip-off is that most lenders don't pay any interest on these monies—so they get to keep your money for a year interest-free. Our advice: see whether you can pay the taxes and insur- ance yourself.

Biggest Myths about the Mortgage Process

Myth #1 *"I'm convinced all mortgage lenders exist solely to rip-off consumers with ridiculous fees and outrageous requirements."*

In defense of mortgage lenders, many of the hoops lenders make consumers jump through are not only for their protection but also for yours. If you take on a mortgage that is beyond your ability to pay back, who wins? Nobody—you might lose your house to foreclosure, and the last thing the lender wants is to own your house or evict you and try to sell it to someone else.

Most of the lender's requirements are mandated by state and federal guidelines—the lender is simply following the law. If there is any point on which to criticize lenders, it would have to be on the very poor job they've done to educate consumers about this process. Many of the fees lenders charge are passed through to third parties. Take the appraisal, for example: banks require an appraisal to make sure the house is worth enough to justify the mortgage. A $100 to $350 fee is collected from the consumer and sent directly to the appraiser. The lender doesn't take a cut. But all consumers see is this money coming out of their pocket and going to the lender (if only temporarily). A good lender should tell you exactly where every penny is going.

Myth #2 *"I assume that the private mortgage insurance premium insures me against defaulting on my mortgage. If I can't make the payments, doesn't this insurance protect me?"*

Sorry, that's not how it works. The private mortgage insurance (PMI) protects the lender, not you, in the case of a default. That's right, you must pay the lender's insurance bill. And unfortunately, it's not an insignificant sum. PMI effectively adds 1/8% to 1/4% to your mortgage's interest rate—which means hundreds of dollars a year (and thousands over the life of the loan). If you fail to pay the mortgage, the PMI bails out the lender. You get soaked.

The reality is that you would have to pay this insurance bill anyway. If it were not paid directly, the lender would probably raise the interest rate on your loan by the same amount as the PMI. The insult is that PMI is zapped into your mortgage every month, a constant reminder that you're picking up the lender's bill. The "in-your-face" aspect of this charge is probably most offensive to consumers.

Blame lenders again for failing to educate consumers on PMI—many consumers are left with the false impression that PMI protects them. Perhaps lenders are embarrassed to tell the truth. The only way to avoid PMI is to put down more than a 20% down payment—not an easy task for today's pressed home buyer. Another strategy is to shop around—lenders have different loan "products" that have varying amounts of PMI. Finding a mortgage with a smaller PMI is an important shopping criterion.

Money Bombs: Rip-Offs to Avoid.

Construction Loans

Money Bomb #1: Builders who hold the money cards.
"My friend had a nightmare experience with the builder. By controlling the construction loan, the builder took large draws to pay his own profit long before the house was completed. He drained all the money out of the construction loan and then skipped town—leaving an unfinished house and a devastated family."

We wish this never happened. The reality is that is does and you, as a consumer, must take steps to protect yourself. It's simple: control the money (construction loan), doling out just enough to satisfy the subcontractors' and the materials suppliers' bills. At the end, the builder gets his profit. We realize that this is the "perfect situation." In the real world, consumers can't control the money builders use to build tract houses or spec homes already under construction. If you can't hold the "gold," you still have control over the "paper" (the contract) and the "scissors" (private inspectors and other quality-control aspects). Just remember this: all the money spent to construct your house must be paid back by YOU, not the builder. Making sure that money (your money) is not mis-managed is one critical step in getting a quality house.

Money Bomb #2: Inexperienced inspectors signing off on fraudulent draws. *"Our so-called reputable builder took us for a ride. The foundation was faulty, the roof installed wrong, the framing a total disaster. Now we have a half-built house and $125,000 in damages. To make matters worse, our construction loan lender approved $10,000 in draws to the builder on work that was not completed and materials that weren't even delivered to our house."*

That's a true story from an unlucky home buyer in Spartanburg, South Carolina. We analyzed this case and found two key problems with the construction financing (not to mention the incompetent builder). First, the bank gave money to the builder based on a "per-cent-completion" basis. Instead of the sub-contractor bills being paid directly to the subs after the work was finished, the *builder* received money based on "estimates" of work completed.

The only problem was that the loan officer was inexperienced (to put it charitably). He had no training in construction. Zip. Consequently, when the builder claimed the roof was 50% completed or certain materials were delivered, the loan officer took builder's word for it. Now the consumer owes $52,000 to the bank for a seriously defective, half-built house—and the kicker is $10,000 of that money was given to the builder for work that wasn't even done. The bottom line: you're on the hook. Search for a lender that will protect your rights (the percent-completion method has major rip-off potential) and a loan officer with construction knowledge and experience.

Money Bomb #3: The "double invoice" and billing errors from hell. *"We caught a $7000 error on our house—the window company billed us for our windows twice!"*

Mistakes do happen. Occasionally, the invoice for work done on your house will be incorrect. For our house, we caught one bill for lumber delivered to another house down the street. Obviously, checking the bills for accuracy is critical. If you're building a custom or semi-custom house, an architect may offer this service. If you're doing this yourself, check with the builder to confirm bills. A little "slip" could cost you thousands.

Money Bomb #4: "Quit claim" deeds. *"We couldn't get a construction loan to build a home on a lot we own. The builder suggested we 'quit claim' the lot to him and he would get the loan. Is this kosher?"*

Watch out—a quit claim deed gives the builder the title to your lot during construction ... a potentially powerful development. Depending on how your contract is written, if you fire the builder, he may still own the lot. If you can't get financing, this may have to be your last resort. Be careful and seek the advice of a real estate attorney on the best way to protect your rights.

Permanent Mortgages.

Money Bomb #1: Surprise fees and 11th-hour disqualification. *"My wife and I qualified for an 80% loan (20% down payment). At the last moment, the lender changed his mind and only offered us a commitment for a 75% loan. The sudden change forced us to put up another $7500 in down payment. Ouch!"*

Loan requirements do change from time to time—and they always seem to get tougher. The best tip is to get a commitment letter from a lender as quickly as possible. Note that this is not a lock on mortgage rates, but is just a general commitment to loan you a certain amount of money at or below a certain interest rate. Another major rip-off is unscrupulous mortgage brokers who surprise you with last-minute fees. The fact is that federal law requires mortgage lenders to provide you with a good faith estimate of fees and charges within three working days after the mortgage application is submitted. Hence, any last-minute charges could be illegal. Consult with your attorney and consider giving the lender an ultimatum—fly straight or you lose my business. Be prepared to switch lenders—even if this means delaying your closing.

Money Bomb #2: Monster adjustable loans. *"We call our adjustable rate mortgage (ARM) a bungee-cord loan. At any moment, the rate seems to spring from one point to*

another. The result is we get hit with higher payments."

Adjustable rate loans are just that—adjustable. While the payment changes every year, the interest rate can be adjusted as often as every *month* on some ARMs. Hence, if interest rates are rising, you could have the dreaded "negative amortization"—where your loan balance actually increases despite regular payments. Some ARMs are tied to extremely volatile indices such as Treasury Bills. The slightest quiver in the markets can set off a steep rise—or fall. The bottom line is your mortgage is your biggest life investment. An ARM holds tremendous risk—go into this with your eyes open.

 Money Bomb #3: Real estate broker "referral fees". *"A real estate agent strongly recommended we use a certain mortgage lender. One advantage he cited was a faster application process—the agent is hooked up via a computer. As he started typing in our application, he mentioned that he would have to collect a $300 'referral fee' that would be charged to us! We were shocked!"*

We find these "relationships" between brokers and lenders to be a major rip-off. Many real estate brokers try to charm home buyers into getting a mortgage this way, claiming this "one-stop shopping" deal will save time and hassle. The reality is that their computer is hooked up to only ONE lender. That one lender can lock out competitors that are offering lower rates or costs—as a result you could end up losing thousands of dollars for this "time-saving convenience."

How many consumers are duped like this? A recent survey by the U.S. Department of Housing and Urban Development found that a whopping 40% of all home buyers choose a lender based on a recommendation from a real estate broker. Many mortgage lenders are aggressively trying to recruit real estate agents to do this computerized scam. Even more scary is the fact that a new federal ruling has taken the caps off such referral fees—now agents can rake in any amount of money they please to "refer" you to a lender via a computer hookup.

And sometimes the "referral fees" are not disclosed to the consumer. Illegal kickbacks from mortgage brokers to their "friendly" real estate agents are widespread in areas such as California, the Southwest, the Midwest and the Philadelphia/Washington, D.C. corridor. A recent federal probe called the problem "epidemic." The result (whether the referral fee is above or below the table) is higher mortgage costs passed on to consumers.

The best advice: shop around to several mortgage lenders. The rate survey by HSH mentioned earlier in this chapter is a good place to start. And be suspicious of that smiling real estate broker who strongly suggests you use his "favorite" mortgage lender.

 Money Bomb #4: Lenders with loose lips. *"We just completed the loan application for a new $250,000 home. During negotiations with the builder over a few items, we*

suddenly learned the lender had leaked to him our financial information. Now, the builder's balking at the concessions because he thinks we're rich! What happened?"

You've just encountered a lender with loose lips. That's right—some lenders actually give your sensitive and confidential financial information to the builder or the builder's real estate agent! This could destroy any advantage you have in negotiations, as you might imagine. Builders who know your annual income, net worth or other goodies may decide you're too wealthy to get any concessions.

You should insist that your lender keep any and all information on you TOP SECRET. Even lenders who give away your qualifying "ratios" (such as the mortgage payment is only 18% of your monthly income) are dangerous—any dip with a calculator could plug in the numbers and figure out your finances. Lenders should merely say that you're "qualified for this particular house" and NO MORE.

Incredibly, we've heard this story several times. If you are using a buyer's broker to help you negotiate the deal with the builder, ask the broker for intelligence on lenders with loose lips. You'll want to avoid them like the plague.

The Fun Begins: The Mortgage Application

A typical mortgage application has 10 sections, six of these are discussed in detail below. The Uniform Residential Loan Application is used by two quasi-governmental agencies that back mortgages, Freddie Mac and Fannie Mae (these are acronyms that stand for names only a bureaucrat would love).

Interestingly, a statement at the top of the application says this is "designed to be completed by the borrower(s) with the Lender's assistance." The point is well taken: don't be afraid to ask questions. Leaving a section blank or guessing as to an answer is foolish—you raise the odds that processing will be delayed or, in the worst case, that you may be turned down.

Section One: Type of Mortgage and Terms of the Loan. This area asks for the type of mortgage applied for (VA, FHA, conventional, FmHA or our favorite, "other") and the "amortization type" (fixed rate, graduated payment, adjustable rate, or "other"). While this is rather straight forward, this section also includes questions such as the loan amount and the interest rate—two things you can only guess at at this point. Ask the loan officer for tips on what amount he or she thinks you can qualify for.

Section Two: Property Information and Purpose of the Loan. Now we're getting down to business. Besides the address, you'll also need the legal description of the property: the lot number and subdivision filing. The builder or real estate agent may be able to give you this

New Rules Force Mortgage Brokers to Play Fair

Mortgage brokers have been operating on an uneven playing field and the federal government is doing something about it. For years, brokers have been able to skirt disclosure requirements to consumers. Since 1993, consumers have had new power in dealing with these folks.

To understand how these rules affect you, you have to realize how powerful mortgage brokers have become recently. As you read earlier, there's an important distinction between mortgage bankers and mortgage brokers. The bankers actually generate mortgages out of their own funds and then sell them to so-called secondary markets. The result: bankers are under strict requirements to disclose all the charges to you, the consumer. They also must disclose all the fees and profit that the bank receives.

That's nice if you deal with a mortgage banker, but mortgage brokers exist in a gray area. They don't originate loans in their own name—it's usually another investor or lender. Money from the investor (not the broker) is used to fund the mortgage. The upshot: brokers haven't been subject to the strict consumer protection rules that must be followed by other lenders. Many brokers provide absolutely no disclosure of fees and charges—even at closing. Incredibly, many states don't even license brokers, leaving the door open to scam artists. The combination of no state regulation and little federal scrutiny is what spurred the feds to take action.

"Federal officials complain that brokers' compensation is poorly understood by consumers," said Kenneth Harney, a columnist with the *Washington Post* Writers' Group. For example, brokers may receive "yield premiums" when they dupe consumers into getting mortgages that are higher than the current market rate. This "premium" is cash paid by the investor and can be as much as $1000 to $2000—that's money that ultimately comes from your pocket.

Another source of money is "servicing rights." The right to service your mortgage (sending you those coupon books, collecting the cash, etc.) is a money-making operation for some companies. And they will pay the broker a fee to get their hands on the servicing of your loan.

The new disclosure policy from the Department of Housing and Urban Development essentially levels the playing field—brokers must disclose all the same stuff that other mortgage lenders, such as S&Ls, do. Now, "all charges imposed upon the borrower" by the broker must be disclosed in the "good-faith estimate" of costs within three working days after you submit the application. New regulations require that the consumer receive two good-faith estimates, one from the lender and one from the broker.

Since the country's 15,000 mortgage brokers are now responsible for nearly half of all new mortgages, this is important consumer protection for the home buyer. While many reputable brokers can truly shop to find you the best deal, all brokers must disclose all their fees and the money they make from you. Ultimately, this will enable you to more realistically compare and shop for a mortgage.

The Lock Game—The Pressure to Get the Best Rate Causes Move-In Headaches

One of the toughest challenges for home buyers is the question: to lock or not to lock?

Most lenders offer 30- to 60-day locks to insure that you get an interest rate you can live with. If rates go up in that time frame, you get the lower rate—as long as you close within the lock period.

And there's the rub. We've met many home buyers who locked too early and subsequently tried to rush closing because interest rates climbed. However, if the house isn't ready, the lender may very well refuse to close—forcing you to re-lock at the newer, higher rate.

Some lenders could care less—you can move into a mostly finished house. The problem is the builder will receive most if not all the money at closing. Hence, his incentive to finish the house to your satisfaction might be diminished. Sadly, some builders will only perform when that giant carrot (your money) is dangling in front of them.

Therefore, the worst-case scenario is locking too soon and then interest rates rise significantly in that 30- or 60-day period. The pressure to close early and move in could be excruciating. Of course, less scrupulous builders realize this and might try to slip sloppy or slapdash work by you.

The best advice is to build in a buffer zone. If the builder says the house will be done August 1, you might want to lock July 1 with a 60-day lock. That way you have until September 1 to close on the house. Then, if the builder comes to you in late July and says that delays will push back closing, you won't have to panic. Gauging how accurate the builder's closing date estimate is can be tricky—ask your private inspector (or architect, if you have one) about how the house is progressing.

We found that our builder was about two weeks off in his projection, based on advice from our own construction manager/inspector. Hence, we planned for a later closing than the "estimate." When the actual closing was delayed, we weren't shocked.

As for figuring out which direction interest rates are heading, good luck. No one really knows. Check out the *Wall Street Journal* for predictions from the "experts" on the direction of future mortgage (and all interest) rates. And then flip a coin.

---

information. If you are getting a construction or construction-permanent loan, you must provide information on the lot: year acquired, original cost, amount of existing liens, present value, and the cost of any improvements. Curiously, this section also includes a few stupid questions—such as the "source of down payment, settlement charges and/or subordinate financing." For fun, you could list "a money tree." What a silly question!

Section Three: Borrower Information. Name, rank and serial number—this section asks basic information such as Social Security number, years in school, and present and previous addresses for the borrower and co-borrower.

Section Four: Employment Information. Basically, where you work, your title, and the number of years on this job and in this line of work/profession.

Section Five: Monthly Income and Combined Housing Expense Information. This is where the rubber meets the road—the section that counts. Here you will face a chart that looks like this:

Gross Monthly Income		
	Borrower	Co-Borrower
Base Employment Income	_____	_____
Overtime	_____	_____
Bonuses	_____	_____
Commissions	_____	_____
Dividends/Interest	_____	_____
Net Rental Income	_____	_____
Other*	_____	_____
TOTAL	_____	_____

*Other income might include child support or separate maintenance income, although this does not need to be disclosed if you don't intend to use this money toward your housing expenses.

Speaking of housing expenses, an adjoining table asks you to compute these figures:

Monthly Housing Expenses		
	Present	Proposed
Rent	_____	_____
First Mortgage *(Principal & Interest)*	_____	_____
Other Financing (P&I)	_____	_____
Hazard Insurance	_____	_____
Real Estate Taxes	_____	_____
Mortgage Insurance	_____	_____
Homeowner Association Dues	_____	_____
Other	_____	_____
TOTAL	_____	_____

Given your comparison of rates, you should be able to get a quote on the estimated principal and interest of the mortgage payment from your lender. An estimate of hazard insurance for your house would be available from any home insurer. For real estate taxes, the lender could provide an approximate figure—or a real estate agent could tell you what similar houses are paying in taxes (this information is conveniently listed for every house for sale in the Multiple Listing Service [MLS] book). Mortgage insurance is something your lender will quote. An estimate of homeowners association dues should be readily available from the association's office. The bottom line: a good lender should be helpful in filling in these blanks.

It's no accident that your income is tabulated right next to your proposed housing expenses. Lenders are looking to make sure you fall within a "magic ratio" of income to payments. This number varies, depending on the type of mortgage you're considering, but generally ranges from 28% to 33%—that means your payment cannot be more than 28% to 33% of your total monthly income. Hence, if your total available income is $4000 per month, your total housing payment cannot exceed $1200.

So what does that mean in real life? Let's assume that $150 of that monthly payment goes to property taxes and insurance. That leaves $1050 to pay principal and interest. Here's how much of a mortgage you can afford at different interest rates:

If Interest Rates Are:

	8%	9%	10%	11%	12%
Your Possible Mortgage Is:					
	$143,000	130,500	119,650	110,250	102,100

Note that if interest rates change by just 1%, the amount you can borrow changes by about $10,000. Put another way, you might be able to qualify for that house at 9% interest rates, but that won't happen at 10%. To figure out how much you can afford, given your income and prevailing interest rates, we recommend you order the Homebuyer's Mortgage Kit, available from HSH Associates (described earlier in this chapter).

Section Six: Assets and Liabilities. This area is just as important as the income section—that's because even if you have income out the wazoo, lenders will turn you down if you are already in debt up to your ears. Determining this debt level is a scientific process in which they take a device to measure to see whether the debt actually reaches ear level or just your neck... just kidding.

Lenders actually compare your assets to liabilities and look for one of those fun ratios again. For assets, the application divides this category into liquid assets and non-liquid assets.

Liquid assets include the cash deposit toward the purchase price that you may have already paid a builder. You also throw in all the money in checking and savings accounts, stocks and bonds and life insurance (net cash value). Non-liquid assets cover the market value of real estate owned, a vested interest in a retirement fund, the net worth of businesses owned, automobiles and other assets.

For liabilities, the application asks for all loans, the monthly payment and the unpaid balance. Alimony/child support/separate maintenance payments and job-related expenses such as child care or union dues are added in to get your total monthly payments. Subtract the total liabilities from the total assets and voila! There's your net worth. Hopefully it's a positive number.

Total monthly debt payments (the mortgage and all other loans) must not exceed 33% if you put down a 10% or less down payment. Put down 20% or more into the new house, and the maximum allowable debt payments is 36% of your income.

Sections Seven Through Ten. From here, it's all downhill. Section seven is the "Details of the Transaction" that asks for purchase price, estimated closing costs and other costs. Section eight is a series of questions such as whether you've declared bankruptcy within the past seven years (if the answer is yes, you're toast). Section nine is a bunch of fine print that basically has you pledge you didn't lie. Section ten is a voluntary disclosure of race/national origin and gender.

Step-by-Step Strategies.

 Step 1: **Determine your needs**. Is a permanent mortgage all you need, or are you interested in construction financing as well? Using some of the sources we've recommended, roughly calculate the mortgage you can qualify for.

Step 2: **Shopping**. Get some of those rate surveys we recommended above and start shopping. Call a few lenders on the phone and gauge their interest in your business. Set up appointments with the final three to five contenders.

Step 3: **Interviews**. Meet with at least three lenders. Be thorough in your evaluation—ask all the questions mentioned earlier and raise other issues you have questions about.

Step 4: **Paperwork.** This phase includes the application itself. For construction financing, you may have to ask your architect/designer or builder to complete a cost estimate on the project.

Step 5: **Hassle.** After all the paperwork is submitted, get a commitment from the lender on the approval date. You may have to hassle them to make sure they hit this deadline—call once a week to see how things are going. A good lender will keep you informed on the process.

Step 6: **The construction closing.** If you are getting construction financing, there will be a "closing" for this loan. Basically, you sign a lot of paperwork and the account is established.

Step 7: **Draws.** During the construction process, you may meet with the lender once a month or so to complete the "draws." These are payments to the builder, subcontractors and suppliers to reimburse them for work done on your home.

Step 8: **Permanent closing.** Finally, the home is finished and the

Doin' the Two-step: The Hot New Mortgage

What's the latest craze in mortgages and country music? If you answered the "two-step," you'd be right on both counts.

Two-step mortgages were introduced in 1990 and quickly have become one of the most popular new mortgage "products"—about 10% of all new mortgages are doin' the two-step.

So what is the two-step? It's a twist on the adjustable rate mortgage (ARM). Most traditional ARMs offer a low rate for just one year. After that, the interest rate can soar, along with your payment. If you get a one year ARM with "2/6" caps, your payment can rise 2% per year, with a lifetime cap of 6%. In year one, that attractive mortgage is just 7%. But in the second, the rate on your mortgage could jump to 9%. And what about year four? You could be looking at a mortgage with a (yipes!) 13% interest rate.

In real life, that means your payment (principal and interest) on a $150,000 mortgage could jump from $997 at the beginning to $1659 in four short years. That's a 66% jump! You can see why traditional ARMs scare the living daylights out of most homeowners—you only win if you think interest rates will decline over the coming years (a risky bet).

The two-step mortgage, however, locks in a low rate for five or seven years—not just 12 months. For example, when fixed-rate mortgages averaged around 8%, you could get a "7/23" two-step for 7%. That means the interest rate is "fixed" at 7% for the first seven years of the mortgage. What happens at the end of seven years? Well, some two-steps convert into ARMs, while others allow you to "convert" to a fixed-rate mortgage at somewhat above the prevailing rate. (Some lenders charge a conversion fee that ranges from $300 to $800.) An alternative to the 7/23 is the 5/25—where the rate is fixed for five years and then is adjusted for the remaining 25 years.

What's the advantage? If you go for a 7/23 for a mortgage of $110,000 at 7% (versus the fixed rate of 8%), you would save $14,000 in interest payments over the first seven years.

The fact is most home buyers will live in their home for less than seven years. Hence, it makes sense to lock in the low rate for five or seven years, *if* (and this is a big if) you anticipate moving to another home in that time frame anyway. Of course, if you see yourself living in this house for more than five or seven years, it may make more sense to lock in at the lowest fixed rate available. That way, if interest rates rise, you won't be hit with an increased payment at the end of five to seven years.

What's making the two-step popular is the flexibility—providing a low interest rate for several years (not just one). Of course, the spread between two-step ARMs and fixed-rate mortgages will vary from lender to lender—shop around to get the best deal.

closing of the permanent loan is held. We strongly urge you to have an attorney review the closing documents. Another wise tip: have your accountant review the closing statement, which calculates pro-rated taxes and other items that come out of your money. Most accountants will do this for a small fee (less than $100).

Closing Costs: The Good-Faith Estimate.

One of the better euphemisms in real estate is the "good-faith" estimate of closing costs. The federal government requires all lenders to provide such an estimate within three days of submitting the application. One wonders, if the feds didn't force lenders to give a "good faith" estimate, what type of estimate would it be?

Anyway, it's important to understand just what closing costs are, since they can zap you for thousands of dollars. These costs are divided into two categories: closing fees and prepaid charges and escrows. Here's a brief explanation of these costs.

Closing fees *may include such stuff as:*
- The loan origination fee: This ranges from nothing to 1% of the loan amount. Basically it's the pure profit lenders say they need to "process" your loan.
- The loan discount points: As explained earlier, this is prepaid interest. More profit for the lender.
- Appraisal fee ($200 to $350): Just to make sure the property is worth what you say it is.
- Credit report (about $60): To check your credit history.
- A final inspection fee (about $100): To make sure the home is still standing.
- Settlement fee (less than $100): Profit for the closing service/ title insurance company.
- Document preparation fee (another $100): Ditto.
- Tax certificate (about $10: When purchasing land, this certificate verifies that the real estate taxes on the property have been paid.
- Recording fees (usually less than $50): To record the deeds at the county courthouse.
- State documentary fee: Essentially, a tax on property transfer— usually about 10¢ per $1000 of the sales price.
- Survey/improvement location certificate: This certifies that your home was built on your lot. About $100 to $200.
- Underwriting fee: More profit for the lender. Roughly $100.
- FHA Mortgage Insurance/VA Funding Fee. For FHA loans, buyers may be required to pay a premium for mortgage insurance. The funding fee for VA loans is just money for the government.
- Danish charge: Just kiddin!. In most states, buyers don't have to pay for any pastries served at closing.

Prepaid and escrow charges are advance payments the bank would like you to pay up front, thank you. For example, you may be asked to

The Special Hell Mortgage Lenders Have Reserved for Self-Employed Persons: Welcome to America

If the American Dream is to own a home, then the Son of the American Dream is to own your own business. To be your own boss. To be self-employed. To be free. (Music fades in.)

It appears that no one has told this to bankers, because next to people convicted of violent felonies, self-employed persons are held in the same esteem as slugs.

To understand why this is, you must realize that mortgage lenders are more conservative than Rush Limbaugh. Speak the word *risk* in their presence and they break out in hives. And that's the rub—self-employed individuals have *risk* stamped all over their foreheads.

Lenders much prefer folks who get a regular paycheck from a big company—just like themselves. Understanding the ups and downs of the income of the self-employed person overloads the lenders' small minds.

Hence, lenders make self-employed individuals jump through many hoops. Instead of providing tax returns for the past year, two years' records are needed. They also want a financial statement for the current year from an accountant. Any wide variations in income must be explained in writing.

All the extra documentation wouldn't be so bad if lenders actually understood what they were looking at. For example, every self-employed person knows that their "gross adjusted income" on their tax return is not their real cash flow. That's because there are many legal deductions self-employed persons can take (such as home office expenses, depreciation, etc.) that artificially lower their income.

Hence, you may have more income to qualify for a mortgage than your tax returns really show. Sadly, lenders often can't understand this concept.

If you find yourself in this situation, here are a couple of tips. Pay an accountant to do "revised" profit and loss statements as well as a balance sheet. Instruct the accountant to show your true cash flow, before all those tax-related deductions. The result is a fatter bottom line, increasing the odds that you'll qualify for that loan.

Another wise tip is to seek out lenders who specialize in making mortgage loans to self-employed individuals. That's right—a few lenders out there have recognized the potential market in making mortgage loans to self-employed people, who often are rejected by traditional lenders. In recent rate surveys in newspapers, we've noticed a few lenders that are advertising "self-employed applicants welcome."

pay 30 days' interest in advance. You also may be required to pay the first year's homeowner's insurance and private mortgage insurance (PMI) up front. Finally, the lender may ask you to cough up six months of property taxes at the time of closing.

Tip: Ask the lender whether you can do your own escrows for taxes and insurance, thus avoiding all this up-front cash at closing. Some lenders may offer to waive the escrows for a fee, ranging from $100 to one-quarter of a point of the mortgage amount. Other lenders have no fee to waive the escrows.

Here is an actual good faith estimate of closing costs for a $120,000 home:

Loan Origination Fee	$1040.00
Appraisal Fee	250.00
Credit Report	55.00
Final Inspection Fee	100.00
Settlement Fee	85.00
Title Insurance	200.00
Document Preparation Fee	100.00
Recording Fees	35.00
Improvement Location Cert./Survey	85.00
Underwriting Fee	100.00
Realty Tax Service Fee	66.50
TOTAL CLOSING COSTS	**$2116.50**
Estimated Prepaid/Escrows	
Prepaid Interest (30 days)	$812.06
1st Year's Homeowner's Insurance	490.00
Taxes (6 months)	600.00
TOTAL PREPAIDS	**$1902.06**
GRAND TOTAL CASH NEEDED AT CLOSING	**$4018.00**

That's right, if you were buying this home, you'd need to cough up an additional $4018 in addition to the down payment. It's important to factor in these costs when doing your budget.

We should also note that if you are purchasing the land separately and then financing the building of the home with a construction loan, you will actually endure *three closings:* one for the land, another for the construction loan and a final one when the home is completed. In this case, be sure to ask for a good-faith estimate of costs for all three closings. A buyer's broker (we'll introduce you to these guys later) or title company will be able to help you on the costs for the land, while the construction lender should provide figures for the building loan. Finally, the permanent mortgage lender will give you costs for the final closing.

Source for Further Reading

The Mortgage Book (Consumer Reports Books). A complete primer to getting a mortgage—must reading for any serious home buyer.

3

The Building Team

There are no solo performances when you build a home—it's strictly a team effort. From the workers who pound the nails to the bankers who lend the money to buy the nails, you are joined on the house-building journey by all sorts of folks.

But exactly who should be on your team? Who's the opposition? Who are the referees? Getting a quality home begins with assembling a quality building team. Here are the key players.

The Designer: **The Rodney Dangerfield of Home Building**

Architects often get a bad rap in this country. Fewer than 10% of new houses are designed by an architect who's working directly for the consumer. Why? Perhaps it's the pervasive myths about architects that some buyers still hold today. Talk to folks out in the real world and you often hear the following myths.

 Myth #1 "*Architects are too expensive— only rich people building huge houses can afford them.*"

Builders like to repeat this myth as a way to scare buyers. The truth is that architects, on average, charge between 6% to 8% of the construction cost to design a typical home. Sure, famous architects' fees in large cities can be 10% or more. But the reality is that an architect's fee for a $200,000 home is likely to be about $14,000. In expensive cities like San Francisco, the fee will probably be more such as $20,000 to $24,000.

That may sound like a lot of money, but consider what you get in return: professionally drawn plans, complete specification lists, and (with many architects) bidding and negotiation services. Many architects also serve as watchdogs to monitor the construction.

Myth #2 *"Architects are just wild-eyed dreamers who design pretty but EXPENSIVE houses."*

In fact, architects who specialize in residential design are most interested in building an attractive, yet *affordable* home. The scary truth is a good architect will probably *save* you money. Instead of getting an overpriced, poorly built production home, you're more likely to get a custom home with quality construction.

By bidding out the project to several builders, you can get the best value for your dollar. Most important, an experienced residential architect is an expert at materials costs and efficient designs.

Some of this misperception is fed by the large number of architects who specialize in commercial projects (schools, office buildings, shopping centers, etc.). Occasionally, these guys will design a house—usually with less than desirable results. Their lack of residential experience shows.

Myth #3 *"Architects only draw a set of plans. I can hire a designer or buy a plan from a book for less money."*

Architects CAN simply draw a set of plans for you, but typically their involvement extends much further. As you'll see later in this chapter, they become the consumer's advocate during construction as well, overseeing the work of the builder and making sure the plans are followed.

A design from a plan book (available through bookstores) is less expensive—about $300 to $500 for a set of blueprints. However, you get (or don't get) what you pay for. The quality of these plans varies dramatically—some are more detailed than others. Furthermore, you have to fit a generic design to your needs and building site.

Some home buyers also try to save money by hiring a designer or drafting services firm. As you'll see in Chapter 6, there are several problems with this route as well. While the level of detail is better from drafting services than plan-book blueprints, they still can't match a careful architect. They don't provide the construction supervision or the engineering expertise.

Myth #4 *"My builder told me he can approximate most of what an architect can do. So, what do I need an architect for?"*

This is a myth that borders on an outright lie. In general, builders are great at building things. But design? To put it charitably, they should stick to building.

With years of training, an architect sees a house as a series of spaces; a builder sees a house as a pile of bricks and wood. While builders have some understanding of the mechanics of a house (basically how it works), a design professional takes the long view. How does it fit your lifestyle? Does it have room to grow?

Architects try to design a house in which people can function—if you frequently entertain guests, a spacious kitchen area is a must. If you spend time in the bathroom relaxing, a bath that is roomy, sunny, and luxurious is more appropriate than a small closet a builder might design.

We can always tell a home designed by a builder versus a professional architect. The builder-designed house is generic and boring, with features often thrown in as an afterthought. The doors, windows, faucets—basically everything—are the cheapest stuff the builder thinks he can get away with.

So, what can a good architect do for you? Think of the architect as an advocate on *your* side (and payroll) who will help navigate the choppy waters of zoning restrictions, building codes, profit-hungry builders and a myriad of design options and cost trade offs. Not only will they design the house of your dreams, but they also will help make sure that dream doesn't turn into a nightmare, by supervising the actual construction.

Sources for an Architect.

1 *American Institute of Architects (AIA), 202-626-7351.* The national headquarters can refer you to local AIA chapters—most will be able to provide a list of local residential architects in your area. Also, the AIA has pamphlets, booklets and a video that may be helpful in choosing an architect. To order, call toll-free, 1-800-365-ARCH and ask for the "Investing in a Dream" package (number T-100). The cost is $21.95 plus shipping.

2 *Word of mouth.* Next time you see a house you like, ask the homeowner for the name of his or her designer. If they used an architect, find out whether the architect was easy to work with.

3 *Parade of Homes.* These annual events for charity are a great way to see the work of architects and builders. Most of these high-priced mansions are designed by residential architects, not by builders. And don't be dismayed by the Parade of Homes palaces—most Parade architects also will design houses in a more realistic price range.

4 *Architecture schools.* Local colleges or universities that have architectural schools are a possible source of referrals. They might recommend an alumnus or perhaps a group of students who might take on your home as a class project.

The Two Types of Architects.

Mention the word *architect*, and the first name that pops into your mind is probably Frank Lloyd Wright, the designer of the Guggenheim

Museum in New York (with its neat, curving staircase). Frank did design other things besides museums, including quite a few homes and even furniture. His craftsman style made many of his homes design classics.

Yet, Wright didn't design those houses to meet any home buyer's tastes—the designs were purely Wright's whimsy. In this sense, Wright is the ultimate *"signature architect."*

While it's nice to admire the work of a signature architect, most consumers have more practical concerns when it comes to home design. Frankly, you need an architect interested in designing a home to fit your lifestyle—a *"customer-driven architect."*

Fortunately, most residential architects fall into the customer-driven mold. They look at you, your family, and your lifestyle before they begin designing a house. They ask all the right questions and develop a design *with your input.* In our opinion, this is the most sane and rational way to go.

Of course, that doesn't mean you won't run into a few signature architects out there. Such designers specialize in a certain style of home—if you don't like that design, it makes no sense spending your time visiting with them.

Architecture by the Numbers

There are 17,000 architectural firms in the U.S. Only 10% of all the money architects make is derived from residential construction—the rest comes from commercial projects such as office buildings or schools. Now you can see why young architectural students are encouraged to go into commercial rather than residential work.

About one-third of all architects are "sole practitioners." These folks are more likely to specialize in residential construction than are large firms with lots of employees. It's not that big firms don't design new houses, it's just that they tend to focus on bigger projects for bigger bucks—like shopping centers. You should compare and contrast the service you get from one-person operations with that from larger firms to see who's right for you.

The use of architects by home buyers to design new homes also varies by region. Architects seem less popular in the Upper Midwest and the Great Plains states such as Iowa, Minnesota, the Dakotas, Nebraska and Kansas. Another area that sees a lower use of architects for new homes is Texas and the surrounding states of Oklahoma, Arkansas and Louisiana.

Meanwhile, in the Pacific Northwest and California, architects are more in vogue for new homes. Another area where architects are hot is the mid-Atlantic states of New York, New Jersey and Pennsylvania.

In the process of researching this book, we interviewed several home buyers who found it more challenging to find an architect in rural areas. This doesn't mean you can't find a good residential architect in a small town in Kansas—it just means you might have to look harder or see whether you can find one in a nearby town or city.

Getting Started: How Far in Advance?

Leave plenty of time for interviews, visits to the architect's past projects, proposals and reference checks. This takes about 30 to 60 days—you can do this while shopping for your mortgage. Considering that the design process itself can take one to three months and construction another four to six months, it makes sense to start looking for an architect about nine to 12 months in advance of when you want to move into your new home.

What Will It Cost You?

The three ways architects bill for their time are:

1 Percentage of construction costs. If a full-service architect charges an 8% fee and your home budget is $225,000, the charges would total $18,000. Many architects use this method, but critics point out a few problems. If you're billed as a percentage of cost, what incentive does the architect have to keep costs down? Consider this method carefully before going with it. If this is the only option, ask the architect to put a cap on the cost of the house—if the architect is a pro, he or she will know costs and be able to design within your budget. Of course, fees vary depending on the service. Expect to pay 3% to 5% for bare-bones design only. You may pay as much as 15% for full service (builder negotiation, construction supervision, etc.) in major cities, although the average in the U.S. is about 6% to 8%.

2 Dollars per square foot. Here you pay the architect a certain fee per square foot. A 2000-square-foot home at $3 per square foot would run $6,000. The logic here: the more square feet, the more work for an architect to design. By not scaling the fee to construction cost, an architect has more incentive to keep costs down, so the theory goes. As one architect explained to us, "Why should I get more money if you put in a fancy Kohler toilet versus an inexpensive one? It takes the same amount of time to draw the toilet on the plan anyway."

Overall, per square foot charges could range from $3 to $12 per square foot—that's for everything from design to actual construction management. The best architects will break down per square foot fees depending on the phase. For example, one architect we visited told us his fee for design development was $350 plus 65¢ per square foot (for a one-story house). Construction documents were priced at $350, plus 75¢ per square foot.

3 Hourly fee. A flat, hourly fee is the third alternative. Putting a cap on the total hours that can be billed makes sense. Some like this method since it completely divorces your home's size or cost from the architect's compensation. Few architects offer this, but it may be worth seeing whether you can negotiate such a deal.

4 *Other costs.* In addition to the basic costs, architects may charge for additional services. These may include fees for an assistant project supervisor, revisions (drawings or specs), work caused by change orders, and evaluation of substitutions made by the contractor. Other optional services also may include providing financial feasibility studies, planning surveys, or site evaluations.

Some architects combine different payment options. For example, one architect we spoke with charges an hourly fee for design schematic and a lump sum for design development, construction documents, and bids/negotiations. Administration or supervision of the construction is an hourly fee. This architect's hourly fee varies depending on whether she does the work or has one of her assistants do it ($95 per hour for architect, $35-$45 for staff).

The AIA contract breaks down payment into five phases: schematic design phase, design development, construction documents, bidding or negotiation, and construction phase (more on these phases later in this chapter). One sample breakdown could be like the following:

Schematic Design Phase	10%
Design Development	15%
Construction Documents Phase	60%
Bidding or Negotiating Phase	5%
Construction Administration Phase	10%
Total Basic Compensation	100%

For example, if the total architect's fee is $10,000 on a $150,000 house, then a payment of $1000 would be made at the end of the schematic design phase and so on.

We should note that other residential architects charge fees during the preliminary work (such as 25% for the schematic design phase, 10% for the refined schematic design phase, 35% for the preliminary construction documents, and, finally, 30% for the final construction documents). Then, bidding/negotiation and construction administration are done on an hourly fee basis.

Because of the complexity of compensation schedules, you should get a written and detailed fee schedule at the outset.

Reality Check

Certainly architects aren't a necessity for every project and many people on tight budgets will be tempted to forgo an architect in order to add a few more amenities. However, there are several fundamental elements you must consider—curb appeal, a sound foundation, a properly designed roof. While it may be tempting to cut corners on these items to add a whirlpool tub or upgraded carpeting, think twice. If the roof leaks or the foundation sinks, your home's value goes to zero—no matter how nice the carpeting.

Going Naked: Make Sure You're Covered

One of the key questions you should ask an architect is whether he or she has professional liability insurance to cover "errors and omissions." This insurance, called E & O, is an important protection for home buyers.

Why? Well, nobody's perfect. Architects can and do make mistakes. Since the builder will NOT take any responsibility for defects in design, such a defect rests on the architect to remedy.

For example, let's take your new home's foundation. Your architect makes a major mistake—undersizing the foundation footers that support the house. No one catches the mistake, including the builder and the county building inspector. You move in and soon find that your foundation settles to China. Walls crack, floors bow, and tile pops off bathroom walls. The damage could be catastrophic—the cost to jack up the house and repour the footers to correct size is estimated at $20,000. The resulting damage to the home's interior is another $20,000. Who's going to pay this bill?

That's why architects carry E & O insurance. Theoretically, you put in a claim to the insurance company and they pay to fix the problem. Now, if you've ever dealt with any insurance company, you probably realize that reality may not be as simple as this. Insurance companies have experts on staff to make sure they swiftly collect premiums and deny claims with equal swiftness. However, if you can document that the problem is the result of the architect's error or omission, you stand a much better chance of recovering if the architect has E & O insurance.

In a perfect world, all architects would carry such insurance. The reality is that half of all architectural firms in U.S. do not have professional liability insurance, according to a 1992 survey by the American Institute of Architects. In industry jargon, such architects are "going bare," an apt description.

Even more frightening: three out of every four sole practitioners are going bare. That's right, the architects that are most likely to design new homes are also the most likely to be without professional liability coverage.

When would you not use an architect? One possible scenario: building a very simple house on a flat lot. If you use a builder's design, make sure he or she has consulted with an engineer to determine that the foundation is well designed. Several inspections by a private inspector to supervise the construction would be quite prudent.

Another possible case where you may forgo a design professional is a "kit home." For example, several companies sell kits for "do-it-yourselfers" to put up a log cabin house. The pieces are clearly marked and the instructions are usually detailed enough not to need an architect (again, consult with an engineer about the foundation). As you noted in the introduction to this book, however, we aren't fans of the do-it-yourself option.

As you might expect, the larger the firm, the less likely they're going bare. For architectural firms with two to four employees, the percentage without insurance drops to 56%. Only 11% of companies with 10 to 19 employees go bare. We suppose if there is any argument to go with a larger architectural firm, it may be the fact that more carry this important insurance.

One major reason architects don't have E & O is the cost—the average firm pays $21,400 per year for this insurance. However, this figure varies widely depending on the size of the company. Sole practitioners only pay an average premium of $5200—that typically buys more than $350,000 (per total claim in a year) in coverage for errors and omissions. Considering the peace of mind to you, the consumer, that seems reasonable.

In addition, architects can also purchase errors and omissions insurance for a specific project or additional insurance for a particularly large or expensive home design. If the architect you're considering cannot afford "full-time" coverage, this might be a good compromise and well worth your peace of mind.

As a side note, some builders also carry E & O insurance. One builder in California told us that his insurance company threatened to cancel him unless he removed the word *designer* from his business card. Why? The builder wasn't really a qualified designer: he had no experience or credentials. Hence, insurance companies also tend to police the industry by refusing to insure so-called professionals who don't really have the relevant skills or credentials.

With all this discussion of mistakes, you may wonder "how often do architects goof?" Well, that same survey by the AIA revealed that only 13% of all architectural firms reported a claim on their E & O insurance in 1990. That means 87% of all firms had no claims. Even more encouraging: 94% of sole practitioners who carried insurance had no claims.

Of course, this is little comfort if you fall into that other 6% and have a serious mistake on your house. For you, the error rate is 100%. Hence, it's best to play it safe and find an architect or designer that carries this insurance . . . just in case.

Step-by-Step Shopping Strategies for Finding a Good Architect.

 Step 1: *Initial meeting.* Discuss the general parameters of your project. Bring magazine pictures with you as well as some ideas of your likes and dislikes. Discuss your lifestyle as candidly as possible with the architect so he or she can get a feel for your needs. Also at this meeting, look through the architect's portfolio of past houses to get an idea of his or her capabilities and style. As important as any other aspect of the architect is your personal chemistry—make sure you like him or her.

Step 2: *Visit actual houses and job sites.* Get a list of residential projects the architect has done and visit them (the architect may need to

set these visits up for you). If he or she has any jobs in progress, this is the time to take a look at them as well.

Step 3: *Get a proposal with fee estimates.* At this point, you should have narrowedyour choices. Now's the time to talk turkey. What would a project like the one you envision cost? If the architect uses a combined payment fee like we discussed above, be sure to get the details of each phase. This will decrease any future confusion.

Step 4: *Ask for references.* If you're worried the architect will just give you the best three projects he's ever done, ask for the last three projects he's completed. When you call the references, ask "yes or no" questions such as:

- Did the architect listen carefully to your needs and wants?
- Did the project cost more than originally estimated?
- Did the architect meet his own deadlines for the design phase?
- Did the architect accurately estimate costs of materials?
- Was the architect an effective advocate for you during the bid/negotiation phase with the builder?
- Did the architect adequately monitor the construction?
- Did the architect get along with the builder?

Also in this step ask for and call financial references such as banks. Later in Chapter 6, "Designing the House," we cover more steps in the design development process.

 Questions to Ask an Architect
(The source for this section is the American Institute of Architects' "Questions to Ask Your Architect" handout.)

1 *Who will design my project? With whom will I be dealing directly?* These are important questions because many architects have staff and assistants who actually do some of the drafting. If an assistant will be drafting and designing your home, the cost should be less than if the architect does it. A clear understanding of who your liaison will be is important. And its' a good gauge of how committed the architect is to your project—if you're farmed out to an inexperienced assistant, other projects may have higher priority.

2 *Given your current workload, can you meet our time frame and deadlines? How much time should we schedule for the design process?* In the real world, most buyers have deadlines. A candid and frank discussion of the architect's schedule is crucial.

3 *How are the fees established? What will be the fee for my house? Are you willing to accept an hourly fee with an overall spending cap?* No matter what method the architect uses to determine compensation, you need a bottom-line estimate for comparison.

4 *What is the payment schedule?* There are all kinds of possibilities, so make sure you have all the details. Confirm with your lender regarding the possibility of financing the architect's fee—the lender may have certain requirements for this.

5 *What are the steps you'll follow in the design process for my house? How will you organize it?* A systematic and organized approach to this process is a mark of a professional. (Chapter 6 discusses the design process in more detail.)

6 *What is your experience and track record with cost estimating?* If the architect has a contractor's license or has spent time in the building field, he or she may have a better idea of costs. Keeping your new home within your budget will be directly related to the architect's knowledge of current construction costs.

7 *If the scope of the project changes (such as reducing the square footage or increasing the size of a deck), will there be additional fees?* Get an idea up front what additional costs you may incur.

8 *Do you offer any construction supervision services? What is the scope of such services? If you don't offer this service, can you recommend a construction manager or private inspector?* Monitoring might include only three inspections (foundation, framing and finishing), but most likely will involve many more visits to the site. (In chapters 9 and 10, we provide you with a detailed breakdown of possible inspection points.)

9 *Describe to me your philosophy of house design.* An experienced pro should have a well-thought-out answer. Look at pictures of past and current projects. Any professional should have such a portfolio available for you to view.

10 *Can I see examples of the architectural plans?* You should see plans that include several elevations, a detailed framing plan, foundation plan, specifications and more. The level of detail often separates less skilled designers from experienced architects.

11 *Do you see any potential conflicts of interest on this project? Do you have a relationship with the builder?* Some architects may design production lines for area builders. Such a previous or current relationship represents an obvious conflict of interest—how can the architect be your advocate when also receiving money from the builder for another project?

A related question is: Does the architect sit on the board of an architectural control committee in your subdivision? This can be a plus or minus, depending on the level of political infighting in the homeowners' association.

12 *What type of insurance do you have? Does this cover errors and omissions? Can you provide me proof?* An extremely important question—see the previous box for more information on this topic.

The Private Inspector/Construction Manager

What is a private inspector? A construction manager? These are important watchdogs who make sure the construction is going according to plan. If you don't hire an architect or are using an architect only to design your house but not to oversee the construction, we recommend hiring a private inspector or a construction manager. For large or expensive houses (over $200,000), it may pay to have both an architect and a construction manager/private inspector to oversee construction.

Who can be a private house inspector? Unfortunately, just about anyone who prints up a business card. Almost all states do not regulate this growing business, so some inspectors are top-notch and others are idiots. Texas and Oregon are the only states that license independent inspectors at the time of this writing—so you need to be careful.

The best inspectors are retired contractors or licensed engineers with residential construction experience. Such individuals would be most likely to spot problems with new construction. We should note that some inspectors specialize in existing homes and do cursory, "cosmetic" inspections—obviously, not who you want to evaluate your new home.

There are several key points in the construction when you should have a private inspector look at your new home—the pouring of the foundation, for example. We discuss these in detail in chapters 8 and 9. Here is a brief outline:

 ### Key Inspection Points.

Foundation: Layout and footings inspection. This can be divided into two parts: when the hole is dug (to check for proper depths of footings) and after the foundation walls are up.

Framing: Rough-in of plumbing, electrical, and mechanical systems. Framing inspection should also gauge the correct use and installation of beams.

Finishing: The details that make a house a home, such as trim, carpet, cabinets, drywall, etc.

Closing: Prior to closing, a final "punch-list" is created of any items the builder needs to repair or install.

A construction manager is typically a contractor or retired contractor with years of building experience. The construction manager usually supervises day-to-day operations at the building site, overseeing the construction in your interests. While construction managers are most often seen on homes of more than $400,000 when an architect isn't involved in administering construction, this may be an option to consider for your house.

Now, at this point, you may be wondering—why do I need a private inspector or construction manager? Isn't the builder supposed to supervise the construction? Yes, in theory, the builder is supposde to diligently supervise your home's construction. No shortcuts are ever taken and the correct materials are always installed in a professional manner. The reality for many home buyers is, sadly, quite different. Supervision is spotty or non-existent. Unsupervised subcontractors are an invitation to disaster. Furthermore, some unscrupulous builders try to pull a fast one on home buyers—passing off substandard work or substituting inferior materials. That's why you need a private inspector or construction manager working for you—you're basically evening the odds.

Are all builders incompetent and out to rip you off? Of course not. But ask yourself—could you tell whether a main beam was installed incorrectly? How about the plumbing? Roof trusses? Even some competent builders get stretched too thin and fail to supervise their homes properly. Unless you're intimately familiar with construction, you should have someone on your team whose sole job it is to protect your interests, not the builder's. Builders may want you to "trust" them; your motto should be **"TRUST BUT VERIFY."**

Getting Started: How Far in Advance?

Hire a private inspector or construction manager after you choose an architect but BEFORE you hire the general contractor. This timing is optimal because the inspector may be able to offer his or her opinion on the building practices of the builders you're considering. If the inspector isn't familiar with a builder's work, consider visiting some of the builder's jobs in progress with the inspector to evaluate the quality.

What Will It Cost You?

Charges for a private inspector could range from $25 to $100 per hour. Assuming the average home requires about eight hours of inspection, the total tab could run $200 to $800. For extensive inspections or in large metro areas, the total bill may be closer to $1000.

Construction managers can cost between 3% and 5% of the total construction cost. Hourly fees are also sometimes charged at a rate of $50 to $100 per hour. For an average $150,000 home, you could expect to pay $4500 to $7500.

Sources for Finding a Private Inspector.

1 *Two national associations can refer you to local inspectors.* The *National Association of Home Inspectors* (800-448-3942 or 612-591-4555) has more than 1000 mem-

bers. You can get the names over the phone or a list of inspectors in your state sent to you by mail.

The American Society of Home Inspectors (ASHI) (800-743-2744 or 703-524-2008) has 1400 members. According to an article we read, ASHI requires inspectors to perform 250 inspections before they can be a member. We contacted ASHI to get more information about their standards but they failed to call us back. This goof didn't impress us.

Nonetheless, be aware that many associations don't require rigorous testing or certification of their members. While they do require members to subscribe to a code of ethics, you're still on your own to check references carefully.

2 *State associations.* Many states, including Florida, California and Texas, have state real estate inspection associations. In your local library, you may want to check out the *Gale Directory of Associations* to see if your state has an association of inspectors.

3 *Architects.* These folks work with inspectors and engineers frequently. In fact, when an architect doesn't have structural engineering training, he or she often subcontracts out the foundation plans to a qualified structural engineer. The engineer may offer inspection services as part of his or her package.

4 *Homeowners associations.* For example, the *North Carolina Homeowners Association* (919-859-2711 or 919-460-6131), a grass-roots consumer group, can recommend home inspectors who are skilled in evaluating home construction. Other consumer housing groups across the country (even in your own town) may be able to recommend similar inspectors.

5 *Real estate attorneys.* Lawyers might know inspectors and engineers who have been used as experts in law suits involving faulty construction in your area.

6 *Yellow Pages.* A last resort. Look under the categories Engineers-Foundation, Engineers-Structural, Engineers-Geotechnical/ Soils, Building Inspection Service, Inspection Service, or Construction Management.

Why Municipal Building Inspectors Can't Be Trusted

One of the biggest myths that new home buyers fall victim to is the belief that city or county building inspections will protect them from getting ripped off by unscrupulous builders. "Home building is one of the most regulated businesses in America," builders are fond of saying. "Municipal inspections protect the consumer from defective construction."

Wrong. In researching this book, we found a clear pattern of evidence that indicates just the opposite—home buyers *cannot* count on city or county building inspections to save them from rip-offs.

To understand why, you must first realize what those municipal inspectors are actually enforcing—the building code. What is a building code? The code is a series of rules typically enacted at the state level to ensure construction meets a *minimum* level of standards. Counties and cities occasionally stiffen the code to adapt to local conditions—such as coastal areas that must brace for hurricanes.

What are inspectors NOT enforcing? Your contract. These inspectors are not there to make sure the work is done in a professional manner. For example, vinyl flooring can pass inspection for code violations even if it is poorly installed without a subfloor, leaving "lumps" in the floor. Government building inspectors are not there to certify that there are zero defects or that the work was done in accordance with your agreement. All they're looking for are those bare minimum standards outlined in the building code.

Sadly, you can't always count on building inspectors to even do that job. We found five reasons that government building inspectors are a miserable failure at protecting consumers:

1   **Corruption.** The *Cincinnati Post* reported in May 1991 that a television station had videotaped building inspectors "playing golf, going shopping or conducting personal business when they were supposed to be working. The station said employees falsified time sheets, inspection logs and mileage records." Later the same station aired reports that showed "a county building inspector admitting homeowners were often allowed to move into new houses that had not been given a final building inspection. The report also showed a building contractor, who refused to be identified, saying that 'inspectors often tagged houses as inspected when they never examined them.'"

Think that's an isolated case? Think again. In Frederick, Maryland, building inspectors were found to be moonlighting as subcontractors for the very same builders they were inspecting. In an editorial in the *Frederick Post*, the paper noted wryly, "Can we assume that someone goes out to inspect a construction site, for example, says it's wonderful and then we discover the same person is also working on that site? It would be like the inspector is inspecting his own work. Bet it passes inspection."

In New York City, 14 employees of the city Buildings Department were indicted on charges of "squeezing $150,000 in bribes from builders and owners over a five-year period," according to the *New York Daily News* in April 1991. The corruption was described as "systematic, widespread, high-dollar and driven by supervisors." In Philadelphia, corruption in the building department has a long, colorful history that goes back to 1951—the year the Department of Licenses and Inspections was created. The *Philadelphia Inquirer* quoted the mayor of Philadelphia as saying that "ever since I've been with the government—from day one—I've heard about the passing of $10 bills and $20 bills to inspectors to speed up a building permit or overlook an inspection of some kind."

You can spot a telltale sign of possible corruption from examining building permits that are posted outside homes under construction. The permit lists each inspection, date and any corrections needed. "Be very suspicious if the card has only approvals and no citations for needed construction," said Dr. Don Jacob, a consumer turned activist in New York who was saddled with $30,000 in repairs from a defective new home. "Some inspectors sign off cards for their contractor friends and never look at the construction. They may only drive by the construction site. In one city, builders were bringing cards to inspectors in a local donut shop and getting them signed off. Inspectors were never going to the construction sites."

2 *Incompetence.* Even if municipal building inspectors aren't corrupt, they may very well be incompetent. You'd think that cities and counties would hire inspectors with engineering or construction backgrounds. The reality is quite different—requirements vary widely from area to area. While some departments may require a college degree, it could be in basketweaving or some other relevant field.

The training and certification inspectors receive also varies from the barely adequate to the incredibly abysmal. Some departments hand out inspecting positions to political cronies of the mayor or city councilors. You can see a prescription for disaster coming: instead of well-trained inspectors with engineering and construction experience or schooling, the inspector in charge of making sure your new home is free from dangerous code violations may be a bureaucrat's crony with as much construction knowledge as . . well, you can fill in the blank.

Some states and counties are better than others. But the best building codes in the country are worthless if the people left to enforce them are idiots. The scary thing is there's no way to tell whether the area where you're building has competent or incompetent inspectors. Unless you're convinced otherwise, assume the worst and take the precautions outlined in this book to heart.

3 *Time pressures.* Let's assume the municipal building inspector for your house is neither corrupt nor incompetent. Unfortunately, you're not home free. There's yet another enemy facing you: time.

Many building inspectors are overworked at best, forced to do a staggering number of inspections in an eight-hour day. This problem is especially acute in areas that have housing booms.

In Atlanta, Georgia, more than 120,000 new homes have been built between 1986 and 1991. In an article on shoddy builders across the country, the *Los Angeles Times* reported that "Cobb County, Georgia's 10 inspectors 'take about 15 minutes per house call,' said Bob Harrison, manager of inspectors. That's an improvement over the nine minutes harried housing inspectors took three years ago but falls way short of the 40 minutes it should take to inspect the framing of a home, he said."

It should scare you to no end to know that the inspector who really needs 40 minutes to thoroughly evaluate the framing of your house—the critical structural element that literally holds up your walls and roof—is giving it only 15 quick minutes.

Even if the area where you're building isn't booming, the inspection department can be woefully understaffed. Governments put a higher priority on visible services such as police and fire protection. Building inspections to protect consumers are left on the back burner.

Housing markets can shift quickly from "cool" to "hot," with the boom resulting in increased new house construction. Suddenly, three inspectors who could have handled the load in normal times are swamped with four times the number of inspections to do in the same period of time. An overworked inspector who is doing rushed inspections is just as dangerous as an incompetent or corrupt inspector.

4 *Laws with no teeth.* Some communities have housing laws with holes big enough to drive a truck through.

North Carolina again comes to mind. While the state requires contractors to be licensed to build a new house, the penalty for not doing so is a whopping fine of $50. That's it, $50. We're sure unlicensed contractors who are building $100,000 homes are quaking in their boots when faced with this type of punishment.

Incredibly, in some areas of the country, there is no systematic check to determine whether contractors are licensed or not. Therefore, unlicensed contractors can "pull a permit" to build a house and dupe consumers into thinking they're legitimate.

Loopholes in laws also let contractors build houses without a permit. A few states allow unlicensed contractors to build houses without a permit if the house is for their personal use. Some builders use this loophole to claim they're building a house for themselves, only to quickly turn around and sell it.

Of course, some communities have tougher codes. Lake Forest, Illinois, requires 17 to 20 inspections to enforce a detailed code that calls for quiet plumbing and jiggle-free floors. Of course, you pay for all those municipal inspections through expensive permit fees that can top $5000 per house. The reality is that Lake Forest is the exception—many areas have toothless laws that are enforced by bungling inspectors.

5 *Political influence.* Builders and developers are big-time contributors to political campaigns. Their big money contributions can buy them a sympathetic ear at city hall. How does that affect so-called impartial building inspectors?

Who do you think pays the salaries of building inspectors? Yes, it's the city or county that is the boss. While inspectors may be certified and trained by the state, their paychecks are in the hands of local politicians.

Hence, we've seen cases of blatant political influence, in which builders and developers ask their friends in government to "ease up" on enforcement of the building code. "Hey, we're choking under all this government regulation," the builders' cry, "why don't you give the businessman a break?"

In the Southeast, we found at least one case of a building inspector who was fired after he refused to "ease up" on contractors who were blatantly violating the state's building code. He found another government job, but was ordered by superiors (county bureaucrats) not to speak to reporters about the situation. As you can see, it's hard to get rock-solid proof on this phenomenon but many inspectors admit off the record that it's a common occurrence.

The bottom line. You as a consumer must take responsibility for making sure you're getting a quality home. Relying on inspectors employed by government building departments is dangerous at best. If the inspectors aren't corrupt or incompetent, they're often overworked. Even if the inspectors are fine, the consumer protection laws for new homes can be riddled with loopholes or watered down by political influence.

The best path is to use your own "scissors" to poke the builder into building a quality new home. Those scissors are private professional inspectors with experience at evaluating new construction. Later in this book, we'll discuss the critical inspection times (it's more than just a closing inspection).

Questions to Ask the Inspector or Construction Manager
1 *What is your level of experience in evaluating residential construction? How long have you be worked in this area?*

2 *What credentials do you have? Do you have a contractor's license, an architect's license, or an engineering degree?* Since most states don't regulate inspectors, thisis critical—avoid anyone whose education or experience is limited. As a side note, you may want to ask if they belong to a national association of inspectors.

3 *Have you worked for this builder in the past?* Conflicts of interest may arise if the inspector or construction manager has ever been employed by the builder in the past. As with architects, any inspector or manager who has been paid a salary by the builder may be less willing to work on your behalf.

4 *What are some common problems with new construction in my area?* Experienced answers might cite low-quality lumber grades, foundation problems, etc. The answer to this question should be in plain English and clearly understandable—jargon is a no-no.

5 *Can I see a copy of one of your reports?* When studying the report, note whether the inspector simply has addressed cosmetic problems

(paint nicks, unfinished trim work) or has made a more detailed exam-ination. Some inspectors use a checklist, while others prefer narrative reports— we like the latter for new construction. If a checklist is used, check to see how detailed it is regarding common problem areas such as foundations.

6 *Is there a guarantee of prompt service?* If something is wrong, you need to have a written report to back up your claims in a timely fashion. While the builder probably will fix a problem without written evidence of a goof, it's nice to establish a paper trail in case a major problem develops down the road.

7 *Do you take photos?* Most inspectors don't, but you might as well ask. A picture of defective construction is strong proof to present to the offending builder/subcontractor.

8 *Do you offer to fix any defects?* If they answer yes, it's a big red flag—an ethical inspector should never profit from defects he or she uncovers.

Money Bombs with Inspectors

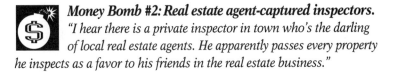

Money Bomb #1: Greenhorn inspectors.
"My friend just bought a home and hired an inspector who did a lousy job. The inspector was new to the business and only did a brief, cosmetic inspection that missed several problems."

These are the inspectors who just got into the business by printing up business cards. Usually, they have no experience and little knowl-edge of common problems such as soil conditions. Be sure to ask for references and check them out. Ask the inspector about his or her edu-cation or certification.

Money Bomb #2: Real estate agent-captured inspectors.
"I hear there is a private inspector in town who's the darling of local real estate agents. He apparently passes every property he inspects as a favor to his friends in the real estate business."

Real estate agents often are the "gate-keepers" of potential clients for inspectors. Many inspectors receive as much as 80% of their busi-ness from real estate agents. What does this mean for you?

Nearly all real estate agents are working for the seller, not the buyer. If an inspector turns up problems that are detrimental to sell-ing a house, the real estate agent may be inclined to stop recommend-ing that inspector. The inspector knows who butters his bread and may give passing grades to projects in order to get repeat business.

Therefore, whatever you do, don't hire an inspector recommend-ed by a real estate agent working for the seller/builder. This is why real estate agents weren't listed above under sources. Use one of the other sources and check references carefully. (The exception:

recommendations from a buyer's broker are more credible. More on buyer's brokers is in chapter 5.)

Be aware that many private inspectors get "bad" reputations among real estate agents because they become too good—that is, too good at ferreting out defects and problems with new homes. If a real estate agent fears a particular inspector, that's exactly the person who should be inspecting your home.

 Money Bomb #3: Construction manager conflicts of interest. *"We were about to hire this construction manager until we learned he was a former employee of the builder. Isn't that a clear conflict of interest?"*

Two situations might occur if you use a construction manager who knows your builder too well.

1 ***They're too friendly with one another.*** This might occur if the manager used to work for the builder or if they just happen to be friends. The whole reason for hiring a construction manager is to keep a tight rein over the builder. If they're buddies, the manager may be unlikely to enforce your wishes.

2 ***If the construction manager and the builder are stiff competitors and don't like each other.*** This situation could lead to many more hassles than you bargained for. After all, the manager is not supposed to be an ogre in this process, just an advocate for your interests. Excessive conflict on the job site is never helpful.

The solution to both these problems: hire a construction manager who doesn't work in the same area as the builder. For example, choose a manager who works in a nearby county or subdivision, but doesn't know your builder or the neighborhood intimately.

 Money Bomb #4: Builder's excuses that block your inspector. *"My builder told us we could not have a private inspector look at the house under construction. He cited some wild excuse, saying his insurance company prohibited it for liability reasons."*

What a joke. Some builders will do anything to keep consumers from looking "under the hood" of their homes. Sure, some builders will allow an inspector to see a home after it is finished—and well after any potential problems with the foundation or construction are covered over with dirt, concrete or drywall. Builders may invent all kinds of excuses about this—a favorite is to say that their insurance company forbids anyone (you or the inspector) from coming onto the property during construction. This is a great bluff.

Challenge the builder to present a written copy of the policy with that provision. Even if such a provision exists, ask the builder if you can call the insurance company to confirm this prohibition against inspectors. Ask the insurance company for a waiver for your inspector. If the builder refuses to cooperate, consider buying another home.

Real Estate Attorneys

How does a real estate attorney protect your rights as a consumer? It's up to the attorney to review all the contracts you will be asked to sign as a part of your new house. Specifically, he or she should pay special attention to your rights, especially regarding warranty coverage (warranties will be explained more fully in Chapter 8).

Builders stack the odds in their favor by having hordes of lawyers on a leash. Seminars sponsored by local builder associations give builders insights on how to avoid "liability problems" (translation: problems from constructing defective houses).

Since most contracts used in new home purchases are written by the builder or his attorney, you can be darn sure every word is crafted to favor the builder. Other, less sophisticated builders pursue an opposite course: their contract may be so ambiguous or poorly written that you're in danger of falling into the "verbal promise trap." Such builders make wonderful verbal promises to you, but later no one can remember who agreed to do what.

Sources to Find a Real Estate Attorney

Local lawyer referral services: Practically every city has some sort of lawyer referral service, a free service designed to match up consumers with local legal experts. Some radio stations also offer "Ask a Lawyer" nights for local consumers who have legal questions. Contact your local bar association for information.

Other professionals: Architects and accountants also may come in contact with good real estate attorneys. The key to a good real estate lawyer is finding one with new construction experience.

What Will It Cost You?

Lawyers ain't cheap. Face it—the cost of a lawyer to merely review your contracts can be as little as $75 in small towns up to as much as $200+ per hour in larger cities. It shouldn't take much more than an hour to review any contracts.

If you want the lawyer to be present at closing, as well as to review the closing documents, you'll have to pay for another hour or two. The total tab could be anywhere from $200 to $500. Consider placing a cap on the lawyer's "billable hours"—get it in writing that the lawyer won't exceed the cap without your written permission.

Money Bomb #1: Lack of construction experience.

"My brother is an attorney who said he could help us with the construction of our new home. However, he seemed to be clueless when it came to the legalities of new construction."

Many real estate lawyers are well versed in dealing with closing documents and contracts on "used" homes, but may not be as experienced with new construction situations. Some real estate attorneys

specialize in construction-related matters, while others focus on buying and selling aspects.

 ### Money Bomb #2: Conflict of interest with builder.
*"When we hired a local real estate attorney to help us with
our new construction contract, we didn't know he was friends
with our builder. When we had problems with the builder, the lawyer
was unwilling to help us out. Now we have to find a new lawyer to
represent us."*

In small to medium-size towns the reality is there often
aren't that many attorneys who specialize in real estate or new construction. Hence, the attorney you choose to represent you also may
have represented the builder at one time. Again, the builder
can bring the attorney more repeat business than the one-time
home buyer.

In the book *And They Built a Crooked House*, author Ruth Martin
describes her family's traumatic experience building a home
in Cleveland. A conflict of interest with their attorney cropped up
as a major problem. Although the attorney revealed at the beginning
that he had worked with the builder, he downplayed any conflict.
Then when a serious dispute occurred, the attorney backed out of
representing the buyer—claiming that his relationship with the
builder was too valuable. The resulting chaos was a contributing
factor to the disaster.

Other Possible Team Members
Think about one or more of these professionals to add to your
dream building team.

1 **Interior designer.** To consult on choices for carpets, paint, tile
and other finish work. Some interior designers are architects
who specialize in interiors.

2 **Buyer's broker.** A buyer's broker is a special type of real estate
agent who works for you, the buyer. (More on this later in
Chapter 5.) We recommend using a buyer's broker to purchase the lot
or building site (if you are building a custom home) or to negotiate on
a tract, semi-custom or new spec home in an existing development.
That way you guarantee the agent is representing you and is on your
side. Many consumers aren't aware that real estate agents are working
for the seller (or builder)—not the buyer.

3 **Insurance company.** A "hazard" insurance policy that guards
against fire and other perils will need to be in place at the time
of closing. You may want to ask your insurer whether they have any
construction-related policies to protect in case of a fire during construction (if you own the lot).

Who Is NOT on Your Team?

1 *Real Estate Agents (for the house).* If they aren't a buyer's broker, they aren't working for you. That's about 99% of all agents out there. Whose team are they on? Frankly, their own—most agents are fixated on that commission. Technically, they are legally and ethically bound to get the highest price and best terms for the builder. It's amazing that agents are getting 5% to 7% commissions for merely introducing you to the builder. Whoopee.

2 *The lender.* While lenders are technically working with you, they are most worried about their money. Most couldn't care less whether you get a quality house. While some lenders may be able to help if a dispute occurs between you and the builder, few really care. Making sure they get your payments on time is their major concern.

3 *Mother Nature.* Weatherforecasters on TV can't seem to guarantee the weather in the next hour, so don't expect to have smooth sailing with Mother Nature throughout the building of your new house. Not only can bad weather delay construction, but it may delay pre-construction activities (such as a soils test) as well. If the builder tells you it will take three months to build your house, add another month to the estimate. This way, if it pours rain or dumps snow, you won't be disappointed when the house isn't finished on time. And if the weather is perfect (along with everything else), you'll be pleasantly surprised when your house is finished early.

4 *Homeowners associations.* In "covenant controlled" communities (condos and townhomes and, increasingly, with single-family homes), homeowners associations often control the kind of houses that can be built in the subdivision.

In fact, many associations set up separate architectural control or review boards to comment on and approve building plans. They may even have monitors to keep an eye on your house while it is being built to make sure it complies with the community's covenants.

The political infighting in these associations can be intense—and your home may get caught in the crossfire. For example, we've spoken with homeowners who were forced to add extra windows, change the paint color for their exterior, or reposition their house on the lot before their house was approved. Some houses are rejected for ambiguous reasons, prompting an expensive redesign.

Check with the association for the community you want to live in *before* you decide to buy a lot and build. Get a copy of the covenants and speak to homeowners in the area to discover any potential problems. Also, let your architect know what the "standards" are in the community so you don't waste money and time altering a rejected design.

5 *Labor shortages.* In "hot" building regions, the supply of construction labor may be very tight. The lack of subcontractor availability can double the amount of time it takes to complete a house. What took four to six months in a normal market may now take seven to nine.

In one community we studied, framers were especially hard to come by. Some houses stood idle for a month or longer after the foundation was poured.

Some markets can turn from "cold" to "hot" seemingly overnight. If you plan to build in such a market, be prepared. Recognize that labor shortages could add weeks or months to the builder's optimistic schedules.

6   *Labor strikes.* Although they may not be as common as labor shortages, labor strikes do occur. For example, a drywallers strike in California in the summer of 1992 significantly slowed new construction.

7   *The scam artists.* When you build a house, you deal with dozens of people and companies. Some are more ethical than others. Scam artists might be subcontractors who intentionally do inferior work. In other cases, a smiling salesperson may sell you products that don't live up to manufacturers' claims. Choosing a builder who is reputable helps raise the odds of getting good subs—but there are no guarantees. Having an inspector on your side is the only sure way to guarantee that inferior work is corrected.

If your builder or architect suggests trying a product you aren't familiar with, do some research before agreeing to use it. For example, thousands of houses were built in the 1980s using an experimental plastic pipe system, instead of copper, for the plumbing. The folks who bought those houses have since discovered incredible leak problems. In fact, the manufacturer has a special division setup to deal with the problems caused by these plastic pipes. A little advance research might have helped these consumers avoid such serious problems.

8   *Delays.* The biggest enemy of any buyer is the seemingly inevitable delays. The wrong materials arrive at your home site. Subcontractors don't show up when scheduled. Or at all. And so on.

Here's an example of what delays can do. One builder we knew had scheduled the carpet installation for a Tuesday. Instead of showing up at 8:00 a.m., the carpet installer sauntered in at 5:30 p.m. This threw off the entire schedule—delaying the final inspection, cleaning and closing of the house.

The builder's biggest headache (and the reason you don't want to build a house yourself) is the scheduling of the subs. Like an expensive and time-consuming game of dominoes, one delay can cause another, which leads to a cost-overrun. The result is a vicious circle that raises the frustration level beyond description.

Like most home buyers, we had dozens of delays on our home—

some major and others minor. For example, a wrong kitchen cabinet was delivered (the manufacturer's mistake), delaying the installation of countertops by a week. However, the house ran only two weeks late in the end—being the cynics we are, we planned for a delayed closing months earlier.

What about the builder? Whose team is he or she on? Gee, it would be nice if every builder were on your side. The reality is the builder is also trying to make a profit at the same time he's trying to make you happy. Unfortunately, some (critics would say most) builders let their thirst for profits win out over your interests. To boost sagging financial fortunes, some builders and developers get desperate, taking home buyers down with them. You should probably pretend that you and your builder are on the same team, but, at the same time, take steps to protect yourself.

 Call for updates! By calling our special hotline, you'll hear the latest news on building a new home! 1-900-988-7295 (See the back page for price information).

4

If Dirt Were Dollars

Finding the Right Location for Your New Home

So, where exactly are you going to put this new house? Finding just the right location for your new home is going to involve a good amount of searching, compromise and trade-offs. Also, you must become your own detective to uncover the past history of the lot—discovering that the "dream location" for your new home was once a toxic waste dump *after you buy it* could ruin your whole day.

Basically, there are four types of potential sites for a new home:

1 *"No Competition" Lots.* These are sites in existing developments that are owned by one builder. You want the lot? Then you also must hire that builder. Many tract-style developments are run this way. Hence, the quality of such homes can range from "passable" to "your worst nightmare." Even more expensive lots in "exclusive" communities are sometimes sold this way. We've heard horror stories from consumers who fell in love with a lot—only to discover later that the builder/developer was an expert at building defective homes. Occasionally, some of the "no-competition" lots will let you choose your own architect or designer. At least this gives you a little more protection.

2 *"Managed Competition" Lots.* Many communities of tract or semi-custom homes allow you to choose from a list of "approved builders." Often, you can pick your own designer or architect and bid out your plan to these builders. Of course, the only problem may be that none of the approved builders has the skill or experience to do your home. Developers of these communities claim they have screened "approved" builders...yeah, right.

Here's the best strategy: ask the homeowners association or developer whether you can get an exception to the rule. Approved builder lists are often done to keep "tract" style builders from building in exclusive communities. The reality is you may be granted an exception if you can prove that your home design (by a professional designer or architect, of course) and builder are up to the so-called standards of the community. It may be well worth the effort.

3 *"Free Market" Lots.* These building sites are not "attached" to any builder. You buy the land and then use any builder you desire. Obviously, the flexibility of this arrangement is its chief advantage. Of course, most areas don't have many "free market lots." You may have a long search—and choose a location farther from town. Some of these sites have services such as natural gas and city sewers—others are more "rustic," requiring septic systems and the like. Don't let the "undeveloped" nature of such lots scare you off, however.

4 *Partially-Built Spec Homes.* In some cases, you may find a partially built home that is still on the market. (In jargon, this home is a "spec" since it was built on speculation, instead of presold to a buyer.) The advantage, of course, is that the builder has already picked a spot, obtained financing and started construction. On the downside, that "spot" may not be the best for you. Furthermore, there is significant risk in buying a partially built home—for example, you can't check the foundation since it already has been poured and the footings are buried. Insisting on a complete set of plans and specifications as well as independent inspections by a private inspector will help, but it's still a gamble. Nonetheless, you will still use the same "location analysis" techniques to determine whether it's the right place for you.

Step-by-Step Strategies to Scoping out a Location: Phase I.

 Step 1: Narrow your search to a general area and determine it's zip code. Go to your local library and find the *Sourcebook of Demographics and Buying Power for Every County in the USA.* This book answers the following questions: What percentage of families in that area have young children? Which area has the highest per capita income? This book provides the answers for every county in the country.

Step 2: If you have a computer, check out Supersite on the Compuserve network. You can find out demographics, income, housing, education and employment for any zip code in the U.S. Compuserve also has various forums where you can quiz people living in certain cities about the best neighborhoods.

Step 3: Identify two to three possible neighborhoods that have new home building sites available. You can determine this by simply driving around, checking your local paper, or asking a buyer's broker for hints.

Step 4: Score each neighborhood on a 1 to 10 scale for the following quality-of-life measures: school district, commute time, access to highways, and other things important to you.

Step 5: Check the availability of various services. How close is the nearest grocery store? Other shopping? Where's the nearest recreation center? How far away are the elementary, junior and senior high schools?

Step 6: Evaluate the neighbors. Are the lawns well taken care of? What types of cars are in the driveways? For kids, do the "Big Wheel" test—see whether any toys are left outside (the tell-tale sign of children). Get out and walk around. If you're looking on a weekend or in the early evening, chances are you can visit with potential neighbors.

Step 7: Give the potential lot a "once over." Visit it during rush hour—how's the traffic flow? Are you on a sleepy cul-de-sac or a busy thoroughfare? How's the traffic noise? If you're near an elementary school, how loud is it during recess?

Step 8: Locate a buyer's broker (see Chapter 5 for tips). Direct the broker to look for available lots in your target neighborhoods.

Step 9: Check zoning for nearby empty land with your city/county planning department. That lovely meadow just down the street may be slated for a giant, smelly factory. Or a high-rise condo building.

Step 10: Who can build on the lot? Any builder? Just three? One? Can you have your own architect? See Chapter 7 for tips on evaluating "tract" or existing development builders.

Step 12: If it looks like a go, do some sleuthing on the "history" of the lot. See the box called Environmental Detectives for more information.

Step-by-Step Strategies to Scoping Out a Location: Phase II

 Step 1: Bring the architect and/or builder out to the lot for a "look-see." Have them walk around the lot before you buy it. The goal is to identify any possible problems—is that wet spot a drainage problem? Is the lot's slope going to add significantly to the cost?

The architect or builder may do this for free or they may charge you a nominal hourly fee. Whether the lot looks challenging or simple to build on, it may be well worth the effort to have an "expert" give an opinion before you buy.

Step 2: Confirm the site's available "services" (or lack thereof). This includes access to a municipal water and/or sewer system, natural gas lines, electrical service, cable and phone lines. Much of this information is in the Multiple Listing Service listing for the property. However, don't take a real estate agent's word on the availability of services—call the utility company and confirm electrical or natural gas service at that address.

The lack of services could mean significant extra cost. No cable TV may mean installing a satellite dish—factor that cost into your decision. If the area is undeveloped, you may have to pay a significant fee to the utility company to bring in service. If you have a home office, make sure the phone company will let you install multiple lines to your home (for a fax, modem, etc.).

Step 3: If you're buying a "free-market lot," the next step is to do the "tests." Depending on the area you are building in, you may want to do all or none of these—ask your architect or builder regarding the norms in your area.

Here's a rundown of the possible tests:

- *A Soils Test:* This is done by an engineer or geologist who drills several small holes 12 to 15 feet deep in your lot. Core samples are taken to determine the "sub-soil conditions"—basically what's underneath the dirt. Is there clay? A layer of rock-hard limestone? The results will influence the type of foundation (including the need and size of footings) and the excavation costs. This test costs $250 to $350. Add in engineering for the foundation and the total cost can soar to $1000 to $1500—some builders consider this too expensive and skip this crucial test, a potentially dangerous decision.

  (Note: In some areas, soils tests are replaced by an "open hole inspection": after the foundation is dug, a soils engineer comes out to look at the hole. He or she checks the rock and makes sure the planned foundation is adequate.)

- *Percolation Test:* Also know as a "perc test," this is done for lots that don't have access to a municipal sewer system and, hence, require a septic system. A perc test is done by digging a hole, pouring in a certain amount of water and timing its disappearance. This is done to determine how quickly water will drain from the future septic field. The depth of the hole for the perc test varies, depending on local code. In northern climates, a perc test may only be possible when the ground isn't frozen. If the test has already been done, get a copy. In cases where deep perc holes are required, this test also may determine the soil condition. Cost: $125 to $200.

Environmental Detectives: Sleuthing the Sludge

It's everyone's biggest nightmare—you move into your dream house and suddenly discover an odor in the backyard. You go to investigate and find a green ooze seeping up from the ground.

Alarmed, you call the health department and learn your home sweet home was a toxic waste dump in a previous life. Or a landfill. Or perhaps it's all those gasoline tanks down the road—have they spilled any gas that could seep into your yard?

Think this only happens in Love Canal? Think again. Dozens of homeowners in Fairfax, Virginia, recently discovered the worst when they found a toxic brew of petroleum by-products leaking into their basements. The culprit? A nearby collection of gas tanks that had a history of leaks. Many of the homeowners faced bankruptcy when they couldn't sell their homes because of the problem.

While this sounds discouraging, it's not impossible to find out the past environmental history of your home site—and the surrounding area. We discovered a company called Environmental Risk Information and Imaging Services in Virginia that offers "ERIIScan" to help you make an educated decision about the site you're considering. The basic report costs $75 and the company accepts credit cards. To order, call 1-800-989-0402.

We saw a sample of the report and were impressed. You give them the address and a nearby cross street and the company scans five government databases to find environmental problems within a one-mile radius of your home. The report details problems at or near your site in five categories:

 The most serious hazardous waste sites near your proposed home, if any.

 Known or suspected waste sites under investigation.

 Facilities that do NOT comply with federal regulations governing the manufacture, storage or transportation of potentially hazardous chemicals.

 Companies or plants that release (or have the potential for release of) toxic materials.

⑤ Facilities that manufacture, store or transport hazardous chemicals.

■ **Water Witch Test:** What's a water witch? In areas where there is no water service, a well may need to be dug. But where should you dig the well? Enter the water witch, who divines the best place for a well with a special twig. We realize this sounds nutty, but it works and people who've dug successful wells swear by it.

Step 4: Check zoning for certain prohibitions. For example, some

The report tells you everything nearby that could be a possible environmental hazard, from a little dry cleaner store to a nuclear power plant. If a truck carrying hazardous chemicals spilled in a traffic accident on a nearby highway, you'll know it.

If the Fairfax homeowners had spent $75 for the ERIIScan report before they bought their homes, they would have discovered the subdivision was right next to a gasoline storage facility that had a long history of leaks—saving themselves untold amounts of grief and money.

Some potential problems can look rather harmless—a nearby gas station or dry cleaner store is required to be registered by the EPA since they use or store hazardous chemicals. Hence, if they've had a spill or any other problem in the past, you have a chance to learn about it *if* it was reported to the EPA.

And that's the biggest potential shortcoming of ERIIScan—it can't pick up problems that have not been reported to the government. Hence, if your neighbor installed a diesel gas tank underground and didn't report it to the state or federal environmental officials (as required by law), this report would miss it. While it obviously isn't foolproof, it's better than nothing.

ERIIScan also notes whether there are any old fire insurance maps or aerial photographs for your site. The photos go back to the 1920s and some fire insurance maps date back to the 1870s in the larger cities. If you suspect your home site was more than just a corn field 50 years ago, you can use these photos to see what was on your lot back then.

Let's say you get a report on your potential new home site and some problems are turned up. (ERIIScan told us some "dirty" sites can have reports exceeding 25 pages.) What should you do next? To determine whether you have a serious situation or not, you probably need to hire an environmental engineer to do a site evaluation. In addition to the Yellow Pages, you can also get a referral by contacting the Environmental Assessment Association at (602) 483-8100.

How bad is the problem? "Some 40 million Americans live within four miles of one of the 1235 sites that have made the U.S. Environmental Protection Agency's Superfund National Priority List—sort of the most wanted list of hazardous waste—and about 50 to 100 new sites turn up each year," according to a June 1992 *Money* magazine article entitled "Home Sweet Toxic Home."

We strongly recommend you check out your home site before purchasing. Discovering your home is built on a hazardous waste site after you move in is not worth the risk.

communities that are still stuck in the Dark Ages prohibit home offices. Height restrictions and other regulations could nix your plans for a grandiose home.

Step #5: Determine the association/government fees for building on the lot. Certain community associations may ask you to put down a "deposit" to guarantee you will obey their covenants, conditions and restrictions. If you play by the rules, you get your money back. Associations sometimes also charge a "submittal" fee to review your plan to make sure their architectural rules are met. Municipal building departments may have certain "fees" to have your plans reviewed and make sure they're in compliance with building codes. These fees may be in addition to the cost of getting a building permit. Knowing all these costs up front is obviously important in evaluating one site over another.

Step #6: Consider a survey to determine just what you're buying. Do you know how big your lot is? Just because there is a "pin" or "marker" indicating each corner, how do you know that it is correctly placed? They may have been put there by a previous lot owner who was merely guessing at the site's dimensions. More blatant fraud occurs when the pins are placed in knowingly wrong locations or are moved, creating the appearance of a bigger lot. The fact is, unless you have a formal survey done, you may not know exactly what's on your lot and what's on your neighbor's. Some lenders require a survey, which costs $150 to $300, before you can get a construction loan.

Step #7: Adjust your bid to the lot conditions. Now you're ready to offer some money to the lot owner. Your bid should be based on what you're buying. That perfect lot may have a rock-hard layer of bedrock under the surface, forcing an extra $1000 in excavation costs. If you know all the facts before you negotiate, you can make a more intelligent bid.

What Will It Cost You?

The "general rule of thumb" is that the lot should cost 25% to 35% of the total price (lot plus house). The reasoning is simple—you don't want to put a giant, expensive house on a cheap lot with awful views or a tiny backyard. Similarly, a cheap house on an expensive piece of land doesn't work either. Obviously, rules are made to be broken—if you find the perfect location, go for it. In some areas, land is so expensive that you may have a hard time hitting the 35%—lenders may be willing to make an exception. In California, the land may account for 45% of the total price.

When you acquire land, the costs include:
- ***The actual land price.***
- ***Tests.*** Most of the costs are the buyer's responsibility. The seller may already have completed a survey or percolation test in some cases.
- ***Tap fees.*** These costs are to "tap" into the local utility lines (electrical, natural gas, sewer, water and so on). Some lots have the tap fees paid already.
- ***Consultant fees.*** You may want to pay for an hour of your architect's or builder's time to visit the potential site to give you their opinion about it's suitability.

To pay for all this, you have several options:

- *Cash.* The old standby.
- *Bank loan.* Occasionally, you may find a lender to loan you about 50% of the lot's value.
- *"Seller carrybacks."* In some areas, the seller may take back a note on the property. You put down a down payment and make monthly payments to the seller. You can use a short-term carry-back (one to three years) to finance the land while you go through the process of preparing to build on the lot.

Siting the House

Finding the right location is just the beginning. Now you must decide where on the lot your home should sit. "Siting" the house should not be a quick, haphazard decision. Here are some thoughts on this process:

1 *What views do you want to see?* Anything you want to avoid? Positioning the house on the lot to take advantage of any view is a delicate task.

2 *Check zoning and any covenants.* Certain rules may dictate how far back your home can be from the front, back and side property lines. These may be county or city zoning "set-backs" or community covenants. Height restrictions and other regulations are also an issue in some areas.

3 *Consider hiring a landscape architect for particularly challenging lots.* If you have a flat lot with few trees, siting the house may not be difficult. However, if the lot slopes or has lots of little hills and valleys, you may want to call in a pro. If you have an architect, he or she should be able to recommend a landscape architect to help you site the house. The landscape architect will maximize the view from the street and the position of the house relative to potential landscaping.

4 *Curb appeal is the goal.* The key to having a quality house with strong resell appeal is to understand how the house will look from the curb. This first impression is crucial if you plan to sell the home later. A facade that's dominated by a giant, ugly garage may detract from the home's value, despite how beautiful the inside is.

5 *Solar "views."* In cold climates, southern exposure helps warm the home through "passive solar energy." Some folks like the morning sun to shine into the kitchen or breakfast nook. In areas where the summer heat is intense, a room with a large expanse of windows that faces west could be difficult to cool. Many homes in the South that have no southern or western exposure are considered desirable. The same logic applies to driveways—in cold climates, driveways that face the north or are shaded by trees and get little sun are a negative (the snow doesn't melt as easily).

The determination of the best solar siting of your home is tricky. If you visit the lot in June, the sun will be high in the sky—much different than in the dead of winter. In cold climates, if you can view the lot in the winter, you may have a different perspective on where to place the home and driveway. The point is to think through these issues carefully.

6 *Driveway.* In snowy climates, a driveway should be level and a straight shot to the garage. Ask anyone who's tried to negotiate a driveway with a sharp turn that's covered with 10 inches of snow and you'll understand why—slow down to take the turn and you're toast. Similarly, a driveway with a "negative slope," where the driveway slopes down to the garage from the street, is a major no-no ... you can easily slide down an icy surface into your living room. A driveway that snakes its way through lots of trees might be nice to look at, but impossible to plow.

In climates with heavy rain, you want rainwater to drain naturally off the driveway into the street—not pool near your garage. "Negative slope" driveways can cause problems in these areas as well.

Questions to Ask

Some of these questions can be answered by a buyer's broker. Others require an expert opinion from an architect, builder, or engineer. A few questions are for you to ask yourself.

1 *Are there any impact fees?* In our "money bomb" section we explain this new tax on home buyers. Impact fees for new schools, parks, or environmental protection range from $1000 to $30,000 and are usually scaled to the home's square footage.

2 *What are the property taxes?* A buyer's broker should be able to give you an estimate for property taxes, given a certain size home.

3 *How much are association fees and annual dues?* If your lot is part of a homeowners association, you may have to pay "submittal fees" to submit your plan to the group's architectural control committee. Annual dues cover any common amenities such as a pool or clubhouse, private police protection/security, or the association's administration.

4 *What school district is the lot in? Which elementary, junior high (middle school), and high school do kids attend? How far away are they? What is their quality relative to nearby schools? Is there "open enrollment" where you can choose another public school?*

5 *Describe the lot's topography.* Most Multiple Listing Service listings will include a description—the lot could be flat, gently sloping, or severely sloping.

6 *Is the lot insurable?* Some lots in a flood plain may require special flood insurance. Ask an insurance agent for information on this.

7 *How much site preparation will be required? Will trees have to be cleared?* These costs should be estimated by a professional architect/designer or builder.

8 *What's the zoning? What uses does this allow or prohibit? Can you have a home office? Could you get a variance or a zoning change if the current zoning isn't residential?*

9 *Are there any easements?* An easement is a right or privilege of someone else to use your property. Common easements are for utilities to run lines across the back of your property. The phone company may have an easement to put a junction box at one corner of your lot. Most easements are marked on a subdivision map—ask to have any and all easements revealed to you before you buy. If you have a survey done on the property, make sure all easements are located.

10 *What is the access to the lot? Is there any legal "ingress" across another lot?* You may have the right to share a driveway with a neighbor.

11 *Are there municipal water and sewer available? What about electricity and natural gas? Will you have to use propane or heating oil?*

12 *Are there any building moratoriums?* Some communities restrict growth by banning a water/sewer tap for new homes. Others slow the permit approval process. Ask a buyer's broker for the latest news in your area.

13 *What are the conditions of the trees?* In some areas, an infestation of pests or insects may have killed all the trees on your lot. Some trees may look healthy but still be infected. Call a county forester or the agriculture department for information.

14 *What's the soil condition?* A soils test tells you what you're building on—a crucial protection for you.

15 *Do you really like the neighborhood?* This may be a tough question to answer, but go with your gut feeling.

16 *Are there any restrictive covenants?* These can be put on the property by a previous owner or a homeowners association. If you have your heart set on a two-story home, but the association's height restrictions only allow one-level homes, you're going to be very disappointed. Know the facts before you buy.

17 *Can you get clear title?* Make sure there are no liens on the property—in most states, you can purchase title insurance. This guarantees the title will be clear of any liens or other encumbrances. The title insurance company does a search to make sure you'll get good title. If title insurance is not used in your area, have an attorney do a lien search to make sure the property is free and clear.

18 *If the land purchase is contingent on financing, can this be written into the contract?* Making the purchase contingent on loan approval gives you an out in case the lender says no. Adding the conditions that you can obtain "market rate" financing also protects you.

The Hamburger Theory of Neighborhoods

A college professor of mine once described the process of determining the right site for a home as "the hamburger theory": Different lots (just like cuts of meat) have different quality and prices.

Just like a side of beef, neighborhoods or subdivisions have various "cuts" of locations. There are the hamburger lots—these may have less-desirable locations such as on a busy street. Sites that back up to a highway or major thoroughfare are not much fun—traffic noise is a big negative for most folks. Low-lying lots that flood during rain storms are also definitely hamburger.

On the other hand are "filet mignon" lots. Depending on your tastes, such a location may be on a quiet cul-de-sac. The lots with the best views or nicest topography always sell for a premium. Locations that are next to golf courses or "greenbelts" (dedicated open space) are also top spots.

Of course, you may want a filet mignon location in the subdivision but you've only got a T-bone budget. The challenge for any new home buyer is to buy the very best location that your budget allows.

Nothing is black or white, either—many locations don't fall clearly in the hamburger or filet mignon categories. There are many different cuts of meat in between—ground chuck, rib-eyes, T-bones, etc. Such locations may be a mix of negatives and positives. A lot on a quiet cul-de-sac may be selling at a lower price since it doesn't have easy access from the subdivision's entry.

In a perfectly free market, the price of certain locations would be scaled to their attractiveness. Yet pricing is often part art, part science. Hence, some hamburger locations may be underpriced, while the filet mignon lots are over valued. If you take the time to search, you may be surprised to find bargains.

Money Bombs

Money Bomb #1: Building your house on fill dirt.

"We didn't have a soils test on our lot. Boy, did we regret it. After we moved in, we discovered our house was built on 'fill dirt.' Now the house has settled and caused thousands of dollars in damage."

If you are building a house, get a soils test. If you are buying a "spec" or tract development house, ask to see a copy of the soils test. If the builder had an open hole inspection by an engineer instead of a soils test, you'll want to see a copy of the engineer's report. The goal: to make absolutely certain your home is not built on "fill dirt," dirt that's brought in to fill in a ditch or low spot. Or maybe your home site was filled in with stumps and various debris. Either way, you're inviting trouble—without a stable base your foundation could sink ... taking your home (and life savings) with it. Treat any builder who says such tests or inspections "aren't done in these parts" with major suspicion.

There is one exception to this rule: areas where the soil has a high clay content. In this case, the foundation hole must be overdug by a specified number of feet. Then, "structural" fill dirt is brought in and compacted to provide a base for the foundation. If this is the case in your area, ask to see a copy of the "density test." This test, done by a qualified engineer, confirms the soil is appropriately compacted.

Money Bomb #2: Impact fees

"We were looking at land in a fast-growing community. Wow, we were shocked to learn that we would have to pay a $10,000 impact fee to build there."

Impact fees are an insidious tax on new home buyers. The theory goes that new home buyers put extreme pressure on schools and other public services (parks, etc.). "Impact fees" are allegedly used to build new schools to accommodate an influx of newcomers. And they aren't insignificant amounts of money—in California, impact fees for a single new home can top $20,000.

Governments have grown fond of impact fees as a "painless" way to raise revenue without raising taxes on everyone. It's easy to tax a new home buyer, who has yet to even move to the area. It's also taxation without representation—how can you voice an objection to a tax when you're not around? Builders simply pass along impact fees in the form of higher sales prices for new homes.

Does the new home buyer solely benefit from new schools or parks? Of course not—existing citizens will also use these facilities, essentially for free since they don't have to pay any impact fees. What if you don't have children? You still have to pay an impact fee for local schools.

Impact fees also tend to raise the price of existing homes, a boon to existing property owners. If a new home now costs $2000 more to build, it tends to raise the value of similar, existing homes—a free bonus to those homeowners.

The simple fact is that impact fees are taxes to restrict growth. They also have the dual effect of making housing less affordable. An impact fee of $1700 on a median-price home ($120,000) prices 12,000 people out of the housing market.

Unfortunately, courts have upheld impact fees as constitutional. The result is that home buyers must pay if they want to live in a certain community.

The Bizarre World of Homeowners Associations

If you don't think the process of building a house is complete insanity, you probably haven't encountered a homeowne's association yet.

Just what are these creatures? When subdivisions or communities are established, the developer may incorporate a series of "covenants, conditions and restrictions" on the lots. Most covenants are there to ensure a quality residential neighborhood. The rules may establish everything from how far you can build from your property lines (set-backs) to the minimum square footage allowed for new homes.

But who will enforce these rules? Enter the homeowners association. The association establishes a review board to look over future home plans to make sure they square with the rules.

Now, in a perfect world, this would work wonderfully. Covenants would be there to protect your property value—to prevent your neighbor from opening a truck stop. Benevolent associations would work diligently to enforce the covenants in a fair and consistent manner.

Unfortunately, this isn't a perfect world. The problem usually starts with the covenants—rules that are sometimes quite hysterical. Here's a sampling:

- Pornographic films, books or magazines in your home are prohibited by a Phoenix, Arizona, homeowners association.
- "Fat dogs" are outlawed in a Huntington Beach, California community. Only pooches under 20 pounds are allowed.
- Basketball backboards must be the same color as the house, according to a Mission Viejo, California, association's rules.

As you'll note, California is a prime example of homeowner's associations run amok. "Orange County, CA has the distinction of having more homeowner associations than any place else on earth," said a recent article in the *Orange County Register*.

But the problem isn't limited to California. Twenty-nine million Americans live under the rules of homeowners associations. The phenomenon is growing like a weed out of control—at last count, the U.S. had 150,000 homeowners associations.

When you build a home, you may enter the world of the association's "design standards." These are enforced by the omnipotent architectural review board or control committee. Fasten your seatbelt—here's what you might expect to encounter:

- *Ambiguous design rules:* Here's an actual rule from a Colorado homeowners association's design standards: "A house must be in harmony with itself and its surroundings." Now what the heck does that mean? The ambiguous nature of many design rules may mean your home is rejected because it is not "harmonious." To comply with the above "rule," the association often asks home buyers to put in windows in their garages—at your expense, of course. How garage windows make a home in harmony with itself is beyond us.

- *Arbitrary enforcement:* With all those ambiguous rules, the door is left wide open to arbitrary and capricious enforcement of the rules. In one case, an architectural board rejected a home because a board member didn't like the realtor involved in the project. The sheer volume of rules can sometimes lead to inconsistent decisions—many standards look like mini-books. Unfortunately, special exceptions to the rules are often granted to those with political pull.

- *Volunteer "control":* Most associations are run by volunteer homeowners, not paid professionals. This volunteer nature leads to high turnover of association officials. One result: inconsistent decisions on which houses are approved or rejected. Depending on the current political climate, your home could be rejected because of the roof color—despite the fact that a similar home was approved one month earlier. The reason? The new board has decided to enforce an obscure provision in the design standards. In some cases, the architectural review board has wide latitude to interpret the covenants.

How can you survive this process? First, find out what the covenants (sometimes also called declarations) are *before* you buy. You can get a copy from the homeowners association. Since these are also recorded with the county clerk, your buyer's broker can get a copy, too.

In addition, make sure you get a copy of any design standards or rules for new homes. At least that way you know what you're getting into before you invest money in a lot and design. Another wise move: Get a copy of the association's budget (usually available from the association's board members or management office). Is the association operating in the red? Are there proper reserves for emergencies? Associations that are losing money or have little or no reserves could be problematic.

Work the association like a smooth politician. Schmooze with the association's board members. Find out who's on the architectural review boar and introduce yourself. Make sure they realize you're a nice person. Tell them you decided to build in the community because their covenants are a good protection for homeowners (they love hearing this).

Do some homework—if the association has a reputation for turning down homes (your buyer's broker should have some intelligence on this), ask the board the most common reasons why homes are rejected. Make sure your architect/designer understands the rules and the potential pitfalls—this lowers the chance of a rejection and the expense of revising your plans.

Despite the fascist and draconian tendencies of some homeowners associations, the fact is most buyers like communities that are governed by some type of covenants and restrictions. If you plan to resell your home sometime in the future, potential buyers may be reassured that their big investment will be protected to some degree.

Unless, of course, the buyer has a fat dog. But at least they'll like your garage windows.

5

The Ugly Truth About Real Estate Agents

Helping Hand or Scum of the Earth?

O n your home journey, it is almost a guarantee that it will happen. When you least expect it. At the moment you are most vulnerable. Yes, odds are you will run into ... A REAL ESTATE AGENT.

Yes, it's the world's second oldest profession. A group of people actually held in lower esteem than Congress or the media. Real estate agents pray for the day they are trusted as much as used car salesmen.

Slithering through the tall grass and slinking out of back alleys, there are over one million real estate agents in the U.S. That's more than the entire population of Montana. And they all have a singular goal: to separate you from your money. In a typical year, agents will rake in $22 billion of commissions on home sales. That's billion with a B.

The home buyer's undoing usually begins in an innocuous way. By chance, you run into an agent and commit the first goof: You admit you are thinking about buying a home. Suddenly, the agent's eyes light up. As he whips out a business card, he can barely keep from drooling on himself from all the excitement. If you could see through his eyes, you have just transformed from a human being into a fat commission check.

"Oh come on", you say, "it's not that bad. I can handle the agents," you argue. Think again, oh naive one. Agents take classes, attend seminars and pore over the latest scientific data—all in the end-less pursuit of your wallet. They'd run over their own grandmother with a truck to get you to sign on the dotted line.

And, of course, they don't care what you buy as long as you BUY. Whether they sell you a cracker box built on a toxic landfill or a quality-built custom home, do you think they care? Nope, their overriding concern is that you spend the largest amount of money possible, since their salary is tied to your naiveté.

Of course, you obviously care about what you're buying since you have to live with this thing for years—from the moment you wake up to the time when you fall asleep, you live, eat and breathe this home. If it's riddled with defects or poor construction, you're trapped inside it like some carnival funhouse ride from hell.

This ride usually starts when home buyers succumb to the biggest myth of all about real estate agents. Let's put this into bold caps.

Biggest Myth about Real Estate Agents: The Agent Is Working for You.

Myth #1 "We looked for a new home with a local real estate agent. She asked for our price range and income level. Later, when we found a house, we were shocked when we learned that the agent had disclosed this personal information to the builder! Wasn't the agent representing our interests?"

Wrong. In almost all cases, real estate agents do NOT work for you. Their boss is the seller—the builder in the case of a new home. The builder pays their commission.

So what does that mean in the real world? Despite how sweet the agent is to you, they are LEGALLY and ETHICALLY required to do the following:

- Negotiate the highest price and best terms for the ***builder.*** Your goals mean nothing.
- Disclose all known financial information about you to the builder. If you tell them you can really afford a $175,000 home but you'd like to bid $165,000, the agent must tell the builder you can really spend more. If you tell the agent your annual salary or net worth, that information is also passed right to the builder/seller.
- In some states, the agents are not required to tell you about any defects or negative aspects about the home. While most agents are required to be "fair" to both builder/seller and buyer, they don't have to tell you that a school down the street is about to close. Or that the home's foundation was designed without an engineer. Or that the builder has lost several lawsuits over defective construction.

Did you not realize this? You're not alone. A 1983 study by the Federal Trade Commission revealed that 71% of new home buyers thought "their" real estate agent was representing their interests. A

Consumer Federation of America survey in 1990 showed that "only 30% of American adults know that real estate agents usually legally represent the seller only." That means two out of every three home buyers are being duped into thinking the agent is working and negotiating for them.

As one observer told the *Wall Street Journal* recently, working with an agent is "like working with an attorney who represents the defendant—and you're the plaintiff!"

The Dangerous Consequences of This Myth
Believing this myth is hazardous to your health for two reasons.

1 *You may disclose sensitive financial information to the agent.* Only a fool would reveal information that could damage your effort to negotiate effectively with a builder. But that's exactly what millions of Americans do when they talk with real estate agents. Reveal your income to the agent (who relays this to the builder) and the builder may hold out in the negotiation because she thinks you're too rich.

2 *You may be duped into spending too much for your new home.* As we'll explain later, if you use a typical real estate agent, you'll add $8000 to the price of the average home and get absolutely nothing in return. The agent has an economic incentive (that is, a higher commission) to get you to pay the most amount of money possible for the new home.

How This Myth Spread
The myth that real estate agents are on your (the buyer's) side has become entrenched in consumers' psyche for several reasons. To understand why 70% of consumers misunderstand this crucial point, you have to have some background on how this sorry situation developed.

1 *First, for all practical purposes, there are two types of real estate agents: a listing agent and a selling agent.* The listing agent does just that—lists the property. It's his or her name who is on the sign out in front. This agent works with the seller/builder, getting all the information on the home and perhaps providing a few marketing tips, pricing advice and so on.

Of course, getting a house listed is just half the battle. The goal is to sell it. Enter the selling agent. That's the agent that finds and "works" with the buyer. He or she may show you several prospective homes. If you decide to buy, the selling agent presents the offer to the builder's listing agent and helps with the paperwork.

The selling agent is often called a "subagent" or "cooperating agent": that's because the selling agent is "cooperating" (a nice euphemism) with the seller/builder.

You may note at this point that the score is 2-0. The seller has two agents working for him. You've got zip—no one to negotiate on your behalf and look out for your interests.

Both agents essentially split the commission on a new home, which runs a whopping 5% to 7% of the sales price. On a $150,000 home, that commission in real dollars is $7,500 to $10,500. What does all that money buy you? We'll tell you later in this chapter. (Hint: not much.)

2 | *Lax enforcement of disclosure requirements zaps consumers.* Did you know that 43 states have laws that require real estate agents to disclose to you that they are working for the seller? If this is so, how come only 30% of home buyers know this?

The answer lies in the *type* of disclosure that a state requires. The Consumer Federation of America (CFA) recommends that the disclosure requirements meet four tests:

- **Written.** "Verbal disclosures are not adequate because, among other reasons, their absence can rarely be proved, so that there is no way to ensure compliance with the requirement," CFA says.
- **On a standard form.** This "assures that a written disclosure is not made in complex legal language that is unintelligible to most home buyers."
- **Signed by the home buyer.** If you have to sign it, the theory goes that you might also read it.
- **Made at the first substantive contact or meeting.** If agents could wait until the closing or some later date to tell you they work for the builder, you may unknowingly disclose important information about yourself early in the game. Forcing agents to disclose their true allegiance up front is the only way to level the playing field.

So how many states require such "complete" disclosure as recommended by the Consumer Federation of America? Only seven. New York, Louisiana, Massachusetts, New Hampshire, Texas, Idaho and the District of Columbia are the only states that have disclosures that meet the above criteria.

The other states fall somewhat short. Wisconsin is the second best, requiring all of the above except that the disclosure must be signed. Typical of the remainder is Colorado, which requires disclosure but there's no standard form or required buyer signature. Agents also aren't required to do this at the first meeting. When we posed as buyers and spoke to real estate agents in Colorado, we found most did not disclose that they were really working for the seller. Hence, weak disclosure laws are often as much protection as nothing at all.

Speaking of which, there are seven other states that have NO disclosure whatsoever. Watch out if you live in Arizona, Arkansas, Kentucky, Michigan, New Jersey, North Carolina or Oregon—these states do not require agents to disclose they're working for the seller.

(To be fair, we should note that Colorado changed it's disclosure law in 1993. Now the state requires written notification that must be signed by the buyer. Critics point out that the wording on the disclosure notice is filled with "legal-ese" and may not be completely clear to buyers.)

3   *The propaganda war.* Real estate agents have been working overtime to convince home buyers that they MUST use an agent to purchase that new home. Or else, they will catch the black plague and die a slow, painful death.

Chief architect of this strategy is the National Association of Realtors, one of the most powerful trade groups in the country. The group has 750,000 members (known as Realtors)—that's almost two-thirds of the country's 1.2 million real estate agents.

The Realtors have an impressive batting average—nearly 80% of all new homes sold in the country involve a real estate agent. (The balance are bought by homeowners directly from builders or sellers.) The association and the country's top realty companies crank out slick promotional brochures that try to convince you to use a real estate agent, preferably a Realtor.

One reason real estate agents are so effective: their monopoly over the Multiple Listing Service (MLS). The MLS is essentially a catalog of all the homes, townhomes, condos and vacant land available for a certain county—and nearly every county or city in the U.S. has an MLS.

Guess who runs the MLS? Your friendly local board of Realtors, who are part of the National Association of Realtors. As you might imagine, in many cases only members of the realtor association are allowed access to this crucial listing of available property.

The bottom line: builders are blackmailed into using agents. Many have told us so off the record. Negative comments about agents are always off the record, since builders live in perpetual fear of having the source for three out of every four customers dry up.

You can easily see the dilemma that builders face. If you have a spec home for sale and want to list it in the MLS, you must hire an agent. If 80% of new home buyers are using agents, why fight it?

Builders simply pass along the agent's hefty commission as higher prices. That translates into thousands "built" right into the home's price. But what does that money buy you from a consumer's perspective? The biggest rip-off of all new home rip-offs—the $8100 "taxicab ride."

Money Bombs

 Money Bomb #1: The $8100 taxicab ride.
Yes, it's the mother of all new house scams. The $8100 that you pay for, essentially, a taxicab ride.

First of all, you might ask, where did that $8100 figure come from? That's how much an average 6% commission translates into in real dollars for a $135,000 new home. Nearly all builders pass along every penny of that $8100 in the form of a higher sales price.

You may be asking, what exactly do real estate agents do for that money (which comes from your pocket)? Good question.

Do they negotiate with the builder to get you a better deal? Nope, the typical agent is bound by law to get the highest price for the builder, not for you, the home buyer. Does the agent make sure the home is designed and built with quality materials and labor? You're daydreaming if you believe that. Most agents have absolutely no knowledge of new construction—they couldn't tell a floor joist from a roof truss. Is the foundation designed correctly? What do they care? They wouldn't know a proper foundation if it hit them in the face. Do agents visit the site to check or inspect the construction? No way. The only time you see an agent is at the closing—to collect the commission check.

The only thing agents really do for you is give you a ride to meet the builder. The agent may give you a tour of the builder's model home or show you some of his previously built homes. Whoopee. If you can drive, you don't need a real estate agent to find a builder. Take the real estate agent's bait and you've just spent $8100 for a taxicab ride.

The Free Upgrade Dance

Astute readers at this point may wonder, if I don't use an agent, will builders lower their price accordingly? The answer is yes and no. Greedy builders will want to keep the agent's commission. You obviously want all the commission—either in a lower sales price or in "upgrades" that equal the commission. And there's another factor—if word gets around town that builders are selling directly to consumers at lower prices, they will be history. Agents will collectively string up these builders and leave them for dead at the edge of town. And for the average builder who gets 80% of his buyers through agents, giving consumers discounts directly is a dangerous development.

This situation often comes up with semi-custom homes under construction in existing developments, or if you find a partially built "spec" house by a custom builder. If you're going the "custom" route (buying the land, hiring an architect and a builder), it's doubtful you'll have a real estate agent involved.

The first "step" of the Free Upgrade Dance is to learn the "creative accounting" maneuver. Since a builder can't lower the price, perhaps he could give you $8100 more house? That way the builder still sells you the house for the "list price," albeit with nicer stuff inside. Now you've started what we call the Free Upgrade Dance.

A builder may offer you a series of "free" upgrades. Essentially, this is a cat-and-mouse game where you haggle over possible options—upgraded carpeting, a garage door opener, ceiling fan, programmable thermostats, etc.

Be careful. Shrewd builders may try to take advantage of your naivete. If you don't know how much a basic ceiling fan costs, they may try to convince you the ceiling fan is worth $400. This becomes like a bizarre version of "The Price is Right." If you do your homework, you know the average ceiling fan costs about $175. Unless the builder is giving you an expensive brand such as Casablanca (these cost $300 or more), you should haggle the price down closer to $175.

Oh, sure, the builder may say that cost includes "installation." What the builder doesn't tell you is that he may buy the fan at wholesale. How you win the Free Upgrade Dance is to do your homework. Call a local store that sells ceiling fans and find out how much the builder's brand costs. If you can't find the same brand, get a comparable price for similar features and quality. If the store offers installation, find out how much that costs.

It's easy to determine the true costs of some upgrades. Programmable thermostats are available at any hardware store, for example. Other upgrades are more difficult to estimate—if the builder offers to finish part of the basement, how much does that cost? This common upgrade costs about $15 per square foot—hence a 1000-square-foot basement would run $15,000 to finish. Of course, finding out these prices is a little tricky (you may have to call other builders or remodelers for cost estimates).

Would you like to move a wall to make a bedroom bigger? This is even fuzzier in terms of costs. If you have a doubt, ask the builder to show you a bill from a subcontractor that shows how much the "upgrade" costs. It's fair for the builder to add in a certain amount of profit to the sub's bill—10% to 15% is fairly common.

The key is that you must not use an agent. Let's put that into bold caps: **DO NOT USE A REAL ESTATE AGENT TO BUY A NEW HOME.** (The exception: buyer's brokers, whom you'll read about shortly. You can hire one on an hourly basis if need be to negotiate with a production or semi-custom builder.) If a real estate agent merely introduces you to the builder at a cafe, the agent may demand a commission from the builder. We believe that $8100 belongs in your house, not in the agent's bank account.

 Money Bomb #2: Builders who use "exclusive" contracts with agents. *"We saw a 'spec' home that is under construction. Can we approach the builder directly and save the real estate agent's commission?"*

Well, yes and no. While the Free Upgrade Dance sounds easy to master, there is another hidden "money bomb" in the process: the "exclusive" contract some builders have with real estate agents.

Basically, an "exclusive right to sell" listing means the broker gets a commission *even if the builder sells the home directly and the agent plays no role.* The listing agent rakes in the entire commission, since there is no "co-op" or selling agent involved! Isn't that a great deal? Now you see why many real estate agents steer clients toward their own listings—big-time profits.

The key to avoiding this money bomb is to simply contact the builder directly (the building company sign should be in front of the home—if not, check the building permit, which must be posted on the job site). If the builder gives you the bad news that the home is under an "exclusive" contract and he can't sell it to you directly with free upgrades, move on to Plan B.

Offer to buy the house with the agent getting a lower commission, say 3%. Keep the price the same, just have the builder throw in upgrades to equal the other 3% of the commission. (Ask what the commission rate is—it can range from 5% to 7%.)

This is a fair compromise since that's about what the listing agent would get if you were a "standard" buyer who came with another agent. Of course, the real estate agent will probably squeal bloody murder. "How can you do this?" they'll shout with arms flailing wildly.

Reasoning with the agent may be difficult, depending on the market. You might point out that if the agent would like, you could go out there and find another agent to share the half of his or her commission. If all else fails, use a "buyer's broker" agent, which we'll describe later. If you must pay full commission, you should at least have someone on your side of the negotiating table.

We should note that not all builders have "exclusive right to sell" deals with agents. Some builders use "exclusive agency" deals. "What's the difference?" you might say. "They sound the same."

Actually, there's a big difference. "Exclusive agency" contracts give the builder the right to sell the home directly to consumers and pay no commission to the agent. A small semantic difference, but a big difference to you. "Open listings" also let the builder sell the home directly to you.

Be aware that many builders and agents don't know the difference between these terms. Therefore, when you approach the builder, you may want to forget the technical jargon and simply ask whether the contract with the agent allows the builder to sell you the house directly without the agent getting a commission.

Money Bomb #3: Illegal kickbacks.

"We used a real estate agent to purchase a new home. He strongly recommended we use a certain title company and mortgage broker. Later, we learned the agent was getting a kickback. The result was we got bilked out of $2000."

Ever wonder why real estate agents "strongly recommend" you use a particular title company, mortgage broker, or inspector? Agents love to tell you that they have "special" relationships with lenders and title companies that will speed a mortgage application or get your home special attention.

Federal authorities and scammed consumers are now discovering just how "special" those relationships are. Illegal kickbacks to real estate agents are bilking consumers out of thousands of dollars in "under the table" deals.

According to a *Washington Post* column by Kenneth Harney in October 1992, "institutionalized kickbacks are so blatant, according to one federal official, that [illegal payments] are the accepted way of doing business at some firms."

Here's how they work. Mortgage brokers face "routine demands ... to split a portion of their fees with individual realty agents who recommend them to home buyers." The agent gets one-half to one point of the mortgage. For a $150,000 mortgage, that could mean a $1500 kickback to the broker. Who pays for this extra "point"? Who do you think?

Of course, these kickbacks never show up on settlement or truth-in-lending disclosures—a blatant violation of federal law. Another version of the scam are agents who demand kickbacks from title companies. "In one case, a title company admitted paying $120,000 to $130,000 under the table to the head of one real estate brokerage firm over the last several years. The [title company] explained that 'It was the only way we'd get the title work,' according to the investigators."

How widespread is the problem? Well, federal investigators have uncovered so many violations in one area (Philadelphia south to Washington, D.C.) that they issued over 100 subpoenas to real estate agents and others. "Loan brokers in California, the Southwest and the Midwest have reported similar, aggressive [kickback] demands."

The whole reason this happens is the real estate agents' incredible power to hypnotize buyers. Many lull you into submission by repeated references to their "professionalism" and "expertise." Access to the Multiple Listing Service gives them a powerful tool to lure buyers. Agents get quite "chummy" with you as you look at property over several weeks. As the gate-keepers for consumers in the new home market, real estate agents have big power to recommend one loan broker or title company over another. Sadly, some abuse that influence by demanding kickbacks.

Consumers pay for these kickbacks in higher fees for mortgages and title company services. Does every agent get kickbacks? Of course not. But the widespread disease of kickbacks by shady agents has one clear message for consumers: do not solely follow the advice of the agent when it comes to a loan, inspection, or title/closing service. Shop around and compare to make sure you're not getting taken for a ride.

Our Recommendation: Use a Buyer's Broker

If you're going the "power home buyer" route (buying the land, hiring a design professional and then choosing a builder), we do recommend you use a real estate agent for one part of the process—purchasing the lot or building site.

Of course, we don't recommend just any agent. You should seek out a "buyer's broker." What the heck is that, you say?

A buyer's broker is a real estate agent who is working for you, not the seller. He or she is legally responsible for the following:

■ Negotiate the best price and terms for the buyer.

- Identify any negatives of the property or neighborhood—beyond what a seller must disclose.
- May offer to do a comparative market analysis to compare this property to others in the area.
- Possibly negotiate for properties that are for sale by owner or not even on the market.

Who pays the buyer's broker's commission? It might surprise you to learn that, in most cases, it's the seller. The commission on a home (that is paid by the seller) is split between the listing agent and the buyer's broker—just like a standard transaction. Some buyers actually prefer to directly pay the buyer's broker a flat fee. This completely eliminates the conflict of interest so apparent in many real estate deals: the higher the sales price, the higher the agent's commission.

We recommend a buyer's broker in the following situations:

1 *If you're building from scratch and are purchasing a lot, a buyer's broker is probably the best source to find available land.* A buyer's broker can dig for facts that might provide valuable negotiating tools—such as what the seller previously paid for the lot. Finding out how long a property has been on the market and how desperate a seller is to sell also will give you an advantage.

2 *If you're moving into a new area and want to buy a new home, a buyer's broker may tell you the truth about certain neighborhoods and builders.* In Tucson, Arizona, a buyer's broker told a retired couple to pass up a certain home after he found out that the neighbor's teenagers enjoyed loud rock-and-roll music at 2 a.m. Moving to a new town makes you extremely vulnerable to unscrupulous seller's agents who will take advantage of your naivete regarding neighborhoods, traffic and anything else they can think of. A buyer's broker evens the odds.

3 *Say you want to purchase a new home, but don't have the time to wait.* Construction on a new home can take three to six months—and that doesn't include the time to design the plans, buy the lot and so on. If you're in a hurry, a buyer's broker can show you new "spec" homes that are nearing completion for a quick move-in.

Buyer's Brokers: What Will It Cost You?

Arrangements vary, but here are some common methods of compensation:

- *A retainer fee.* Some buyer's brokers charge a retainer of $200 to $700—this is a good-faith gesture on your part. This retainer is often "refundable" (or applied toward the commission) if you buy. The retainer fee confirms that you're a real buyer, not a looker. As one buyer's broker told us, the retainer fee is a down payment on your commitment to buy.

- *Flat fees.* You may set the buyer's broker's commission at 2% to 5% of your *target* price range. If you're purchasing vacant land and have a $35,000 target price, a 4% fee to your broker would run $1400. If you're looking for a buyer's broker who can help you purchase an entire new home, a 4% fee on a $150,000 new house would cost $6000. This fee is fixed—if you decide on a more or less expensive piece of property, the broker gets the same amount of money.
- *Variable commission.* Like a traditional real estate deal, in this case the broker gets a percentage of the final negotiated price. This could also range from 2% to 5%—the higher rate applies to lower-priced homes. Most buyer's brokers get an average commission of 3% to 3.5%.

As we mentioned earlier, this fee is usually paid by the seller. In a few cases, the seller may balk and you may have to come up with this money. However, if the broker negotiated a lower price that saved you money, you may still come out ahead even if you pay the buyer's broker's commission from your own pocket.

 ### Sources to Find Buyer's Brokers

Unfortunately, buyer's brokers are not on every corner in the nation. Experts estimate that only 30,000 to 40,000 of the country's 1.2 million real estate agents exclusively represent buyers. While buyer's brokers are popular in states such as California, Colorado, and Florida, other areas are sadly lacking in this important consumer service.

Buyer's brokers are less common in the Midwest and Northeast. A New Hampshire newspaper article in 1991 said agents there are "slow to embrace the idea." There are very few buyer's broker agents in Cincinnati, according to a recent *Cincinnati Post* article. Among the 3000 Realtors in Cincinnati, only 30 agents are members of a national buyer's broker organization. If you think that's bad, only 25 agents in the entire state of Oregon represent buyers, according to the Oregon State Real Estate Agency. Besides Oregon, states that have few buyer's brokers include New Jersey, Michigan, Montana, and Idaho. The popularity of buyer's brokers is spotty even within certain regions— buyer's brokers in Chicago are booming, while there are very few in Detroit, just a few hundred miles a way.

At the time of this writing, there are only isolated pockets of resistance to the buyer's broker concept. North Carolina (which, as you'll notice later, is the Number One Scam Mecca for real estate) is a place were buyer's brokers are not exactly loved. In that state, seller's agents have been known to blatantly lie to buyers, telling them they will negotiate on the buyer's behalf. However, just down the road in South Carolina, buyer's brokers are going great guns.

Of course, just because buyer's brokers are rare in some areas doesn't mean there are none available to help you. It may be well worth the effort to search for them in your area. Here are some sources:

1 **Buyer's Resource (1-800-359-4092).** This Denver-based company has 40 offices in 13 states that specialize in buyer's brokers. If you don't live in one of those states, they also have a referral network of over 500 buyer's brokers across the country. There's no charge for a referral and the company will answer any questions you have about the buyer's broker process. If you want to learn more about buyer's brokers, the company also sponsors consumer seminars in several cities.

2 **Buyer's Broker Registry** is a book by George Rosenberg that lists more than 500 buyer's brokers across the country. Brokers are screened to make sure they are real buyer's brokers. In addition to the listings, several articles teach you about buyer's brokers, including what to look for in hiring a good agent. Cost: $25 plus $2.90 shipping. To order, call 1-800-729-5147. If you don't want to purchase the book, you can get a free referral of a buyer's broker in your area by calling that same number.

Questions to Ask

1 **How long have you been a buyer's broker?** While this is still a relatively new phenomenon, some agents have more experience than others.

2 **What percentage of your business is representing buyers as a buyer's broker?** The higher, the better. The best buyer's brokers are those who do this exclusively—they don't accept listings nor do they ever accept "subagency" commissions, thus representing the seller.

3 **Does your firm take listings from sellers?** Ideally, the best situation is a buyer's broker who works for a firm that only does buyer's brokerage. The reality is that some buyer's brokers work within "traditional" firms that also take listings from sellers. The problem, as is often the case with traditional brokers, is that the broker might only push the firm's listings. The conflict of interest is obvious, and you should steer clear of anyone who claims to be a buyer's broker and then pitches you on his or her firm's seller listings.

4 **Can I have a written agreement?** True buyer's brokers will provide a written agreement covering compensation and their responsibilities to you. Get in writing the broker's commitment to renounce subagency commissions (in which the broker represents the seller).

5 **What are the pluses and minuses of a certain neighborhood?** If you've already identified a few potential locations for your new home, ask the broker about the pros AND cons of certain areas. A true buyer's broker will candidly lay it on the line.

6 *Can you recommend a good inspector who is familiar with new construction, the local building code, and common defects?* This is a trick question—a good buyer's broker should giv e you not just one name but *several* possible candidates. Be aware that finding a good inspector who knows what he or she is doing is a very difficult challenge for many buyer's brokers—there are so many inspectors who are used to rubber-stamping homes in order to curry favor with seller's agents.

7 *What type of negotiation training do you have?* The fact is you're hiring someone to negotiate a very expensive purchase for you—it'd be nice if that person had some professional training in negotiation. Another good question: what training did you have in general as a buyer's broker? Any training in identifying the negatives of a property as well as the positives? Sure, it's easy to talk up the amenities of a piece of land or new home. The real pros are trained to spot weaknesses and talk frankly about them.

8 *Will you keep my financial information and price range confidential?* Of course, this is a trick question. Any true buyer's broker is legally bound to keep this information confidential. However, traditional agents MUST disclose this to a seller. Any alleged "buyer's broker" who says he or she must disclose your information to the seller is not really a buyer's broker. They're frauds.

9 *Could I have the names of three to five of your most recent customers?* Call these past customers to see whether the buyer's broker is fulfilling his promises.

Controversy: Where Should the Money Come From?

There is a split opinion in the buyer's broker ranks as to "where" the money should come from for their services. If you buy a $100,000 home and the buyer's broker wants a 3% commission, who pays it? Does the seller pay this out of the home's proceeds? Or does the buyer write out a separate check?

Philosophically, all the money comes from you, the home buyer. So, we're less concerned with reality than with the semantics. And those semantics are important because they have important financial and tax considerations.

In the real world, the seller pays the buyer's broker commission about 99% of the time. That means your purchase of the $100,000 home is contingent on the seller paying your buyer's broker a 3% commission. This is good for a couple of reasons:

1 *Most sellers don't mind.* Interestingly, more than 80% of sellers think all brokers who work with buyers are "buyer's brokers"! And, of course, they're used to paying for the agent who finds a buyer. The reality is most sellers are happy to talk with any agent (even a buyer's broker) who finds a qualified buyer.

2 *If the commission is part of the purchase price, you can finance it with your mortgage.* If you pay it out of your own pocket, you can't.

Detractors of this practice say it builds a "conflict of interest" into the deal—the bigger the purchase price, the higher the buyer's broker's commission. But isn't that person suppose to negotiate the lowest price for you? Shouldn't the money come from the buyer's wallet, instead of the seller's proceeds?

The reality is that buyer's brokers make their living from representing buyers—if they don't do a good job (say, not negotiating the best price), they don't stay in business long. A buyer's broker would rather trade off the slightly lower commission and get new client referrals from that buyer.

Flat fees and "target price" commissions paid by the buyer are nice but rarely used in the real world. Most buyer's brokers work on a "traditional" commission of the actual purchase price—that comes from the seller. If you find one that offers a flat fee or target price option, that's fine as well.

Granted, you also may be in an area where buyer's brokerage is so new that sellers and their agents are balking at sharing or paying commissions to a buyer's broker. Most nettlesome are greedy "traditional" agents who want the entire 6% to 7% for themselves—refusing to pay buyer's brokers the typical split. They argue, "why should we pay someone working against our interests?" Fortunately, this is the exception and occurs only in a few places.

By the way, there is one exception to the rule of the seller paying the buyer's broker commission: In northern Virginia, buyer's brokers must be paid out of the selling agent's commission (not from the seller, directly).

Money Bombs with Buyer's Brokers

Money Bomb #1: Dual agents.
"We hired a buyer's broker who then tried to pitch us on a listing by another broker at his firm. He said he couldn't act as our broker on that property—he could only be a dual agent. Is this a rip-off or what?"

We believe it's a definite rip-off. A "dual agent" is a new euphemism used by real estate agents when they pitch you a property listed by a fellow agent in their firm. Dual agents (also known as "facilitators," another slick term) allegedly represent both the seller and the buy Are they kidding? This is a hostile negotiation in which the wants to get the highest price and to disclose the least amour ative information. A buyer wants the lowest price and nee all the flaws. How can an agent play both sides? The best buyer's brokers are from firms that do nothing but specialize in buyer's brokerage—they take no listings from sellers.

Money Bomb #2: Turf battles

"A buyer's broker found us a wonderful new home—we decided to make a bid. The builder's agent discouraged the builder from taking our offer, saying that our buyer's broker was corrupt! What happened?"

Welcome to the turf battles in the real estate business. Many traditional agents have resisted buyer's brokers to the point of trying to sabotage deals. This can range from small-time harassment (such as accidentally forgetting an appointment to meet with a buyer's broker) to major damage—actively encouraging builders or property owners to reject bids from consumers who use buyer's brokers.

The fact is that real estate agents have been working overtime to try to kill buyer's brokers. National trade associations have made concerted efforts to "stymie, suppress, and mislead" consumers' knowledge about buyer's brokerage, a leading proponent of buyer agency told us. This attitude filters down to the front line, where a few agents carry this turf battle to absurd ends.

Builders also work to stop buyers from having protection from construction scams. While some agree to pay the buyer's broker's commission, builders refuse to sign documents that acknowledge the agent is representing the buyer. This effectively helps kill any deal.

Money Bomb #3: Counterfeit buyer's brokers.

"When we searched for a new home, we found a buyer's broker who was willing to work for us. After four weeks, we discovered the broker was refusing to look for lower-priced homes on our behalf. He also pitched us on listings from his firm. We fired him."

And you should. The recent surge in popularity of buyer's brokers has flooded the field with "counterfeit" agents who claim they're working for buyers. The reality is that some of these folks have no idea what representing the buyer really means—they just want a quick commission. You can usually spot fake buyer's brokers when they fail to look hard for lower-priced properties. Others will not "dig for the dirt," failing to provide you with potential pitfalls about certain properties. Most counterfeit buyer's brokers will not put your

Money Bomb #4: The shortage of land "specialists."
"We're having a devil of a time finding a buyer's broker who knows anything about local building sites. No one seems to specialize in vacant land."

Buyer's brokerage is still in its infancy and, in some places, it may be hard to find a buyer's broker who is familiar with vacant land or building sites for new homes. Of course, it's sometimes hard to find any buyer's brokers at all—those that are out there may only specialize in existing (read: old) houses.

Another problem is the fact that many building sites or open lots are not listed in the Multiple Listing Service (MLS). Lazy brokers just rely on this book as a one-stop shopping alternative for their clients—hence you may miss some of the best properties. The best brokers are tied into networking groups of builders and developers who may have land available that is not listed in the MLS. Other lots may be for sale by owner—and these take some effort for a broker to identify. Some of the best deals may be for lots that aren't even on the market—the best buyer's broker should have no problem in approaching property owners about the possibility of selling.

That's the secret to the power of buyer's brokers—they can negotiate for property that is invisible to the radar scopes of the MLS. Sure, a regular real estate agent can ask property owners whether they want to sell their house or lot—but this agent must require that the seller pay the agent's commission. This is a major negative for the seller. Buyer's brokers are assured of being paid by buyers, freeing them to go out there and negotiate with any seller.

The bottom line: even though it may be a hassle, you should still try to find a buyer's broker. If you're purchasing a lot or building site, this may be a long search. If a partially built "spec" house is your goal, it still pays to have a buyer's broker despite the roadblocks some builders will try to throw in your way.

Tips for Dealing with Regular Real Estate Agents

Okay, let's assume that you're in Small Town, USA. And, frankly, there isn't a buyer's broker within 200 miles. (Actually, this can happen in big cities as well.) What do you do now?

You may be inclined to contact a real estate agent regarding a partially built home you see in an attractive neighborhood. Or there's a certain development of "semi-custom" homes that hits your hot button. The fact is that sooner or later you may come face to face with a real estate agent. Here are some cardinal rules to remember if you want to survive the encounter with your wallet intact.

1 ***Don't trust them.*** Sure this sounds paranoid, but, hey, it's your money. Treat everything the agent says with extreme suspicion. If the agent mentions that an elementary school is just three blocks away, go and make sure it's still there. And confirm that it isn't about

---

A Brief History of Real Estate Agents

6 million BC: God searches for a planet to establish life. Encounters real estate agent from "Lucifer's Planets & Gardens" who says, "I've got a great deal on a fixer-upper just 90 million miles from the sun."

5.9 million BC: God buys the Earth and, after the closing, discovers it is a mass of molten goo. Angry, God confronts the agent and banishes him to spend an eternity wearing polyester suits.

4 million BC: God creates the oceans and the seas. By accident, a pool of pond scum transforms itself into the National Association of Realtors.

3.5 million BC: God creates Florida.

3.49 million BC: Thousands of real estate agents crawl out of the ocean to scout good condo locations. Market immediately crashes when agents realize that "snow birds" won't be invented for another 2 million years.

3 million BC: A meteor crashes into Earth. The resulting crater creates a giant black hole filled with green ooze. The Multiple Listing Service is born.

2.45 million BC: God makes Adam and Eve. However, delays in constructing Garden of Eden force Adam and Eve to live in an apartment for eight months.

2.44 million BC: Shopping for a move-up garden, Eve visits an Open Garden and encounters a fork-tongued real estate agent who tells her, "Garden, why would you want another one of those? I've got an entire apple orchard you can have real cheap."

2.43 million BC: Adam and Eve become the first humans to truly understand what it means to buy from a real estate agent.

550 BC: Jealous of rising property values, real estate brokers in Greece devise a way to attack Troy by using a Trojan horse.

42 BC: Cleopatra decides to build the pyramids. Real estate agent and builder try to convince her that squares would be much cheaper.

30 BC: Rome touted as "the hottest housing market in Europe." Thousands of buyers flock in.

---

to be closed. Smile politely at the agent, but keep your hands on your wallet. Anything the agent tells you about the house or lot should be viewed as a bald-faced lie until proven otherwise.

Above all, do not take the agent's recommendations for an inspector, title company or mortgage lender. Ask the agent who he or she recommend, so you can *avoid* these businesses.

  Keep your cards close to your chest. Do not reveal your target price range when the agent asks. Simply say that the

29 BC: Rome real estate crashes. Julius Caesar calls a meeting of his advisors to see what can be done. Chief real estate broker Brutus suggests Caesar tours Rome to inspire consumer confidence. "Just lead the way," Brutus says, "I'll be right behind you."

500 AD: Middle Ages bring major real estate slowdown. Agents are forced to take second jobs as undertakers. Scandal breaks out when agents are discovered to be removing gold fillings from dead people.

1308 AD: Real estate agent lists a tower in Pisa, Italy, as a "one-of-a-kind property. Solid building guaranteed not to lean."

1492 AD: Christopher Columbus lands in America. However, he mistakenly believes he's in India, thanks to a bogus land survey provided by a Spanish real estate broker.

1620 AD: Pilgrims land on Plymouth Rock. First colonial real estate agent promises Pilgrims that Massachusetts is "always sunny and warm. Never drops below 70 degrees—I swear."

1621 AD: Giant blizzard nearly wipes out Pilgrims. Real estate agent is banished to New Jersey.

1626 AD: Manhattan bought from the Indians for 100 beads and trinkets. The Indians' real estate agent takes 6 beads as a commission.

1803 AD: Napoleon shocks and angers French real estate agents when he sells Louisiana to United States without an agent. At $15 million, sets record for largest "Fizbo" (for sale by owner) sale in history.

1867 AD: United States purchases Alaska from Russia for 2¢ an acre, after Russian czar is given advice by real estate agent that Alaska is "utterly useless" land with no value at all.

TO BE CONTINUED . . .

house or lot you're looking at now is within your means. Whatever you do, *never* tell a seller's agent what your income or financial status is. Don't reveal any deadlines or time pressures that you face, such as, "I must make a decision by the end of this weekend." The more desperate you look, the easier target you become. Play it cool and give the agent as little information about yourself as possible. We realize it's hard to talk to an agent and not reveal your price range or intentions, but remember that this information is passed right on to sellers.

3 | ***Get prequalified from a lender.*** This is a sign to the agent that "you're ready and able to buy." Of course, don't tell the agent how big of a loan you've qualified for—that gives the agent the opportunity to sell you a more expensive house.

4 | ***Don't let your guard slip.*** The agent may show you several new homes or building sites. Over several weeks, the agent will try to charm the pants off you. She or he may take you out to dinner and loosen you up with small talk. Watch out—the moment you let your guard down and reveal sensitive information, you're a dead duck. No matter how sweet the agent is, he or she is legally required to reveal any information that is wrangled out of you to the seller/builder. Resisting this may take an iron constitution, but the agent's charm factor is a major way consumers later get stung.

5 | ***Answer the agent's questions with questions.*** When the agent asks, "Is this home big enough for you?" you could respond, "Does the builder offer other size options?" You haven't revealed any information about your situation, but have turned the question around.

The only exception to this rule is "qualifying" questions. A good agent wants to make sure you're not wasting his or her time. Hence, the agent may ask whether you've pre-qualified for a loan and how much. You can simply respond "yes," omitting any mention of the amount of loan you've qualified for.

Always ask yourself whether you're being manipulated and controlled by the agent. Answering the agent's questions with questions of your own is a good way to be in control.

6 | ***Keep the agent offbalance with technical questions.*** Most agents have shockingly little knowledge about the properties they sell. You show you're in control when you fire several technical barbs at the agent. Asking questions about the brand names of the heating/cooling system or the windows is a good start. Having the agent comment on the type and adequacy of insulation or the structural soundness of the foundation is something that will make an agent's head spin. This strategy is to keep the agent on the defensive and apologetic ("I'm sorry I don't know the answer to that question, I'll have to ask the builder"). Having the agent constantly justify why the builder has chosen this feature over another keeps them off balance. This works to your advantage later in the negotiations.

By the way, any agent (except buyer's brokers) is responsible if she makes any misrepresentations about the home or property. Ultimately, the builder is liable for these goofs. It's this liability issue that is making builders and sellers more accommodating to buyer's brokers—because builders aren't liable for any statements those guys make.

7 | ***Zap agents with trick questions.*** If you ask the agent about the builder's quality, he or she will almost always reply, "He's the best in the area." You reply, "Is that so? I heard he's had some quality problems and some previous buyers are not that happy." Now you've just set up the agent. He might reply, "That can't be true, those people must be mistaken. Sure, there was one person who wasn't happy with the furnace, but that was fixed by the subcontractor. If you buy from this builder, I'll personally see to it that you're satisfied. If you'd like, I'll arrange for a free upgrade on the carpet." Now you've gotten an implied promise from the agent that he'll help you. Nail the agent with the following: "Is that a promise that you'll help resolve any difficulty? Did the builder switch brands of furnaces after that problem? What type of carpet upgrade?" Your goal is to uncover information he wouldn't normally disclose—notice the furnace confession.

8   ***Treat the agents like dogs.*** Praise them when they do a good deed ("I really appreciate you running down that brand name on the windows for me"). Scold agents when they goof ("You said the basement is 1500 square feet. The literature says it's just 1000—if you continue to give me erroneous information, I'll give my business to another agent I met yesterday"). Test the salesperson's honesty by verifying a known negative about the property ("I understand there's been some flooding in the neighborhood. Is that true?").

9   ***Remember, if you buy a defective house, you're stuck.*** There's no return policy with new homes. If a builder fails to stand behind her work, an expensive legal battle will saddle you with big legal fees and headaches. The agent's only concern is to close the deal—make sure you check out the property and the neighborhood thoroughly. Remember our "paper, scissors, rock" strategy to buying or building a new home to maximize your protection.

 If you have any questions or comments on this chapter, please feel free to call the authors. See the "How to Reach Us" page at the back of this book!

6

House by Design

Considering how expensive houses are today, it would sure be nice if the home actually suited your needs, wants and lifestyle. The process of designing the right home for you can be challenging.

Of course, houses don't just appear on command—there must be a plan. And somebody must draw that plan. Basically, new home buyers have four options today: the builder as designer, plan books, designer/drafting services and professional architects.

1 ***Builder as Designer.*** In our opinion, this is your WORST CHOICE. Left to their own devices, many builders would plaster the country with look-alike homes decorated in mind-numbing earth tones. If you look at many of the cookie-cutter subdivisions that dot this country, you'll discover why builders should be banned from designing.

Some builders actually design their homes by themselves, as opposed to hiring an architect or designer to help them. This would work fine, except for the fact that most builders aren't trained in design. A simple drafting course does not make them a designer or architect, just as a tool belt doesn't make me an expert carpenter.

Many builders simply rely on past homes they've built for design ideas ("It worked the last time—let's do it again"). This inbreeding of design perhaps led to the sorry shape of home design today. Builders may pitch you their own design services more for their convenience than, your benefit. First, it's easy for lazy builders. Second, there's no architect working for you who's looking over the builder's shoulder. No architect means no design elements (such as a fancy archway) that are beyond the builder's skill level.

Other builders hire low-paid design staffs to churn out cookie-cutter "production" homes built with all the care of an assembly-line product.

Imagination? Sparkle? Forget it. You basically get a "home-in-a-box."

Even more scary are builders who simply wing it "in the field." They actually think it's possible to take an empty lot and create the perfect house—all from vague sketches or no plans at all. Once they get a crude set of plans approved by the building department, they then make dozens of "field changes" that could dangerously affect the structural integrity of the home.

For buyers considering a tract or production home, there's little choice—you get the builder's plans and that's that. Semi-custom and custom home buyers have more choices—but beware of the builders who pitch their design services. The resulting design is often just "dimension plans": you get a rough layout of the rooms and that's it. For example, there's an opening specified for a door, but no mention of what type and quality of door you're getting. Dimension plans often are missing separate framing, electrical, and plumbing/heating plans—making the prospect of dangerous and costly field changes more likely. The lack of specifications (what exact windows? doors? faucets? trim?) opens you up to the biggest rip-off of all: substitution of cheaper materials. Want a nicer faucet? Well, there's an "upgrade fee" that you usually find out about late in the ball game.

The bottom line: Builders should build, not design. Our advice is to be wary of any builder who pitches you on his or her design "skills." You appear to "save" the fees that a professional architect or designer would charge (anywhere from 4% to 12% of the final price), but that savings could vanish if any of the following money bombs explode on your house.

A Word about Tract Homes

The tract home appears to be a one-stop shopping alternative where the builder has decided for you what the design will be. The hip trend with tract builders now is to offer you the ability to "customize" the house. Customizing might include changing the size of rooms or adding higher-end options, such as a whirlpool tub.

One builder told us he is willing to change anything in his houses except load-bearing walls to offer customers a choice. Often, however, there is an additional charge for these changes and options—be sure to check on this *before* you make any agreements and get *all* changes in a written contract.

We should note that several of the best tract builders do hire top-notch architects to design their homes. While this may ensure a good design on paper, it doesn't mean it's followed in the field or that you get quality materials.

Money Bomb #1: Hassle-free building.

"We thought it would be so easy to buy a tract-style home in a planned development. Well, it was easy, but we are paying for it now. The builder put in cheap windows—now, just three years later, we have to replace them at a cost of $5000."

Perhaps the biggest reason builders prefer to design houses themselves is because they won't have to contend with an architect looking over their shoulder, correcting anything that isn't according to the plans. Unscrupulous builders like the ability to substitute inferior, cheaper products during construction in order to improve their profit margins—an architect or private inspector will keep that from happening, as we'll discuss later.

Money Bomb #2: Omission by design.

"The builder on our $120,000 semi-custom home implied we were to get top-of-the-line plumbing fixtures and faucets. Unfortunately, the plans had no mention of the exact brand. We later found out the builder put in cheap, builder-grade fixtures."

As is so often the case, the plans provided by the builder are so incomplete that consumers aren't quite sure what they are buying. For example, the plans may not specify whether the builder will use "2x6 construction" rather than "2x4 construction." 2x4 means the exterior walls are about four inches thick. A better option is 2x6, where six-inch thick deep walls allow for more and better insulation. Two-byfour construction might save a little money now, but could cost you money down the road when those heating or cooling bills come in.

Do builders intentionally leave such details off their plans? It's hard to tell whether builders do this because of incompetence or outright fraud. Without the proper training, builders may not be able to delve into the level of detail that a professional can do. On the other hand, such "omissions" may be intentional to keep you, the consumer, in the dark about what you are buying.

All of this contributes to the air of absurdity that goes with buying a new home. Can you imagine spending a similar amount of money on another product that the seller refused to identify?

Money Bomb #3: Charging for changes.

"We got charged $200 for a goof our builder made—he failed to draw the furnace ventilation system correctly on the plans. Halfway through the construction, we got billed for an extra soffit. Ouch!"

The more detail you have in your plans, the harder it is for the builder to make "field changes." Field changes are just what they sound like—changes to the house made after building starts. Because subcontractors may charge builders for such spur-of-the-moment changes to the house, this cost gets passed on to you in the form of a higher sales price.

Complete and detailed plans (we'll discuss what makes plans complete later in this chapter) greatly lower the opportunity for this rip-off.

2 **Plan books.** Visit any bookstore or newsstand and you'll probably encounter plan books. Basically, these publications are page after page of home designs. Each design gives you a picture of what the house is supposed to look like, plus rough layouts of the rooms.

The publishers of these publications don't make their money selling books—the real bucks come from selling the plans, which cost $250 to $500 a pop. But what do you get for that money?

Basically, you receive "complete" blueprints for a new home. This includes designs for a foundation, floor plans, "exterior elevations" (the outside views of the house), interior elevations and cross sections, roof plans and schematic electrical layouts. You may also get a list of general specifications. On the plus side, these plans provide a quick and cheap way to get a home design.

Critics point out that the quality of these plans varies dramatically—some are more complete than others. If you decide to go this route, make sure you get a money-back guarantee. Charge the purchase to a credit card, as well. If you discover the plans are defective or incomplete and the plan book company refuses to refund your money, you may be able to reverse the charge on your card.

Another problem: Most plans are designed for flat lots. In the real world, lots are rarely perfect. The plan may show the house with a window in what looks like a perfect location, but when placed on your lot, it looks onto an ugly, neighboring home.

Also you may want to note the fine print in plan books. If you want to make changes to the design, the books urge you to consult only with an architect for "major changes or alterations." The fact is most buyers who use these plans end up modifying them in both major and minor ways. This seems to defeat the plan books' major selling point that they're saving you all this money in architect fees.

In the real world, we found few architects who modified these plans. Who does the changes? It's often the builder, whose entire design "experience" is basically limited to rudimentary drafting skills. This exposes the buyer to major risks if the builder goofs. And builders often charge you $500 to $1000 for their time to modify the plans. Given these facts, it may make more sense to forget the plan books and just hire a real architect to design a house that fits you and the lot.

 Money Bomb #1: Off-the-rack houses.
"We purchased a house plan from a plan book. The design just had a crawl-space foundation—but we wanted a full basement. The builder ended up charging us another $600 to draw a foundation plan."

The Achilles heel of plan books is the "off-the-rack" house problem. Basically, consumers find they're buying a plan that doesn't fit their needs. The costs to fix or modify it may run more than the plan itself.

3 **Designer/Drafting Services.** What is a designer? How does this person differ from an architect? To understand this, you should first realize that an architect must be licensed by the state in which he or she practices. The licensing requirements vary, but most states require certified training and several years of experience.

Unfortunately, architects aren't the only individuals allowed to design houses. In most states, anyone can design homes and call herself a house "designer" without having a license. The only prohibition is that such designers cannot refer to themselves as architects.

The experience of home designers can vary widely. Some are newly minted architectural graduates working toward certification. Others have taken a drafting course and have grand delusions of being great designers. Occasionally, designers join forces to form a drafting service firm.

Such companies usually offer "limited" architectural services—they basically just draw the plans. It's up to you to find and negotiate with a builder, as well as to monitor the construction.

The chief advantage to these companies is that they're much cheaper than hiring an architect—designers' fees to design a home are about one-quarter to one-half of what an architect charges. Critics point out that you get about one-quarter of the quality that a professional would deliver. And there's more to building a home than just drawing a blueprint—negotiating with builders and monitoring the construction (services most designers don't offer) are key elements as well.

In a few states such as California and Florida, design services are popular alternatives to architects. In Florida, there is actually a state registry for designers.

Some states require an architect and/or engineer to stamp a designer's plans with their professional certification to ensure that the home is structurally sound. Designers get around this requirement by having a friend who's an architect or engineer provide the stamp. Some of these architects will look at the plans carefully, while other simply "rubber stamp" them for a fee.

 ### Money Bomb #1: Lack of expertise.
We heard of one horror story involving an inexperienced designer in Columbus, North Carolina. The designer had just moved from Massachusetts, where she designed and built Colonial-style houses.

She charged the home buyer $1800 for plans and a whopping $6000 for supervision of the construction. The only hitch: she had no experience with North Carolina building customs and procedures. When major problems cropped up, the designer shrugged her shoulders and said "Well, that's not how we did things in Cape Cod, but I guess that's how it's done here."

The result: a seriously defective home that has racked up more than $100,000 in repair bills. The cause: an inexperienced designer and an incompetent builder. After viewing a videotape of this house, we're certain this designer knew little if anything about construction.

4 *Architects.* All of the above options (builders, plan books and designers/drafting services) are poor substitutes for the real thing: the residential architect. After investigating all the alternatives, it's our opinion that the best person to design your home is an experienced residential architect. In a nutshell, here are the key reasons:

- *Experts at design.* This is perhaps the biggest reason people give for using an architect—and it should be. After all, architects go to school for years to learn how to design a functional living space. When you walk into a house designed by a good residential architect, you'll know it. Don't forget about resale value as well—we often see ads for existing homes that tout they are "professionally designed by an architect."

- *Complete Plans.* In contrast to some blueprints provided by plan books, a trained, residential architect will provide a complete set of plans including spec lists, inside and outside elevations, cross sections, etc. The level of detail is often extensive—instead of just drawing a fireplace symbol, an architect will draw the exact fireplace, complete with mantel. Exact door types will be provided instead of just "rough opening" sizes. With most architects, this level of detail is standard procedure. Also, as we mentioned above, complete detailed plans help limit the number of field changes (and change orders), saving you time and money.

- *Consultation with structural engineers for the foundation and structural elements.* This is crucial to ensure a proper foundation for your house. Faulty foundations are at the core of many defective construction horror stories—hence, the more careful the design, the better. Most architects will consult with an engineer to ensure your foundation is designed properly. Some architects have engineers on their staff and still others have engineering backgrounds themselves. Don't underestimate the importance of a proper foundation—forget about the kitchen cabinets or decorator tile. If the underpinnings of your home are crumbling or improperly designed, you're sunk.

- *Periodic inspections of the construction to ensure that the builder is following the plans.* The work of most full-service architects doesn't stop at drawing the plans—many continue to work with you to monitor the construction. Inspections when the footings/foundation are poured, framing is finished and interior finishing is completed are most common. The exact number of inspections varies from architect to architect. Some don't offer construction monitoring at all; others offer the service but, unfortunately, don't have a lot of experience. Depending on the cost of the house, you may want to hire a private inspector to double-check the construction as well.

Money Bomb #1: The occasional house designer.

"A friend of ours is a commercial architect who designs office buildings. He offered to design our home, but the results were disastrous! The home fell way short of our expectations."

Architects who do mostly commercial work and an occasional residence can be trouble. If an architect's business is more than 50% or 60% commercial, look somewhere else. Frankly, unless an architect spends at least half her time working with residential clients, she is going to be out of touch with costs, techniques, technology and trends in residential housing. As a result, the "occasional house designer" may not be able to suggest which materials/designs are cost-effective and within your budget.

Interestingly, architectural schools tend to emphasize commercial work over residential. Some of the brightest architectural talents are steered away from residential design. Other architects find commercial design (schools, shopping centers andthe like) to be more financially rewarding and less frustrating than the tumultuous world of residential real estate. As a result, there are just a few really good and experienced residential architects in most metro areas.

Money Bomb #2: Architects who live on the Planet of Unrealistic Costs.

"We instructed our architect to design us a $150,000 house. A design was completed and sent out to bid with several local builders. We were shocked at the result! The bids all came in at $200,000 or more!"

What happened? You've encountered an architect who spends too much time on the Planet of Unrealistic Costs. Unfamiliar with local costs and trends, he or she whips out a lovely design that's *way* over your budget. The resulting plans must be redrawn ... a considerable waste of time and money for everyone involved.

Of course, understanding local construction costs isn't as easy as it seems. Staying up-to-date on material costs that can fluctuate daily and on new methods that can lower costs is quite a task. Nonetheless, such experienced architects actually exist and are obviously worth searching out.

We recommend you ask the architect how long he's been designing homes in your area and about his experience in estimating costs. How close do the architect's designs hit the budget mark when costed out to builders?

As a professional, an architect has a responsibility to stick with a budget (plus or minus 8%). If an architect blows it and designs you a white elephant, the plans should be redrawn at his expense. Any reputable architect should agree to this in writing.

Money Bomb #3: The out-of-towner.

"We live in a small town and are thinking of building a home. There is one architect in our town and he does nice work ... but, we heard great things about another architect who lives 80 miles away. Are there any problems with hiring an out-of-town architect?"

Most architects live in big cities. If you aren't planning to build in or near a large city, you may find the architectural pickings slim. Hence, some buyers hire an architect who lives out of town—some even contract with professionals who are outside the state.

The problem: A Boston architect may be an expert at building customs, codes and prices in Massachusetts, but may be a fish out of water trying to do a vacation home in Maine. The skill and knowledge level required to pull this off are rather high.

Some architects get around this problem by consulting with local experts. For example, a local engineer who's familiar with soil conditions can help design the foundation plan.

Obviously, monitoring the construction is much more difficult when you're long distance. We have noted this problem in several cases. For example, a Florida home buyer we interviewed hired an out-of-town architect to design her $600,000 beach front home. When problems cropped up, the buyer sided with the "local" builder who convinced the buyer that the architect's design was flawed. Since the architect was 100 miles away, he couldn't adequately defend himself or his design. So the buyer fired the architect.

Big mistake. The builder turned out to be a con artis, whose incompetent construction led to a nightmare. When he finished the home, 19 of the 23 windows leaked. The roof was defectively installed causing more leaks. Giant cracks appeared in the exterior, thanks to a faulty foundation. Total bill for repairs: $300,000.

Not all consumers who hire out-of-town architects have such disastrous results. Hiring a local private inspector (such as a licensed engineer or retired contractor) to monitor the construction lowers the chance of problems (the above homeowner didn't do this). However, our first preference would be to hire a "local" architect before searching out of town.

What Will It Cost You?

Builder/designers will charge anything from $0 to $1000 to develop plans for a new home. If you use a "stock plan" the builder has already designed, the cost is usually nothing. Modifying the plan may incur additional costs for redrafting, etc.

Plans purchased from *plan books* cost from $200 to $450 for one set of plans and up to $550 for seven sets of plans. You will probably need to purchase several sets—one for the lender, three for the builder, two for the building department, and one for your own use. (Ask your builder for recommendations on this.)

One negative about plan books is the extra costs. For example, if you want an itemized list of materials, that's an extra $30. A description of materials for use in obtaining FHA/VA financing is $25, while a surcharge to reverse the plans (so the house is a mirror image of the plan book) is another $25. The "how-to diagrams for suggested framing and wiring" are an extra $12.50, and even postage is another $12 to $15 extra. Add up all the costs and you could easily top $500.

Designers and drafting services charge in the range of $200 to $1000 for a set of plans. **Architects** average about 4% to 15% of the home's cost. The lower figure is for "bare-bones," design-only services. In the most expensive housing markets, a full-service architect could run 12% to 15% of the home's cost. However, the average for full-service (design through construction supervision) runs 6% to 8%. For a $150,000 home, this would cost $9000 to $12,000.

One cardinal rule to remember about new home design is that you're paying for the design one way or another. Even production builders who have "stock" plans are charging you for the design—they've just built the cost into the price of the home. Granted, many production builders spread the cost of one design over 50 or more homes. That's how they can sell those tract homes for comparatively lower prices than true custom homes.

Remember, however, that the quality doesn't necessarily correspond to the price, especially with builder/designers. In one case we researched, a builder wanted to charge $600 for a bare-bones, dimensions-only plan. Only by shopping around for several alternatives will you be able to understand the quality differences. And don't forget the hidden costs of trying to go too cheap—the money you might save could be far out-weighed by future surprises.

Step-by-Step Strategies: Designing the House

 If you're designing a house from scratch and are planning to use an architect or other design professional, here are the steps in the design process.

Step 1: Ideas. Before you meet with a design professional, it's a good strategy to get some ideas of what you like. Home and decorating magazines are excellent sources. Floor plan designs from plan books are too limiting—most designers and architects prefer you to think in terms of "spaces," not boxes. Hence, a magazine picture of a bay window or the perfect kitchen is more helpful than a floor plan. Also, put together a list of "needs versus wants" to help the architect key in on your requirements.

Step 2: Getting to know you. At the first meeting, discuss briefly what your project will be, answering any basic questions. Most design professionals should ask you for a budget. Try to get a feel for the architect's style by asking a few key questions (listed earlier in Chapter

3) and looking at some past designs. Also, ask about the services offered and the corresponding prices.

Step 3: Show and tell. Look at homes the architect/designer has recently completed, as well as homes under construction. Remember that some cosmetic details are often the owner's choice, not necessarily the architect's. Focus on how the spaces in the house are arranged. Is traffic flow logical? Are the rooms pleasant to walk through? How did the designer utilize natural light? From the outside, do the different exterior elements look in balance? How is the "curb appeal," the first impression you get when driving up?

Step 4: Check references. This step is extremely important—don't skip it. When talking to a reference, ask yes-or-no questions like: Did the designer meet your deadlines? Did he or she stay within your budget? How familiar was the architect with local builders? Did the monitoring of construction meet your expectations? Add any other questions that relate to your project.

Step 5: Get a bid. Ask the designer to give you an estimate on the cost of his or her service, including all the necessary construction documents. Extra services such as bidding/negotiation to builders and supervision of construction should be clearly delineated. Ruminate on the bid for a week or so before rushing into a decision.

Step 6: Hire the designer. See Chapter 8, "The Paper Trai,l" for general information about contracts. Our recommendation is to use the contract from the American Institute of Architects (AIA). Architects who are members of the AIA (and even some of those who aren't) should have copies.

Step 7: Lifestyle questionnaire. The next step is a detailed discussion of your ideas about the new home. (This is also known as programming.) Many architects will give you a questionnaire to help you focus on your "needs and wants." Heidi Richardson of Richardson Architects in San Francisco has an excellent lifestyle questionnaire. Here are some sample questions:

- **Site design:** What views are important? What do you not want to see? What's the home's relationship to neighbors in terms of view, noise and privacy? Any outdoor activities such as hot tub, garden, play areas, entertaining?
- **Kitchen/dining room:** How much cooking is done at home and who does it? What kind of entertaining do you do (small or large groups)? Focus on where you are going to eat (nook or dining room) plus whether the use of the dining room is casual or formal. How much storage is needed for food in the kitchen?

- **Living/family room:** What will happen in the living/family rooms? Separate rooms? What furniture do you have that you want to accommodate?

- **Main/master bedroom:** How private? How much time do you spend in it besides sleeping? Should master bath/dressing areas be directly off it? How large should the closets be (compared to your current situation)?

- **Master bath:** Separate shower, tub or special features like bidets? Separate sinks for his-and-her use? Do you use the bathroom just for washing and cleaning or do you spend time in it? Should the closet be off the bath or off the master bedroom?

- **Other bedrooms/bathrooms:** How many extra bedrooms and whom are they for? Size of beds and needed storage? Home office? Does each bedroom need its own bath? Separate powder room near main living areas?

- **Storage:** Will everyone's belongings fit the proposed closets/cabinets? Do you need storage for linens, luggage, valuables, coats, brooms, etc.? (Note: There are regional variations to the storage issue. For example, in Texas, few homes have basements, so storage is usually under staircases or in an attic.)

- **Laundry:** Do you need a separate laundry room? Where should it be? Near the garage, kitchen, bedrooms?

- **Heating/ventilating/air conditioning:** Do you need air conditioning or will passive cooling methods such as shading or ventilation work? What type of heat source is available? Do you have a preference of forced air, wall radiators, or radiant floor (hot water) systems? Any interest in active solar system or passive solar design?

- **Plumbing:** Sewer or septic system? Well or city water? How much hot water do you use each day?

Source: Richardson Architects, San Francisco, (415) 541-7903.

Richardson's lifestyle questionnaire is substantially longer than the questions listed above. The questionnaire is perhaps the most complete of all the architects we interviewed, but most professionals will have some sort of questionnaire to help determine your needs. The goal of this step is to develop specific ideas about what you want and don't want in this new home.

Step 8: Rough sketches or "schematic designs." Schematic designs are intended to give the homeowner some idea of how the house would sit on the lot and how the rooms of the house would be arranged. Also, a good designer will be able to give you a preliminary cost estimate at this time.

Step 9: Design development and refinements. The designer begins to develop a specification (spec) list and provides more detailed drawings of your house. Cost estimates also will be refined at this stage. Give yourself a month to really think about the design. If you have any questions, consider paying for a three-dimensional model or drawings to help you visualize the design better. Remember that change orders are expensive later, so nailing down any changes *before* construction is a cost savings.

Step 10: Construction documents. Once you have given the designer all your input and have come to an agreement on the design, he or she will prepare the detailed drawings that the builder will (hopefully) follow during construction. A detailed spec list is also provided. Keep in mind that to prepare these documents, you will have to make decisions on minute details including light fixtures, trim colors, cabinet finishes and more. Expect to spend some time with the architect or at a home center looking at sample books.

With builder/designers, you may receive an allowance for certain items. For example, the builder will tell you you can spend $16 per yard on carpet. You won't have to pick the carpet immediately in this case—but it is smart to visit a carpet store to make sure the allowance meets your expectations.

Step 11: The bid process. An optional service offered by many full-service architects, bidding and negotiation involves sending the construction documents to several qualified builders. (More on finding a builder, in Chapter 7.) Builders will, in turn, get bids from their subcontractors and suppliers—this could take a couple of weeks. Once the builders' bids come in, the architect negotiates with them to arrive at a final deal (subject to your approval, of course). As a side note, if the architect is experienced at estimating costs, the bids should closely match your budget (plus or minus 8%). If the bid comes in way over your budget, the architect or designer will have to redraw the plans at his or her expense, incorporating any money-saving suggestions the builders provide.

Step 12: Decision time. At this point, we assume the bids are in line with your budget. Basically, you pick a builder and take the plunge. But the architect's or designer's work isn't quite over—many pros offer construction monitoring. This involves visiting the site at several key inspection points to make sure everything is proceeding correctly. More on these inspection points in Chapter 9.

Reality Check
Too-Many-Cooks syndrome. Anyone who's attended a meeting with too many people knows the hazards of having "too many cooks." By the time everyone has expressed his opinion, time is running short. It's hard to reach a consensus. One home buyer we interviewed experienced this firsthand. The original design meet-

ings for her home included her architect, the builder and an interior designer. The result was chaos and the process dragged on for months.

Houses are not designed by committee. You and your architect or designer should really meet one on one. While you should seek the input from a builder or interior designer, they should not be present at every meeting. Designing your home shouldn't be a democracy—it's *your* house, so make it your choice.

Input from your builder is important when it comes to costs—any cost-saving suggestions are obviously helpful. If the builder spots a problem with an early drawing (such as a proposed roof line that might leak), he should have an opportunity to comment. But allowing too many people to cloud the design process with too many voices is counterproductive.

Resale vs. your own quirk.: Is it your dream to own a purple house? What about having a chartreuse master bath with matching tile and carpet? You may decide you want a chartreuse master bath, and, since it's your house, you should have one. But . . . what if you plan to sell your house in five years? Chartreuse is not in the Top 10 Colors Preferred by Most Buyers.

Here's where many new home buyers face a dilemma—they want to customize the house to their tastes, but they worry about "resale potential." The average homeowner lives in a house for just seven years—after that time, it's on to another home. Hence, this dilemma is a real issue for many home buyers.

Our advice: Use restraint. While we don't advocate doing everything in a nonoffensive beige, we do think staying away from shocking colors is a good idea. One strategy is to choose neutral fixtures (like white or almond toilets, tubs and sinks) and accent them with color. For example, you could put a white sink into your powder room, but use an exotic wallpaper to add zing. That way, if a buyer doesn't like your choice of wallpaper, she can come through and put up her something else. Ripping out a bright purple sink is another matter.

The goal is not to box future home buyers into a corner with your color or design choices. The home should reflect your personality, but not in such a way that it destroys any resale potential down the line. An architect or buyer's broker will give you hints on what's in and what's out.

For example, when we built our home, every other home in the neighborhood had a three-car garage. Did we need one? Not really. But we spent the money anyway and now we have a three-car garage. The reason is simple. If we go to sell the home in a couple of years, only having a two-car garage would be a major negative. Most buyers today like the three-car garage for the extra storage space.

Getting Started: How Long Is This Going to Take?

A builder/designer may have a stock plan or design ready to go—this convenience may be a major advantage. If you want to make modifications, this could take one to four weeks, depending on the extent of the changes.

Plan books require at least a week or more for shipping. Overnight shipping is available, but at a premium. If you need time for a builder or designer to redraw these plans to your tastes, add another few weeks.

The average custom or semi-custom home designed by a designer or architect will take about two to three months, while a high-end, luxury home designed by an architect can take as much as six months to a year. And that's before a single shovel-full of dirt is thrown.

Making all the decisions required to design the house that's right for you takes time. Be sure to allow yourself plenty of time to consider each decision—don't be rushed by a proposed moving schedule.

The bottom line: plan ahead. If you want to be in the house by September 1, recognize that construction may take three to six months. Add on top of that the time required for your design method. Many home buyers find they must start designing the home 9 to 12 months before they plan to move in.

Design Trends: What's Hot and What's Not.

Let's be honest—you're not building your house in a vacuum. If you plan to sell your home in the future, it'd be nice if it contained some of the items that buyers want.

To determine just what's hip, we turned to a study of home buyers in the July 1992 *Builder Magazine*, the mouthpiece of the National Association of Home Builders. This study was conducted by market researchers Myril Axelrod and George Fulton, whose excellent studies provided an interesting window into what's happening currently in the new home market.

So, what's hot and what's not? Here's a rundown.

The Three Top Trends for New Homes

1 **Less frills, more space.** Home buyers are forgoing the fancy marble foyers and cherry kitchen cabinets. What do they want instead? More space. More "value." Forget those fancy cathedral ceilings—it seems folks would rather have bigger bedrooms. Buyers walk into two-story entryways and think, "Gee, that space could be a spare guest room." Parents with giant master bedroom closets are perhaps feeling guilty that their children's rooms are tiny boxes.

2 **Forget the power bathrooms.** Here's one sure sign that the 1980s are over—the decline of the "power" bathroom. This trend was typified by master baths with giant, whirlpool tubs and gilded faucets. While these amenities are still in vogue with luxury home buyers, most others see these water-guzzling bathrooms as passe. Buyers in areas with water shortages (such as the West) seem especially guilt-ridden.

3 **Storage, storage, storage.** That's the new byword for new home buyers. This trend is probably driving the "three-car garage" as a standard amenity in some areas. It's not for a third car but for all the important junk folks seem to acquire. In parts of the country where basements are rare, storage areas in inventive places (such as under staircases) are hip.

Top Eight Inexpensive Thrills

Not everything in your new home has to be expensive. Here are several fun, yet inexpensive options that add a little pizazz to your new home.

1 **Built-in ironing board.** Ironing probably doesn't top anyone's list of Top 10 Fun Things to Do, but it's slightly less of a hassle if you don't have to drag out and set up an ironing board. Adding a built-in ironing board for $100 to $400 is quite a space- and time-saver. Most designs have an unfinished oak cabinet that hides the ironing board. High-end models also have a hoo-up for an electrical outlet, light, and a sleeve attachment. We recommend putting your built-in board in the master bedroom closet or your laundry room—think about where you do your ironing before choosing a location.

2 **Laundry chute.** Staying with laundry for a minute, we recommend putting a laundry chute in any two-story house. You have unlimited options as to where you want to locate the chute, as long as it ends in the laundry room. No more lugging baskets of dirty clothes downstairs. The cost: $100.

3 **Motion-sensor lights.** These are a neat idea to help protect against theft and to shed a little light when you come home late and the outside lights haven't been turned on. For about $20, you can attach a motion sensor to your garage lights or any outdoor lights. When something (even as small as a neighborhood cat) approaches within 50 feet, the light turns on. Another nice feature: the sensor automatically turns off the light after a preset time period.

4 **Wiring for housewide stereo.** Here's something you can do while the walls are going up, even if you don't have all the equipment for a housewide stereo system. In a living room, you can wire for a home theater system. You can always hook up speakers later (keep a plan of where the wires end, so you know where they are). The cost: only $30 to $50 per pair of speaker wires, depending on the distance.

Another neat option to consider is a remote-control stereo. In our office, we have a remote-control sensor and set of speakers that are connected to an Onkyo stereo receiver downstairs. The remote control allows us to change stations, fiddle with the volume, and even play tapes and CDs—all without going downstairs. Cost: $80 for the sensor and $200 for the extra speakers. Beats having to buy a separate stereo.

5 *Pet door.* If you have a pet or expect to have one in the future, install that pet door now while the walls are still going up. Framing a hole for the door is much easier now than later. Cost: $30 to $50.

6 *Gas log fireplaces and grills.* Many people want a fireplace in their house, but don't want to fuss with buying or chopping wood and cleaning up ashes. Gas log fireplaces have become increasingly popular in the past five years. They require no maintenance and only need to be switched on—some even have remote controls! And for you eco-conscious folks, gas log fireplaces don't contribute to air pollution and can be burned on "no-burn" days in high-pollution areas.

A new product in the gas log business is a high efficiency (80%) gas log fireplace that is directly vented out the back of the fireplace. The hot air doesn't go up a chimney, but instead circulates back into the room. The cost for one of these is $900 to $1000. You can add a blower for another $125. Basic gas log models start at $500 but aren't as efficient.

Another fun option to consider for folks who like to grill outdoors is a natural gas grill. First, you need a gas spigot on your patio (or wherever you want the grill). This costs about $50 to $100 and is usually installed by the plumber or a licensed gas contractor. Then you buy a natural gas grill, available from your local utility company or appliance store. Prices start at about $250 for a basic model and go up to $500. No more charcoal or filling up propane gas tanks.

7 *Master bedroom refrigerator.* How many times have you been settled in bed and then decided you wanted a late-night snack? You get out of your warm bed, trudge out to the kitchen, and fix yourself a plate of cookies and a glass of cold milk. But, hey! What if you had a mini-refrigerator in your bedroom? This inexpensive option costs only about $100 to $150 and can be built into a bookcase or hidden in a walk-in closet. If you have a baby on formula or medicines that must be kept chilled, a fridge is a great solution.

8 *Weather station.* For all those weather nuts who simply have to know the temperature, humidity, wind chill, barometric pressure, wind speed and direction, and rainfall, a weather station is a great toy to install. Since it has several external sensors that need to be mounted on a roof, an ideal time to buy one is when you're building a home.

We recommend a weather station by Davis Instruments. Several models are available, including the Weather Monitor II. This unit gives you all the above weather observations for $399. A rain gauge is an additional $50, while the external temperature/humidity sensor is $75. Everything can be ordered directly from Davis by calling (800) 678-3669.

The Four Types of Home Buyers

Marketers love to put people in boxes. Some people actually make their living by coming up with catchy words to categorize people like you and me, such as "blue-collar button-downs" and the "young homesteaders." When you talk about home buyers, researchers generally divide folks into four categories: first time, move up, luxury, and singles/couples. Builders think they know how you "tick" and what hot buttons to push to make you cough up your money—understanding these patterns and pitfalls helps you become a smarter consumer.

Here's a brief sketch of the four types of home buyers.

1 | First-Time Buyers

Who are they? The first-time buyer is about 30 years old. Two-thirds of these folks have two-income households that pull in $54,000 a year. Most are singles or couples without children—only 25% are traditional families with children. The major reason first-timers buy? Tax breaks—many are tired of "throwing away" their money on rent and want that mortgage interest deduction. As a side note, a different survey by the National Association of Realtors found that first-time buyers had incomes of only $23,000.

What they want to buy. The typical price range is $117,000 to $153,000, with the average mortgage payment running $945 to $1246. Most first-timers expect two levels (58% compared to 38% who like ranch-style homes). The ideal first-timer house is smaller than 2000 square feet and has three bedrooms and two-and-a-half baths. In some areas of the country, "starter" homes go for $80,000 to $95,000.

Design trends. Resale is the mantra of first-time buyers, who realize this house is just a short-term investment, a stepping-stone to better things later. Hence, an emphasis on items that make the house more attractive down the road leads them to consider practical features and options. More bedrooms than needed, for example, seems to be in vogue.

The biggest features first-timers think should be standard include a refrigerator, a fireplace in the family room, a ceiling fan in the kitchen, and a separate laundry room—all pretty basic stuff. "Value" is the perceived "hot button" for first-time buyers.

Top options that first-timers like are also quite practical—a cable TV hookup, garbage disposal, a self-cleaning oven, and a garage door opener are the most popular. At the same time, many first-timers are torn between the practical and other features/options that are more whimsical. Bay windows are hip, especially in formal living rooms. Never mind that these windows might be enjoyed more in other parts of the house.

What they hate. The cookie-cutter design of most entry-level houses is a major frustration with first-time buyers. "Everything is stamped out," one first-timer said. "Sometimes you enter a house and you already know exactly where everything is." Often using cutesy model names, builders seem to have a condescending attitude toward these buyers.

The neighborhood. That emphasis on resale surfaces again in the consideration of neighborhoods—first-time buyers are acutely aware that subdivisions built right next to less desirable areas can pull down the value of their home.

To camouflage marginal neighborhoods, some builders have been including landscaping as a part of the new home package in many areas. While this helps houses maintain value, most buyers realize that what's nearby their house will influence the value more than a few shrubs. Rental units just down the street from new homes are a major red flag.

Watch out: Scams with first-time homes. First-time buyers want quality—the problem is that they often don't know what to look for. Unfortunately, some builders take advantage of this naiveté.

Take cathedral ceilings, for example. First-time buyers love 'em. However, most folks don't realize the additional utility expense to heat or cool these vast expanses. Nonetheless, builders continue to put these into model home designs and simply say they're responding to customer demand. Of course, there's no mention of the additional utility cost. The obvious tip: Ask for utility bills (12-month averages) from existing houses with that design.

More insidious are builders who substitute the cheapest of the cheap materials. Walk into a typical first-time home and chances are the salesperson won't even mention the brand names of the heating/cooling system, faucets, windows, bath fixtures or flooring. The cabinets are some generic pressed wood instead of solid wood. What type of insulation is in the home? Most salespeople are clueless.

That's because the builders don't want you to know that nearly everything is a "builder's special." The use of low-quality materials is epidemic, in our opinion. While this happens with even expensive homes, the pressure to bring the first-time house in at an attractive price may drive builders to cut corners.

The fact is *you* have to ask about the brand names of the items mentioned above. Then, *you* have to investigate the quality by going to home improvement centers, plumbing supply showrooms and other sources to find out what you're buying.

Another scam that zaps first-time buyers is the "model trap—" builders who stuff the model with expensive furniture and fancy "options" that aren't clearly identified as such. You almost have to have a salesperson follow you to point out what's standard and what's optional and how much each option costs.

2 ***Move-Up Buyers***: ***Who are you?*** Every two out of three new home buyers is a "move up," which adds up to an incredible buying force—and builders have taken notice. The average move-up buyer is 36 years old, and two-thirds are couples with children. Seventy percent of move-ups have two-income households—the average income is $71,000.

What they want to buy. The #1 issue is neighborhood—most move-ups have ties to a certain area and are only interested in moving to another house nearby or in a neighborhood they know is good. Obviously, school quality is a major factor. If the nearby school is a dud, it doesn't matter how fancy the house is.

As for the house itself, move-ups want a four-bedroom, two-story house with two-and-a-half to three baths. Square footage desired by a typical move-up buyer is at least 2350. Price expectations range from $142,000 to $183,000; a reasonable payment is $1076 to $1438.

Design trends. Interestingly, nearly 60% of move-up buyers would rather have a larger house with fewer amenities than a small home loaded with goodies. This group probably most typifies the trend toward space and away from frills.

Of course, this doesn't mean move-ups want no frills at all. Standard features that move-up buyers expect in a home include a separate tub and shower in the master bath, as well as his-and-her closets. In the kitchen, walk-in pantries, grill-top ranges and double ovens are in vogue. Another interesting note: One-third of move-up buyers now expect a home office. "Flexibility" is what the builders think is the move-up buyer's hot button.

The most popular options among move-up buyers include a garbage disposal, garage door openers and self-cleaning ovens. In a sign that they're slightly more savvy than first-time buyers, move-ups also like programmable thermostats and energy-saving showerheads.

Compromise is not a word that move-ups like—hence, they are more willing to consider such upgrades as nicer carpeting, entry flooring (hardwood, tile or marble are popular options), and kitchen countertops.

"Specialty rooms" with defined functions (such as a game room, media room, guest suites or home office) are the new buzzwords.

What they hate. Dinky bedrooms are a major turn-off. Most consider the minimum size to be 12 by 12 feet. Another major negative are dinky closets—walk-ins are preferred. In fact, inadequate storage is a major reason why certain houses lose out.

Move-up buyers realize that open floor plans with lofts and cathedral ceilings aren't very practical. Besides, the bigger heating/cooling bills, these buyers want more compartmentalized home plans that allow them to seal off rooms from noise, traffic and clutter. "Cathedral ceilings now mean to me that you don't have any space in the attic," said a Washington, D.C., move-up buyer. "You can hear everything everywhere in the house," chimed another.

Watch out: Scams with move-up homes. Move-up buyers aren't naive idiots—they've bought a home before and have a better feeling for construction . . . BUT, there are still scams that trip them up.

Listen to what the *Builder Magazine* article says about move-up buyers: "What is surprising is how naive [move-ups] still are in knowing what counts in a house. They judge a builder mostly on appearances." Sure, cosmetic mistakes are easy to spot—such as holes in the moulding left unfilled. However, just because something is "solid," like cabinet doors, doesn't mean it's quality.

And don't think builders don't know this. Clever builders can trick buyers with skin-deep beauty on a new home, such as six-panel solid oak doors. They're nice, but did you notice the inadequate foundation, cheap windows or the exterior siding that wasn't primed before it was painted (this will require repainting in a short year or two, versus several years for primed siding)?

Similarly, move-ups don't pay much attention to brand names. Except for heating and cooling systems, less than half had a brand preference for faucets, windows, flooring, cabinets and so on. Once again, shoddy builders are given a free hand to put in "builder's special" materials with inferior quality for this price level. Of course, the only strategy is to ask for brand names and to research their quality.

Be cautious of salespeople who try to "set the quality agenda" by harping on the quality of certain items while ignoring basic structural elements.

3 ***Luxury Buyers: Who are you?*** As the name implies, luxury buyers have lots of money—the average household income is $104,000. Nearly 60% are couples with children and the average age of a luxury buyer is 40. As you might expect, this is a relatively small percentage of the new home market. The number of households in the country that make more than $100,000 is a puny 10%.

At this point, you might say, "Who cares about these guys?" Well, they're important because they tend to be the trend setters. Their affinity for certain styles or designs often leads tract-home builder to adopt these features (albeit in a watered down fashion).

What they want to buy. A big house, as you might expect. The typical "luxury" house boasts at least 3000 square feet with four or five bedrooms and three-plus baths. All this isn't cheap—the average price is $307,000 to $415,000. Luxury buyers expect their monthly payment to be $1820 to $2445.

Design trends. You'd think luxury buyers would want gargantuan rooms with huge ceilings. The reality is that many find such rooms intimidating—they like space, but don't want to be living in a gymnasium. Giant ceilings in public areas where they might entertain guests or clients are okay, but not for the rest of the house.

Specialized rooms like guest suites with separate entryways are quite hip with the luxury set. Sun rooms, exercise rooms, and libraries are important—more than half said they expect a home office. Privacy is key and individuality is a hot button. This drives many luxury buyers to consider custom homes.

Top features include marble entry flooring (to impress those guests) and French doors. Regular water that commoners drink isn't for luxury buyers—they expect a water purifier as a standard feature. Half of all luxury buyers prefer a three-car garage.

As for options, top-of-the-line heating and cooling systems are popular. This includes zoned heating and cooling plus programmable thermostats.

What they hate. Like Alice in Wonderland caught in some out-of-proportion world, luxury buyers don't like to think they live in a museum. Giant houses built on tiny lots are another no-no; most like a good distance between themselves and the neighbors.

Interestingly, houses built on two-acre lots have a dow side that many luxury buyers discover: loneliness. Alienation is the craze in many luxury communities and such buyers lament the passing of the "good old days" when neighbors visited on a porch or veranda.

Watch out: Scams with luxury homes. Just because a home has a $500,000 price tag doesn't mean you're going to get "half a million dollars quality." We've heard several stories from luxury buyers who got burned when they bought something that was far less than luxurious.

The big problem is with inexperienced builders who are good salesmen. They convince luxury buyers they can build from an architect's exact custom plans. Sadly, some builders get in way over their heads. A unique roof design may be botched by ignorant subs and expert tile work screwed up by inadequate supervision.

Even at this price level, we see the same construction mistakes as with lower-priced homes. For example, inadequate foundations can cause what one would charitably call "catastrophic settling." Another common scam: sloppy installation of expensive materials or substitution of inferior materials—despite what the architect specifies in the plans.

While luxury buyers are more label conscious when it comes to items like windows, most builders realize luxury buyers aren't any more knowledgeable than other home buyers. Once again, cosmetic details are scrutinized, while important quality checks are missed. Granite countertops in the kitchen are considered a quality symbol in California, but many luxury buyers miss an important point—how will the home stand up in an earthquake? Questions about "seismic" soundness are not as common.

4 **Singles/Couples: Who are you?** You know marketers have run out of creative ideas when they start to lump people into a "miscellaneous" category. Such is the case with "singles/couples." This broad group includes newlyweds without kids and retired folks whose kids have moved away. Also thrown in for good measure are singles (widowed, divorced or never married) and a small number of "unrelated" people living together. The average age is 41 (but that, of course, is deceiving) and the household income typically equals $70,000. An important thought to ponder: This group is the fastest-growing home buyer category.

What they want to buy. Seeking anything with "style," most singles/couples feel ignored by builders who seem to churn out houses for "traditional families." That's nice, but most don't fit that mold, and who has a use for four bedrooms, anyway?

The ideal house: a $175,000 home or townhome with three bedrooms and 2100 square feet. About 40% prefer single-level designs, while over 50% like two-stories. A reasonable monthly payment is $1070 to $1457.

Design trends. Just like first-time buyers, young singles see the house as a short-term investment to get tax breaks. Very few intend to live there forever and hence resale advantages such as a quality school system loom as an overriding factor. Meanwhile, the empty-nesters are moving down from oversized homes.

Young buyers like the look of a single-family home, with big entertaining areas. Older buyers, not having to worry about noisy kids, seem to prefer open floor plans.

Hot features that these buyers expect as standard amenities include a fireplace, high ceilings, bay windows and a separate tub and shower in the master bath. Special touches like a spice rack and hot-water dispenser in the kitchen are in demand. The "gourmet upgrades" are quite popular.

Options that singles/couples like are built-in microwaves and self-cleaning ovens in the kitchen, and a glass shower door in the master bath. In a trend that runs opposite of the rest of the country, most of singles/couples buyers want more amenities than space. Still, they won't compromise on storage area—a room off the garage is preferred by half of these buyers.

A place to visit with neighbors (like a common courtyard) is important, as is a small yard—for resale as well as a place to keep a pet. Views and light, airy floor plans are on the top of most of these buyers' lists—hence the popularity of skylights and bay windows.

What they hate. Condos are out, as many singles/couples saw the condo resale market collapse in the 1980s. While "zero-lot line" homes appear hot in quite a few areas, the high-rise condo is a dinosaur in all but a few places.

Gaudy features such as sculpture niches are also out. Anything that smacks of overindulgence reminds yuppies of the bashing they took from the media in the '80s.

Singles/couples are rather depressed by what they see in the marketplace—builders just don't seem to understand them. The lack of customization in townhomes/patio homes irks them, as they see builders bend over backwards to accommodate single-family home buyers.

The matchbox-quality of certain developments is also a source of irritation. While the builders of single-family homes at least try to cover up their flaws with cosmetic bells and whistles, the lousy quality of some townhomes is certainly more "in your face."

Watch out: Scams with singles/couples buyers. Retirees are especially vulnerable to scams. One of the biggest driving forces behind the North Carolina housing scandal that we've cited in this book is a large influx of retirees from the North—easy targets for scam artists. Many buyers who expect houses of the same quality as "back home" are shocked to find the quality standards in "retirement areas" to be scandalously low.

Young singles are also vulnerable to rip-offs. Attached housing like townhomes is often a minefield of defective construction. The root cause? The "let's slap it up as fast as we can" mentality of some builders inevitably leads to problems. An example: inadequate sound-proofing can make living in a town home unbearable.

Source: Builder Magazine's *1992 Home Buyer Survey conducted by Fulton Research of Fairfax, VA.*

ECO-HOUSES: They're Not Just for Granola-Heads Anymore

Drive by any ex-hippy community and you'll spot 'em: 1970s-era versions of "environmentally-friendly" homes. They also had an additional feature: They were god-awful ugly. I mean really *ugly*. The same people who brought us tofu and natural childbirth were also responsible for the ultra-eco-conscious geodesic dome. And they were always brown.

Of course, today these folks don't seem as crazy as they did in the days of Jimmy Carter. We called them "health nuts" then, but later discovered, to our horror, that Big Macs and Ding-Dongs were not extending anyone's lifespan.

So, it is the Revenge of the Granola Heads that today we put "environmentally-friendly" houses right up there with Mom and apple pie (as long as the apples have not been sprayed with Alar). Fortunately for today's home buyers, the eco-house has metamorphosed into something much more palatable than the geodesic dome. Many of today's eco-houses are cleverly disguised to look like real houses. From the exterior, they are normal. Look under the roof, however, and you'll note a few changes.

In Chapters 9 and 10, we highlight several eco-friendly building products with our "eco-alternative" symbol. (As a side note, some of these products have been installed in an experimental "resource conservation house" erected near Washington, D.C., by the National

Association of Home Builders.)

And those products are just the beginning. Many new products are flooding the "green" market every year. How do you find out the latest eco-news? Ask your architect/designer or builder if he or she has a copy of the *Environmental Resource Guide* published by the American Institute of Architects. Another possibility is the *Sourcebook for Sustainable Design*, a catalog of eco-friendly building materials published by the Boston-based Architects for Social Responsibility.

If you would like to use tropical hardwoods in your home (trim, cabinets, doors, etc.), consider using wood with the "Smart Wood" logo. This certification comes from Green Seal or the Rainforest Alliance, who certify "approved" tree harvesters and make sure the harvesting does not have a negative environmental impact on the species.

Drawbacks to the Eco-Home

1 *Unskilled laborers must learn new tricks—at your expense.* Many eco-products require special installation methods. Unfortunately, this is sometimes above the skill level of many subcontractors. As a result, there may be time delays and cost overruns as they learn steel framing or the installation of plastic wood.

2 *A few of these products are still in the experimental stage.* All the bugs haven't quite been worked out from some eco-friendly products. In the real world, you also may not have access to these products in certain areas of the country.

 Call for updates! By calling our special hotline, you'll hear the latest news on building a new home! 1-900-988-7295 (See the back page for price information.)

7

Bring on the Builder

It doesn't take a rocket scientist to recognize a simple rule of new home construction: The quality of your home will be directly related to the builder's competence. A perfect site and expert design plans are worthless if the builder is an idiot.

So how do you "idiot-proof" your new home's construction? The answer: homework. Only by checking out the builder thoroughly will you be able to separate the talented from the pretenders. It probably wouldn't shock you to know that very few home buyers really check out the builder—instead of a thorough examination of the builder's past homes, track record and reputation, many buyers focus on the color of carpet or kitchen cabinets in a model home.

First, recognize the three truths about new home builders today:

1 *You're hiring a builder "team," not a single person.* Looks are deceiving—it may appear that you're dealing with just one person. Actually you're hiring three groups:

- *The builder's crews:* Larger builders may have their own crews that do some or all of the framing and finishing work. These crews work solely for that builder and may construct dozens of homes from the same basic design. Smaller builders may have a foreman or site supervisor who manages the project on a day-to-day basis.

- *Subcontractors:* Many builders farm out the production of their homes to "subs," independent workers/companies. The plumbing contractor may install not only the plumbing but also the heating/cooling system and duct work. The quality of the subs your builder uses will really determine whether you get a quality home or a lemon. Later we'll offer some tips on determining the quality level of the subs.

- *Materials suppliers:* Builders may have certain sources for building materials. If the builder has "contractor's discounts" with certain suppliers for such things as kitchen cabinets, light fixtures and other materials, you will want to know this information. Identifying the suppliers gives you an indication of the builder's quality. Take kitchen cabinets, for example. It's obviously more impressive if the builder has an account with a custom or high-quality cabinet manufacturer than with a lower-end, tract-style cabinet supplier.

2 *Caring craftsmen were long ago replaced by incompetent number crunchers.* Years ago, homes were built by builders who were craftsmen—they tended to build homes one at a time. Sadly, many of these caring craftsmen were replaced by "merchant" builders whose main skill was number-crunching and slick marketing. Craftsmanship was replaced by "volume", in the push to build more homes at a faster pace and lower cost. Hence, builders became more skilled at number-crunching than quality building. Corners were cut on important structural elements like the roof and foundation, while cosmetic details were played up—the "gingerbread" exterior detailing, octagon windows and flashy kitchen cabinets.

Even smaller builders—who focus less on volume and somewhat more on quality—can get caught in this trap. When times are good, some get greedy by taking on far too many homes to supervise carefully.

3 *Quality control is tied to the level of supervision by the builder.* An unsupervised crew or subcontractor is an invitation to disaster. We've seen many new home fiascoes that were built by allegedly quality-conscious builders. The reason for all the defects? The builders spread themselves too thin and couldn't supervise the homes properly. The best builders watch their workers like hawks, personally staying on site for long periods of time. If the actual builder isn't there, a qualified foreman or supervisor should be. Subcontractors should also supervise their workers carefully.

In the real world, however, supervision ranges from adequate to spotty. The builder may be called away from the construction site on the afternoon that the furnace is installed. The sub botches the installation by putting the furnace in the wrong place. Or the wrong trim materials are delivered to the site and are installed by a crew that couldn't care less.

Therefore, one of the best ways to screen for the best builders is to determine the level of supervision you're buying. And you don't want to just take the builder's word for it—visit actual job sites to see what's happening. We'll get to that in just a page or two.

Sources to Find a Quality Builder

1 *Architects.* An experienced residential architect has seen which builders have been naughty or nice. The architect will also have some idea of which builders are best for your particular house—while they rarely admit it, builders often specialize in certain types of homes or price ranges. A builder may be able to build a quality $150,000 three-bedroom "basic" home, but may be a fish out of water on a $400,000 "executive" home. The degree of difficulty in executing the architect's design is an important factor in choosing a builder, as well.

A good architect should offer bidding and negotiation services with potential builders. Even if you go with more bare-bones service from an architect (say, design only), he or she should be able to pass on the names of several reputable builders. BE CAREFUL: An architect's recommendations should not be taken on blind faith. You must still screen the builder thoroughly.

2 *Recent home buyers.* Ask your friends and relatives if they know anyone who has recently built a home. A satisfied customer of a builder is a very important find. Later we'll talk about questions to ask such previous customers or references.

3 *Driving Around in New Home Communities.* If you drive around areas where new homes are being built, you'll no doubt see builder signs. You may also see a builder sign on a vacant lot the builder owns. Of course, just because a builder is building homes in a certain area does not mean they're actually doing quality construction. But at least it gives you the names of several possible candidates.

 ### Not-So-Good Sources.

1 *Professional Associations.* Nearly every state has home builder's associations, which are affiliates of the National Association of Home Builders (NAHB). What does it mean if a builder is a member of a so-called professional homebuilder's association? Do they screen for quality contractors? Are you kidding? Membership in such an association means they've paid dues to the association. That's it. Big deal.

Oh, sure, there's lots of propaganda from the builders that these associations help consumers. Please. An ethic's pledge or a requirement that members be licensed is not very meaningful.

In Florida, we read an article about a builder who was touting the local homebuilder's association's ethics committee. "If a builder screws up, we'll throw them out of our group. And that means they can't participate in the local Parade of Homes." we're sure the scam artists are quaking in their boots at that threat. Frankly, we've found no evidence that homebuilder's associations ever "police" their members or protect consumers. In North Carolina, the *president* of a local homebuilder's association was accused of building severely defective homes, according to a television documentary. Despite the overwhelming evidence against him, he was never censured by the association.

What these groups are good at is political influence. Local homebuilder associations are big political contributors—this money "buys" off local politicians from enacting tougher consumer protection laws. Watering down enforcement of building codes is a major "non-public" goal of some associations.

2 *Real Estate Agents.* These guys wouldn't know a quality home if it landed right on them (a la the Wizard of Oz). What an agent is good at is ferreting out builders who offer bigger commissions. Others steer you to new homes they have listed—that way they get the whole 6% to 7% commission to themselves.

Even honest agents are hobbled by their own ignorance—most have no clue what is sound construction. Just like unsuspecting consumers, they may equate cosmetic details like six-panel oak doors or fancy kitchen cabinets with "quality." Is the foundation engineered correctly? Are the roof trusses correctly installed? A real estate agent is often clueless.

3 *The Newspaper.* Most newspaper real estate sections are pure advertising for builders. Articles disguised as editorial copy are really puff pieces about how "wonderful" and "talented" certain builders are—and the builders pay for this. They may even write their own copy.

Sadly, many newspapers are intimidated by powerful developers and builders, who fill the paper's coffers with big advertising bucks. Most papers are scared to death of offending these big clients. Not only can builders buy positive coverage, they can also kill negative articles at some papers. Complaints about defective homes are buried or not even reported at all.

On the plus side, at least newspaper real estate sections point out neighborhoods with new home construction. Of course, many new homes or available lots are never advertised, but it's a start.

Getting Started: How Far in Advance?
When should you hire a builder? If you're buying a tract or "spec" home, this is a moot point. Your search for location and builder are one in the same.

However, if you're building from scratch or doing a "custom" home on a lot you've located, there are three different ways to go:

1 **Hire a builder before you hire an architect/designer.** Some folks recommend this path, but we see several big problems. If you don't have a home design yet, how can you get a price estimate? How do you know that the builder is really skilled at building your design? What incentive does the builder have to bring your project in at a certain cost? Going this route implies you must trust the builder—and have faith in his or her ability to execute a design no one has yet to see. Frankly, finding someone who you can put that much trust in is a 9.0 on the 10-point difficulty scale.

2 **Hire a builder at the same time you find an architect/designer—but before there is any design yet.** This method requires extreme faith in your architect—they must have a rough feel for the best builder for you even without doing a design yet. The advantage is you bring the builder on board early in the process—he can contribute to the design process by suggesting cost-saving ideas. The disadvan-

tage is there is no "competitive" bid process—you've committed to a builder even before you've gotten a price estimate. Sure a good architect should design a home that's within your budget range—but not all architects are experts at construction costs. Hence, you may get a design that is way over your budget. And you're stuck with a builder that may not be inclined to watch costs.

3 *After you complete the design, bid out the house to two or three builders.* Hire the one who gives you a good bid, *and* seems most interested in your home. This method offers a "competitive bidding process" that provides a builder with an incentive to hold down greed—the competition will get the job if he gets too pricey. The key to making this process work is having an architect draw plans that completely spec out every detail—that way you get "apples-to-apples" bids. What are the disadvantages? In hot markets, builders may not want to go through the hassle of submitting a bid. If you bid the home out to more than three builders, this sends the signal that you're just price-shopping (such a negative in the builder's mind that they might not even want to bid). By not having the builder in at the beginning of the design process, you may miss out on cost-saving suggestions and other insight.

What's the best course? It's up to you. We think the last method is probably the best in most cases. If you are lucky enough to find a talented architect who is very experienced in residential design and construction cost estimating, method two is certainly acceptable. Unless you're convinced you've found the very best builder, hiring a builder first without an architect or design seems less preferable.

The Four Types of Builders:

There's no "IBM" of home building—most home builders are local contractors who build less than 25 homes a year. The nation's largest home builder, Centex of Dallas, built just 7572 homes in 1991—that's less than 1% of all the homes built in the U.S. According to the *Professional Builder and Remodeler* magazine, the nation's ten biggest builders in 1991 accounted for just 51,785 home starts or 5% the total—the other 95% are built by smaller, local builders.

As far as we can tell, those local contractors come in four flavors. Here's an overview of who you will encounter on your new home journey.

1 *The Dog and Pickup Truck Builder.* As you might expect, these guys get their name because all they basically have is a pickup truck and a dog that follows them to work. No fancy office or plush model homes. They tend to build one home at a time. The general contractor is the sole employee and supervisor of the homes.

Some of the best homes we've seen are built by dog and pickup truck builders. And some of the worst homes we've seen are built by this type. Most small-time operators build between one to five homes a year—in good times, they could double that volume. Unfortunately, they rarely have the skill or staff to supervise more than one home at a time.

Best For: Semi-custom homes designed from a plan book. Lower cost homes (less than $150,000 depending on market conditions). If this builder is bold, he may try a few "semi-custom" spec homes. Most other homes they build are "pre sold" to customers.

Worst For: Architect-designed homes—most don't know how to work with or understand architects. Don't expect wonderful design skills from these folks—most have limited drafting skills and churn out plain vanilla homes.

Used To Be: A framer or other subcontractor who recently "promoted" himself into being a builder. While he may have knowledge in one area (framing), he might be clueless about plumbing, roofing, etc. Hence, it's difficult for this builder to judge the quality of certain subcontractors.

Watch Out: Most Dog-and-Pick-Up Truck builders are poorly capitalized—if they fail financially, they could take your home down with them. Lack of adequate insurance looms as another major risk for you—it's rare to find a small-time builder with "errors and omissions" insurance. Others lack worker's compensation insurance—another negative.

2 *The Mini-Tycoon.* This builder has grown beyond the pickup truck and now may have a small office. While the contractor is still the primary supervisor of homes, the mini-tycoon has one to four other employees who help with site supervision, materials purchasing and so on. Most build between 3 and 15 homes in a typical year—up to 20 homes during boom periods.

Quality tends to be a little better since this builder has slightly more experience than the dog-and-pickup-truck builder. At the same time, the emphasis on bigger volume can drag down the quality. Some mini-tycoons specialize in the custom home market and build spectacular homes.

Best For: Move-up homes in the middle to upper price ranges. Some build small communities of semi-custom homes, while others concentrate on the custom, pre-sold market. Occasionally works with architects/designers. The larger mini-tycoons may do both custom homes and "production" (read: tract) homes in a hot subdivision.

Worst For: Challenging designs or complex plans. Difficult sites may also pose problems. With some successful homes under their belts, mini-tycoons may have over inflated opinions of their design skills. They still haven't learned that the best thing for them to do is build, not design.

Used To Be: A dog-and-pickup-truck builder but now has more money. Other mini-tycoons may have worked for a subcontractor or materials supplier and wanted a bigger piece of the action. However, just because he's worked for a kitchen cabinet manufacturer as a rep does not necessarily make them a talented builder.

Watch Out: These folks still have money problems—they often use the profit from the last home to build the next one. Foolishly, they go out and buy land in hot markets to do spec homes, then get caught with no cash and lots of dirt when the market turns sour. Lack of insurance still haunts mini-tycoon builders—while they probably have liability and worker's comp, E & O is beyond their financial grasp. Despite the increased chance of better supervision, these builders must be watched like a hawk on quality issues.

3 *Top-Gun Builders.* These builders have taken home building to the next logical step—forming a professional company with a focused emphasis on a certain market. Usually, that market is either pure custom homes or communities of semi-custom executive homes.

The president of the company has "retired" from field supervision—that's left to teams of project supervisors and site foremen. An in-house estimator does nothing but estimate and bid projects, holding down the construction costs. The general contractor focuses on administration and marketing. As a result, these folks can crank out 10 to 40 homes a year.

Surprisingly, some of these builders are willing to do custom homes in most price ranges. However, most of their customers are building expensive homes designed by architects—hence they get used to building for a certain clientele.

Best For: Move-up and luxury homes. Experience working with an architect makes this builder a preferred choice for home buyers.

Worst For: Starter homes—top-gun builders rarely take on these projects, except in slow markets when they are looking for work. If you don't want to hire an architect, these builders may not want to work for you. They've realized that what they do best is build, not design.

Used To Be: Successful small-time builder—but with financial and managerial skills. They didn't take risks by locking up all their money in vacant land—instead they let clients take that risk in buying the lot.

Watch Out: Since these companies are bigger, the risk of bureaucracy headaches increases. There may be several layers of management between you and the company president. While these builders tend to prodeuce the best quality, they still must be watched by private inspectors and architects to insure unsupervised subs don't botch complex or difficult plans.

4 *Production builder.* These are the builders you see advertised in the newspaper—the builders of large communities of cookie-cutter homes. Many falsely promote themselves as semi-custom builders since you have the choice of "customizing" the carpet color. The reality is that a production builder's main emphasis is just that—production. Quantity over quality. As a result, the largest crank out 5000 homes a year. Smaller production builders may build "just" 50 or 100 homes a year.

Best For: Starter homes and townhomes. If you don't have the time to invest in going the semi-custom or custom route, this may be a viable alternative.

Worst For: Anything with creativity. You basically pick from one of several stock plans. The builder owns all the lots.

Used To Be: A faceless corporation that wanted to diversify into real estate. Or, it is remotely possible that these builders did quality homes at one time. Eventually, that quality-conscious builder sold out to number-crunchers who, with the backing of lots of money, built the company on savvy marketing and luck.

Watch Out: Remember, the goal for the production builder is quantity, not quality. Frankly, you can't do a quality home in just 84 days—corners are cut and worse. Look out for the production builder's contract—a team of lawyers may have worked late nights to find ways to limit your rights. Production builders also have an affinity for 10-year warranty plans, perhaps the biggest rip-off in new homes today. We'll talk about those in the next chapter

Questions to Ask a Builder.

1 ***What do you think about architects or designers?*** Here's a loaded question that probes for builders with problem attitudes. A typical knee-jerk response is, "Architects design pretty houses but they know nothing about costs." A better answer: builders who honestly point out some architects' shortcomings, while praising architects who have residential experience. You may ask the builder if he's ever worked with the architect(s) you are considering.

2 ***How long have you been in business? How many "pre-sold" versus spec houses have you done?*** Builders who do lots of spec homes may not know how to work with custom buyers—they're used to making their own decisions, not having an architect or consumer call the shots.

3 ***Have you or any partner in your company built under any other name?*** This question hits at the heart of a scam that has bilked home buyers out of thousands of dollars in defective construction: builders who change their names and move to another state to avoid angry customers. Be suspicious of newly formed corporations or companies. Later, we'll discuss probing their background to see whether they've ripped off home buyers under other names.

4 ***Could you provide me with a copy of your contractor's license and insurance coverage (both liability and errors and omis-***

sions)? Any legitimate contractor should give you a license number for you to check out. It's not enough to get a promise that the builder has insurance—you must get written proof. As a side note, many insurance companies are dropping builder coverage after a spate of defective construction lawsuits. Hence, only the most reputable builders will probably be able to maintain coverage. Of course, insurance is no guarantee—it's just one piece of the puzzle.

5 *How many projects do you currently have going?* The key here: is the builder spread too thin? If a dog-and-pickup-truck builder has 10 homes under construction, it's not a good sign. At the same time, a builder who's been sitting around doing nothing for several months is suspicious as well. If they aren't working, is it because their reputation is choking off the supply of new customers?

6 *Can I see several of the homes you are working on?* Paranoid builders may not want you poking around, but the most reputable contractors have no problem at all. They're proud of their work. No apologies. Ask if you can visit the homes without the builder to get a more objective look-see.

7 *Would the builder be willing to look at my plans and provide cost-saving suggestions? Do you see any mistakes or missing points in my design plans?* This is crucial to getting an accurate bid. A real pro should spot potential problems—such as a leaking roof or bad site design. Alternatives to expensive materials should be discussed. You can really tell a builder's experience level if he can answer this question well.

8 *Can I have a copy of your contract? What level of warranty is offered—can I get a copy of the warranty?* In the next chapter, we'll talk about the contracts. You want a copy now to see what terms and warranties the builder offers. A builder with an anti-consumer contract loaded with clauses designed to severely restrict your rights is a major red flag.

9 *How will the construction be supervised? Is the supervisor the builder himself, a foreman, or a site supervisor?* This is a critical issue—while you can't expect the builder to be at your site 24 hours a day, there must be a strong commitment to quality supervision or you're in trouble. Unsupervised subs will run amok. Ask for a commitment here—builders who are spread too thin will be nervous about this issue.

10 *How much are change orders?* Odds are that you'll want to change something during construction—it's a fact of human nature. If you want to add a window, how much does it cost (for the window and installation)? Is there one charge before construction

begins and another set of fees afterward? Are there any "administration charges" for changes? If a builder has to track down the price of an added item, this takes administrative time. A small fee ($25 or a small hourly rate) is alright, but a massive charge indicates a problem.

Change orders also can be initiated by the builder. When the builder discovers a problem with the plans, she or he may want to charge you to change it. Watch out: some builders make a killing charging customers "change" fees. These builders nitpick the plans and charge you for every extra screw and nail. Asking the builder how many change orders he typically has is a good way to sniff out this scam. A couple of change orders are expected—20 change orders initiated by the builder are excessive.

11 *Who are your subcontractors? Materials suppliers? Can I have a list of all the subs' and suppliers' phone numbers and addresses?* Let's say you talk to a previous home buyer who complains about the plumbing. If you know the sub who did the plumbing job and the prospective builder's plumber, you'd be able to steer clear if the two names match. Getting a list of all the subs will let you confirm that they've been paid prior to your home's closing. This helps lower the chances you'll get stung in a "mechanic's lien scam": the builder takes your money but doesn't pay the subs, who then promptly file liens on your new home. You then get the thrill of paying for the home twice.

12 *Can you provide me with a bank reference? A business reference (a supplier, for example)? Personal credit report? Financial statement?* The more information they supply, the better you will feel about entrusting tens of thousands of dollars of your money with them. Most builders will at least provide a bank reference. This seems fair—since most builders will ask whether you are "financially-qualified" to buy the home.

It's fair play for you to turn the tables and ensure that the builder is financially-qualified to *build* the home. Those who get nervous at these requests or say it's "none of your business" may be trying to hide shaky financial footing.

13 *Could you provide me with references of buyers with comparable homes?* You need three to five previous customers who have bought between now and three years ago. Make sure at least one or two references have been in their homes more than one year—by that time some construction defects will be more than evident.

Also, the glow of new home ownership has worn off. By the way, we realize that if you get four references from each of three builder candidates, this means 12 interviews. But we know no other way to find out whether a builder is worth his asking price. All the sales talk is meaningless if customers aren't satisfied—and you can't tell if you don't ask them.

An alternative to this would be to ask the builder for a list of *all* the homes he has built in the past five years. Will you contact all these buyers? Of course not. You can pick and choose among several prospects. The goal here is to prevent the builder from giving you a list of just the most trouble-free homes.

"But won't the builder just give me happy customers as references?" This is a reasonable fear. However, by asking for home buyers who have built similar or comparable homes, you're cutting down that risk. The builder can't just pick happy customers at random. Also, by limiting the search period to three years, you prevent the builder from finding happy customers from 1984.

The Square-Foot Price Myth

One of the biggest potential mistakes you can make in searching for a builder is to shop by "square-foot price." How does this method work? Well, if Builder A has a 2000-square-foot home that costs $150,000, thenthes price per square foot is $75. However, Builder B down the street is charging $200,000 for a 3000-square-foot home— the per square foot price is just $67. Is Builder B a better deal than Builder A?

The fact is you can't tell just by the square-foot price. Builder A might use expensive Corian kitchen countertops, top-quality windows and better insulation. Meanwhile, Builder B has cut some corners, using cheap carpet, builder-special faucets and inexpensive doors. The point is that expensive, quality materials will push up the price per square foot. The builder with the lowest prices may be giving you bottom-of-the-barrel quality.

Another problem is location. A big part of a home's price is the land—up to 30% and even 45% in some parts of the country. Lots in bad locations (on a busy street, for example) are definitely cheaper than prime location lots with views, on a quiet cul-de-sac, etc. Homes in less exciting locations will probably have lower prices per square foot.

Don't forget that it's cheaper per square foot to build "up" than "out." Hence, two-story homes are often less expensive (per square foot) than one level, ranch-style homes. Comparing the prices of these two home types is like comparing apples to oranges.

Basically, per square foot prices are only helpful on a large scale. When you analyze such prices on a community, city or county basis, you have a more meaningful comparison to other communities. Hence, all the regulation and high land costs in California make their homes cost $100 to $150 per square foot in some cities. On the other hand, homes in North Dakota may be closer to $50 per square foot.

One builder we interviewed best summed up the "price per square foot" myth by saying that he can build you a home for anywhere from $5 to $200 per square foot. Five bucks buys you a tent, while $200 gets you the Taj Mahal.

Step-by-Step Screening Strategies:

 Step 1: Decide on the design "strategy" for your new home. Will you hire an architect? Use a plan from a magazine or book? Or go with a stock plan from a builder?

Step 2: Identify three to five potential builders from the sources listed above.

Step 3: Setup an interview appointment with each candidate. Leave a good hour or more to ask the above questions. Talk about the builder's past projects.

Step 4: After the interviews, narrow your list to two or three final candidates. Call them back and ask for the following:
- A list of current projects you can visit.
- The names of recent customers (3 to 5) who have bought homes in the past year.
- Other recent customers (3 to 5) who have been in their homes for more than one year and less than three years.

Step 5: Before you go out, check out several "home inspection" books from your local library or bookstore. Familiarize yourself with some basic construction aspects—you're not expected to be an expert engineer, but get a feel for "good" versus "bad" construction methods.

Step 6: If possible, visit the construction sites without the builder. This gives you uninterrupted time to evaluate the home. But remember to stay out of the way of workers. As an alternative, you can visit the home in the evening after the workers are gone and before the sun sets. If the builder wants to be present, don't let him distract you. Take time to look at basements, attics and other nooks and crannies. If you have any questions, don't be afraid to call the builder on certain problems you notice. See the box "Visiting the *Other* Homes: Evaluating Construction on the Fly" for more tips.

Step 7: Call the previous home buyer references. If you can, setup face-to-face meetings. Ask a series of yes-or-no questions to get just the facts. It's a big no-no to ask open-ended questions such as, "What was your opinion of the quality?" Instead, ask the following questions:
- Was the house built on schedule and on budget? Did it start when the builder promised? Were there any delays?
- Were there any problems that the builder had to come back to fix? Did the builder fix these problems quickly? To your satisfaction?
- Does the roof leak? If you have any skylights, do they leak? Is there any water problem in the basement? Are any rooms

hot/cold or drafty? (Add your own questions to this list, given the home you're building.)

■ How is the "warranty" service? Does the builder promptly respond to warranty repair requests? Did the workmen show up when they promised?

Step 8: *As you visit each reference, make notes about the quality of construction and craftsmanship you see.* After each visit, make more notes to yourself in the car about the interview.

Step 9: *Confirm the builder's license and insurance coverage.* Call your state contractor licensing board (the local building department should have this number) to confirm the builder's license status. Ask the board whether the builder has had any complaint and/or license suspensions. If the builder built in another state in the past five years, call that state's licensing board as well. Call the builder's insurer to make sure any liability, workers compensation or errors/omissions coverage is in place.

Step 10: *Do the financial "screens."* Call the bank reference and ask about the builder's account. Any bounced checks? When was it opened? Any other information they can give you? Check the supplier references—what type of credit does the builder have (net 30 or C.O.D.)? Has the builder been current with payments?

Step 11: *Have your attorney do a judgment and mechanic's lien search on the builder.* If the builder has worked under another corporate or company name, search it too. This will determine if he have any unpaid bills or outstanding judgments from lawsuits. The fact is bad builders leave a trial of such liens and judgements behind them— sniffing out this information is extremely important.

Step 12: *Call your local Better Business Bureau and your area's consumer affairs department*. Most new home complaints don't go to the BBB, but it's worth a shot. Consumer affairs departments (which may be separate agencies or part of a district attorney's office) may have a record of past complaints.

Step 13: *In areas with high utility costs, ask your local utility company for a print-out of utility bills (gas, electric, etc.) for the builder's previously-built homes.* So the builder claims she builds energy efficient homes? See if it's true—some utilities provide this information for free or a nominal charge. It's the best way to see whether the builder's promises match reality.

Step 14: *If the builders pass these tests, get cost estimates for your project from the winning candidates.* Have them break down the bid by trade area/subcontractor. Any options should be clearly spelled out in terms of costs. Suggestions for lower costs should also be listed (an asphalt shingle roof is $3000 less than the specified cedar shake shingles, for example). If you've hired an architect, she may assist you in preparing the "bid package" to get an apples-to-apples cost estimate from each builder. Some architects also offer negotiating services.

Step 15: Cross your fingers and pick a builder.

We know this sounds like a major commitment of time, but your new home will be your biggest life investment. Only by thoroughly checking out builders will you prevent yourself from falling into a scam. Remember, the key is to avoid being sold on a builder, but instead to pro-actively buy your house.

Money Bomb #1: No insurance.
"We built a home last year that ended up with serious structural problems—the foundation walls cracked and water damaged our basement. The problem was a 'math error' by the builder. We sued but found we couldn't collect since the builder had no insurance and had just declared bankruptcy."

"Errors and omissions" (E & O) insurance covers just such problems. Unfortunately, few builders have it. And even if they do, it's no guarantee—you may have an expensive legal battle with the insurer to settle the problem. Nonetheless, it's worth the time to ask about E & O. Another type of insurance required for builders in some states is workers compensation—in case someone gets hurt working on your home. Small-time builders may try to skirt these rules—it's basically your risk, however. If someone falls off your roof and dies, the building department may pull the site's permit if the builder was improperly insured. An expensive lawsuit also could drain the builder of cash. All of these possibilities imperil your home. By the way, forget about those "10-year warranty programs" that claim to cover structural defects—they're worthless, as you'll discover in our next chapter.

Money Bomb #2: License loopholes.
"A builder in our neighborhood recently built a $200,000 home without a license. How can that happen?"

Loopholes is the answer. Some states don't require builders to be licensed. Others have loopholes you could drive a truck through—in North Carolina, for example, builders who do a home for less than $30,000 don't need a license. As you might expect, some fudge their numbers to make a $100,000 house look cheaper (by not including the cost of land, for example). Other states let unlicensed builders construct homes they intend to live in—many builders just turn around and sell them a few days after completion. The result: Some new homes slip through the "safety net" system of licensing, permits and

Visiting the Other Homes: Evaluating Construction on the Fly

Let's say you pop by some other homes that a builder is doing. Interestingly enough, you can tell a lot about the overall quality of a builder by judging his subcontractors. Those are the folks actually doing the work. Here are the clues:

- **Supervision.** Is there a supervisor or foreman on the site? Are the subs working unsupervised? Does the supervisor just drive by from time to time and wave from her truck?

- **Beer bottles.** It always amazes us to walk around in a new home under construction and find beer bottles and cans lying about. How exactly can you install a window properly or align something in a straight line if you just quaffed six Budweisers? Any builder or subcontractor who employs workers who drink beer or booze on the job is amazingly stupid. One homeowner we interviewed found an empty Jim Beam whiskey bottle in the basement—it belonged to the plumber, who had just botched the home's plumbing installation.

- **Trash and "stacked materials."** Materials and supplies should be stacked neatly, not strewn around the job site. While most construction sites have some amount of trash, you can tell if it's accumulating.

- **Supplies and materials left exposed to the weather.** Expensive products like windows and fireplaces should be protected from the elements. Floor joists should not be left in the open for more than a few days since they can warp. Sadly, we see many job sites where expensive materials and supplies lie exposed to rain, wind, vandalism and worse.

- **Foundations.** Girders (the main beams under a home) should be centered on the foundation piers that support them. If they aren't, big problems can result. Are anchor bolts installed? These hold the house to the foundation in severe wind storms or earthquakes.

- **Six-inch-deep exterior walls.** This type of construction (2x6, as it's known) is preferable to four-inch deep walls (2x4 construction). The reason: You can stuff more insulation into a six-inch deep wall. This is important in areas with extreme hot or cold temperatures. Why do builders use 2x4s? It's cheaper.

- **Particle board or plywood exterior sheathing?** Particle board is made of pieces of wood glued together, while plywood is a single sheet of wood. "Tongue-in-groove" plywood is the best choice for exterior sheathing, but once again it's cheaper to use particle board. So guess which one builders use? Another note: There should be no gaps between exterior sheets—each panel should be flush.

- **Plumbing.** Here's one good sign of a quality plumber: wiped joints. When two pieces of copper pipe meet, a soldered joint holds them together. See if the plumber wiped the solder to form a smooth joint—that's a pro job. Amateurs don't wipe and leave globs of solder behind.

- **Drywall.** "Sheetrockers," as they're known, are a peculiar bunch who work at lightning speed. Pros screw and glue the drywall to the walls instead of nailing.

- **Paint.** For the interior, professionals can be distinguished from amateurs by their equipment—heavy drop cloths, quality brushes and paint. Also, pros do a lot of prep work such as patching nail holes. Exterior painters who are pros always use a coat of primer before putting on the actual paint—builders often cut out this step to save money, and it's a major money bomb (as we'll explain later). A good paint job means no paint on the trim work or window glass and no visible brush marks.

- *Brick work.* A quality brick mason makes sure the mortar is of even depth between the bricks. Obviously, any cracks or gaps in the mortar are a telltale sign of problems. In areas where concrete block and masonry foundations are common, check to make sure mortar is between each block and brick.

- *Trim work with no gaps.* Look at the corner of the molding that lines the floors—any gaps? Real pros don't do gaps. Good molding or trim work is evenly stained and installed without any hammer marks. Filled in nail holes indicats quality—many builders rushing to complete a project may "forget" to do this.

- *"Seamless" carpet.* Good installation of carpet is almost as critical as the type of carpet itself. If you see a seam, it's not a good sign. Look at the corners, doorways and walls to see if the carpet was professionally installed.

- *Windows.* Most builders install windows and leave the name brand sticker on for a little while. This gives you a clue as to the quality level—ask a local window supplier or home center for information on the brand.

- *Gutters and "smart" drainage.* The downspouts should be extended at least five feet from the home. Even better: black plastic pipe that connects to the end of the downspout and moves water far away from the home. The ground near the home should be graded to drain water away from the home—sadly, most builders pay scant attention to these details. They think that once they finished the inside of the house, they're done. And the home buyer doesn't notice bad drainage until water washes away dirt under a concrete sidewalk, causing it to crack and collapse, or until water floods a basement or garage.

- *Decks.* Most deck posts are placed in cement footings—make sure the post is in the center of the footing (as opposed to on one side—this causes "eccentric loading," which is not any fun). Ask the builder about the grade of deck lumber. For redwood or cedar, two-inch decking is better than thinner options.

- *Driveways.* Check out older driveways from the builder's previous customers—see how they've aged. Proper drainage off the driveway is important—you don't want pooling near your house. Expansion joints for concrete are critical as well. Does the builder reinforce the driveway by use of steel re-bar, mesh or fiberglass-impregnated concrete? Is the soil under the driveway compacted before the driveway is poured? If these steps aren't done, the chances of driveway cracks increase.

As you can tell, professional subs tend to have professional equipment—trucks, ladders, large crews, etc. We urge you to visit homes under construction and look at the subs as they work—you'll either confirm that the builder you're going to hire is professional or you'll be forewarned about potential problems.

inspections. Due to lack of oversight, the homes are often riddled with defects and poor construction.

A parallel "money bomb" in this category is states that have such loose licensing requirements, there might as well be no licensing. In Colorado, the builder's licensing exam is a 20-minute open -book test. On the other hand is Florida. Its grueling five day-exam is the toughest. But builders in Florida have invented creative ways around this— those individuals who pass the test are hired as "front men"—the ace student holds the license but doesn't do any actual building. The building is done by less-than-caring individuals who are still mastering their multiplication tables at press time.

If that weren't enough, some con-artist builders use another contractor's license to get a building permit. Incompetent bureaucrats in some states don't even check to see if the builder is legit before they issue him a building permit.

Money Bomb #3: Inflated subcontractor bids.

"On our custom home, we hired an architect who helped us bid our house to three builders. Each one broke down the bid by trades or subcontractor area. To our horror, we found that one builder padded each sub's bid with extra profit. Then he added another 15% profit onto the bottom line."

We heard this story from one home buyer who noticed part of the bid was for pricey custom kitchen cabinets. In trying to negotiate a better price, the architect called the cabinet maker to confirm their $7000 bid. "$7000?" the cabinet sub sai., "We only bid $5000." When confronted, the builder admitted to padding the subs' bids with extra profit.

While there is nothing wrong with builders making a fair profit on a new home, the subs' bids should be free of "extra padding." The builder can add profit on the bottom line, but nickel-and-diming the home buyer on every sub's bid for a custom home is a cheap shot. This "double dipping" in such a deceptive manner should never happen—but it does. Notice that the architect in the above story discovered the fraud by calling the subs to confirm their bids.

Of course, if you structure the home purchase so the construction loan draws (that you approve) are based on the actual sub's bill or invoice, you also can stop this. In the above case, the builder was in charge of paying the subs' bills directly. Hence the home buyer would have never known what hit him.

Reality Check: Builder/Architect Tension

In a perfect world, builders and architects would work together as teammates on your new home. In the not-so-perfect world of new home construction, there is often tension between the architect and the builder.

Occasionally, home buyers don't have to wait until construction begins to witness this phenomenon. Nope, some builders and architects square off right at the beginning, during the design and bidding process.

Some builders balk at bidding on a home they think is a "leaker." That's defined as any home they *think* might leak because of an unusual roof design. If this happens to you, you should meet separately with that builder and discuss his opinion of the design flaw. A frank discussion with the architect should follow and he or she should justify the design and make doubly sure it won't leak.

Tract Homes: Choosing a Production Builder

As you can probably tell by now, production builders are not the first choice we'd recommend for your new home. The reasons are obvious.

1 **Production builders are focused on just that—production.** Quality and craftsmanship take a back seat to the headlong rush to slap up as many homes as possible. Sure, the prices are low, but so is the quality of materials and workmanship. Everything in the home is the cheapest quality or the lowest cost option.

2 **Cookie-cutter designs leave much to be desired.** You have to live with the prefab design cooked up by marketing consultants who think it's what the American family wants today. Instead of fitting like a glove, the house is a little too big here, not right there, and so on. Considering the prices, settling for a home that doesn't fit your lifestyle or needs isn't a fun prospect.

3 **"Semi-custom" often means just changing the color of paint.** Many builders abuse this term by simply faking it. Real semi-custom builders will change interior walls (except for load-bearing walls, which are part of the structural integrity of the home) and just about any feature. This is more than picking the color of paint, carpet, tile or linoleum from a choice of six samples.

Of course, in many areas of the country, production builders have sewn up 80% or more of the new home market. They've done that by buying up land in giant new subdivisions and then aggressively marketing it. Production builders also have done a snow job on consumers by convincing them that their homes are the only affordable options and custom homes are extremely expensive.

The other major advantage for production homes is time. You can often move into a nearly completed house in just a few weeks, while completely designing and building a home can take six months to a year. If you want a prime location or neighborhood near work or schools, your only choice may be production builders.

So, with those sobering facts in mind, here are some tips on picking a production builder.

Beware the Model Trap

Did you know that production builders actually call those model homes "model traps"? That's because they're designed to trap buyers—first you visit the sales office, which is cleverly plopped into the garage of a model home. Then you exit by another door that leads you to another model home.

The pathway to the model home is designed by scientists to make sure you have the perfect (and most unblemished) view of the exterior of the house. Inside, you'll find the ideal specimen of caring construction—every corner is perfect, every detail is right. The furnishings are designed by an interior designer in such a way as to bamboozle you into thinking the rooms' sizes are just right. Not too pretentious and not too K-Mart, the furniture and window treatments are calculated to maintain the illusion that "this could be your home" (if you never lived in it).

After you finish visiting the model home, a fence keeps you from returning to your car. You must walk back into the sales office to be pitched by the cheery salesperson. Despite the fact that this salesperson really knows less about the home than your cat, she will endlessly try to get you to buy. Today. Right now. This is the "trap" part of the model trap.

But you're smarter than this, aren't you? There are several ways to defeat the model trap.

1 **Ask for a list of options.** When you walk around the model home, drag the salesperson by the neck and have him or her point out everything that's "optional." Wouldn't you know that much of that pretty model home is not included in the base price? In fact, much of the home is "optional upgrades" or "designer touches." Translation: It costs you more money. However, many builders are rather cagey about what's standard and what's not. They stuff model homes with all kinds of goodies, the price of which they spring on you later. It's like buying a car without seeing the sticker to determine all the optional equipment.

You defeat this by getting a list of options up front. If no list exists (it does but it may not be for public consumption), you must determine what you're really seeing. Only the salesperson really knows this—you must drag him or her with you. That way you won't fall in love with the special tile treatment in the master bedroom—after you learn it's a $700 upgrade.

2 **See "real homes."** These could be partially finished homes under construction in the community. Or, even better, check out real homes lived in by real people. If you visit the community on a weekend, chances are you'll find neighbors out doing yard work. Say hello and shoot the breeze—about the neighborhood, the builder and their home. It's amazing how different homes look when they're decorated by real people, not interior decorators. You may be impressed ... or you may run away as fast as you can.

3 **Check out the "model variances."** That's jargon for the fact that models aren't reality. The builder doesn't guarantee that your home will look that good. If you don't believe us, check out the production builder's contract—it usually says in the fine print that your home may vary "significantly" from the model. Grill the salesperson and any other builder representatives for concrete examples of such "variances." Is the trim always oak or do they substitute pine? Do they always use that name brand (window, furnace/air conditioning, carpet, flooring)? What warning do you have of a possible "substitution"? If they can't give you a straight answer, don't buy.

The point is that you don't have to get trapped in the model trap. By taking a few steps, you can eliminate those unpleasant surprises.

Money Bombs with Production Homes

Money Bomb #1: "Builder-grade materials."
"We paid $190,000 for a semi-custom home to discover we got tract-home quality. Everything from the windows to the garbage disposal is 'builder-grade' cheap and has caused us nothing but problems and repair headaches. How did this happen?"

There's not one single building product out there that someone hasn't figured out a way to lower the quality of, in order to sell it at rock-bottom prices. And what do manufacturers call these super-cheap materials? "Builder grade." Makes you wonder. Many companies that make everything from windows to siding to carpet have three grades—the quality stuff for professionals, medium quality for do-it-yourselfers, and the lowest of the low, reserved for your friendly builder.

The problem is most of the "builder-grade" materials aren't built to last much longer than the warranty period on your home (usually about a year). Cheap carpet wears quickly in traffic areas, cheap paint fades fast and builder-grade appliances break down with alarming regularity. You end up replacing the cheap stuff and spending thousands of dollars in the process.

How do you avoid this ultimate money bomb? First, forget about the builder's stock brochures and sales materials, filled with warm and fuzzy references to their great quality. Instead, get brand names/grades on materials used in the home—everything you can think of (especially the big ticket items like windows, siding, roofing, and the like). Some of this information is in plain view, while for some items you may have ask the builder to volunteer this information.

Investigate the quality by going to a home center or calling a professional. For those faucets you suspect are cheap stuff, call a plumber and ask. Ask a home center or roofing supplier about the quality of the shingles. Beware of builders who use obviously high quality items in very visible areas like the kitchen or bath, only to turn around and use builder-grade stuff for not-so-obvious items like windows, shingles, etc.

Money Bomb #2: Deceitful Decorating.

"A model home that we saw the other day was quite slick. In the living room, there was just a love seat. When we got home, we realized our normal-size couch may not fit in there."

You've just discovered what we call "deceitful decorating." Clever builders use all kinds of tricks to make their model homes more attractive. One favorite: using undersize furniture to make a room seem larger. A love seat creates an "optical illusion" of a bigger room. Mirrored walls also make dinky rooms seem cavernous.

Don't be fooled—bring along a tape measure and take actual measurements of rooms. Don't rely on the builder's information: they often "forget" to put room measurements on floor plans or fudge the figures to boost square footage.

Money Bomb #3: Ten-year warranties.

"The builder who sold us our home pitched us on this 10-year warranty program. He said only quality builders can participate and the warranty company will stand behind his work. Later, after we discovered a structural problem specifically covered in the warranty, we got an endless run-around from the warranty company. They refused to fix our home unless it was falling down."

Welcome to the world of 10-year warranties, the biggest rip-off of all with new homes. In the next chapter, we'll tell you how thousands of complaints like this prompted congressional hearings in 1991 on this insidious scam. The bottom line: production builders love to pitch these warranties, but the evidence shows they're worthless. The best "warranty" on your home is confirming the quality of the builder and then subjecting the actual construction to a series of inspections by a private inspector (who works for you).

 ### Money Bomb #4: The incomplete contract and allowance game.

"We got hooked on a semi-custom home and signed a contract. It turns out that the one-page contract gave us no details on our new home. First we found out that the nice oak trim in the model was an option—the standard was ugly pine. Then the allowances we got for lighting and carpet were pitifully low. We ended up shelling out $8000 more to get the quality we thought we were buying in the first place."

It's shocking to see the actual contracts of many production and semi-custom builders. Lots of legal mumbo-jumbo about deposits and payments due to the builder. What's missing? The "specs and materials." This list tells you exactly what you are buying—the type of trim, brand of windows, type of fireplace, type and size of doors, etc. Very few consumers ask for this and most regret it later.

Not seeing the specs and materials list (in some cases, it's a small book) is like buying a car without seeing the price sticker. Do you get a manual or automatic transmission? Air bag? Air conditioning? The last thing you want to do is first buy the car, pay the money and *then* discover what's in there. Sounds silly, but that's exactly how many tract and semi-custom homes are bought today.

Another twist on this scam is the "allowance game." Many semi-custom builders give you an "allowance" toward purchasing flooring (carpet and vinyl), tile, appliances, light fixtures, landscaping, brick selection, and other items. The allowance is money the builder pays for the items—anything over is your responsibility.

As you might guess, the allowance game rip-off occurs when the money really doesn't pay for anything. Here's a sample allowance from a real semi-custom home:

> Lighting fixtures $500
> Appliances..$2000
> Tile, carpet, and vinyl flooring (installed)..........$8500

Now, $500 sounds like a lot of money for light fixtures ... but have you priced light fixtures recently? Basically, $500 might pay for *one* dining room fixture. Don't forget about outside fixtures as well—one of those nice carriage lamps can easily run $100. And you need two of them for most garages. Even if you buy the bare bones, cheapest light fixtures on Earth, you'll be hard pressed to spend less than $500. We fell victim to this scam and ended up spending another $600 out of our own pockets to get semi-decent light fixtures—and that was after shopping at discount shops and catalogs. (We'll pass these names along to you later.)

Be aware of lighting allowances that include "recessed lights." The builder may give you $1000 for lighting, but that might include recessed cans. A basic, no-frills recessed can is $30 to $50. Ten cans could set you back $500 and then you'd only have $500 more for other lights. Overall, lighting allowances range from $500 to $1500.

How about $2000 for appliances? Of course, the first question you should ask is, "which appliances?" Does the builder assume you already own a refrigerator? Trying to stretch $2000 to buy a refrigerator, range/oven, dishwasher, disposal, washer and dryer is impossible. You can easily end up spending $3500 for all the above. Just walk into an appliance store and start taking notes on prices to determine whether the builder is really offering you a deal.

Here's another good question: does the builder have any "contractor discount deals" with local suppliers? For example, an appliance store may give your builder "contractor prices" that are 5% to 15% below retail. Any reputable builder can qualify for these discounts by simply filling out credit forms to get an account.

However, beware of builders who might be getting kickbacks from certain suppliers—they might build this into a price bid. One builder we knew also owned a carpet/vinyl store and "heavily recommended" that his buyers shop there. The prices were quite high. The best tip: shop around to sources not recommended by the builder to make sure you're not getting fleeced on the price. Despite the pitfalls, seeing whether the builder has such discounts or accounts with suppliers is a good money-saving tip.

Strategy for Production Homes: Use That Salesperson

Many salespeople who work for production or semi-custom builders have a vested interest in making sure you're happy—many are given bonuses based on "customer satisfaction" surveys.

Hence, you can often get the salesperson to act as your advocate when things go sour. One home buyer we interviewed had just such an experience. The supervisor on her custom home was an . . . let's, just say "not a very nice person."

The supervisor would lock the home buyer out of the home to keep him from snooping around and finding problems with the construction. Even though the home buyer had a key to the garage, the supervisor would jam the door with a piece of wood. When the home buyer did get inside, she noticed lots of problems. Some of the workmanship was poor, in other cases, their *paid for* "semi-custom" requests were being ignored.

The home buyer discovered the salespeople at the development were sympathetic to her plight. One salesperson left windows of the home open so the home buyer could crawl inside. By complaining directly to the president of the company, she got action. It was the president himself who accompanied her on a final walk-through inspection that lasted two hours. The supervisor no longer works for the builder.

Another lesson from this debacle: make sure your rights to visit the home under construction are spelled out in the contract. You should have a key and the right to visit the home any time without notice or warning. Common sense says you shouldn't get in the way of the workers, of course.

Some builders are quite nervous about letting home buyers into their homes under construction. Their official reasons for denying consumers access: "construction sites are dangerous places and our insurance company forbids anyone but workers from being there."

The real reasons: builders realize that if home buyers see the actual construction, all kinds of problems may be discovered. You may find out that the options you paid for are not being installed. Or the workmanship is not up to their promises. A few builders worry that consumers will want to make lots of costly and time-consuming changes as well.

Of course, if you can't view the home until it's done, you'll be under intense pressure to close and move in—your rental lease may be expiring or you may have sold a previous home. Some con artists know building is a long and emotionally draining process. Many home buyers just want it to be over. Builders know that this pressure or exhaustion might make buyers overlook a few "problems" and close anyway.

Once the walls are closed up, you can't see that warped wall stud that may cause the drywall to pop out later. You also might not see the duct work for central heat/air conditioning that isn't properly connected. Oh, sure, you'll discover this later when a room is too hot or too cold. By that time, the builder will have all your money and little incentive to fix it. Some builders skip town altogether.

We believe total access to a new home under construction is a fundamental consumer right. You are the one who's put down a substantial deposit and it's all your money on the line. You're on the hook for the next 30 years to live with the thing. And, sad to say, the quality of many production homes just cannot be left to chance.

 If you have any questions or comments on this chapter, please feel free to call the authors. See the "How to Reach Us" page at the back of this book!

8

The Paper Trail

Protecting Your Rights with a Good Contract

When you sign a contract, you might as well consider that pen in your hand to be a stick of dynamite. Over the next several months, you will have to live by what's in and—equally important—what's *not* in the contract.

If you ever talk to a home buyer who's been ripped off by a builder (that is, had a "negative home buying experience"), you'll notice one common thread: a bad contract. After you strip away all the incompetent subcontractors, the builder-grade materials, and the outright deception by the builder or salespeople, you'll usually discover that it all starts with a lousy contract that didn't protect the consumer.

How do bad contracts zap good home buyers?

1 *Generic real estate forms.* Surprisingly, many new homes are bought with just the generic real estate "Contract to Buy and Sell." While this might be fine for existing homes, new home construction is another ball game. Although this generic contract does identify the buyer and seller and the amount to be paid, no mention is made of exactly *what* you're buying or *when* it will be completed. Some builders get around this problem with a "new construction addendum," which is nice but runs into the next problem.

2 *Omission of details.* Even contracts written for new construction are devoid of critical details. For example, it's rare to find a completion date and any penalty clause. No specs or materials are promised—just vague wording that says the home will be built in accordance with the "drawings and design plans." If the builder drew those plans, the plans may still omit many details. For example, a door opening is drawn on the plans but no mention is made whether it's an expensive, six-panel, solid oak door or a cheap, pine hollow-core door. And it's like that all down the line: heating/cooling systems, windows, faucets—the plans give you no clue as to whether you're getting quality or trash.

3 ***Verbal promises.*** The final straw of these bad contracts is verbal agreements. The builder may promise a brick fireplace at the beginning, but having no written agreement makes it easier for the builder to say later he never promised that. If you order a change but fail to put it in writing, the builder may fail to make the change. Or the change will be made and you'll be cahrged twice the "verbal" price. Near closing, you may be shocked by huge bills for items you thought were more affordable in earlier conversations.

We do have a prescription to avoid bad contracts. But first, here are three reality checks on this process.

Reality Check
In most cases, the choice of contract is not yours. With production-type homes, the builder will insist you use their contract. There won't be much discussion except for a possible addendum that specifies some details you want in writing. Many tract and semi-custom homes are sold with this "take it or leave it" attitude.

Custom homes are slightly different. In some cases, you (or your attorney) may be able to draft your own contract. Some builders will insist on their own contracts while still others will use a neutral third-party contract such as the American Institute of Architects' standard form (more on this later).

We suggest you pass on a builder who refuses to use a fair contract. Such an agreement includes many of the clauses discussed later in this chapter. One home buyer we knew walked away from a deal on a new home when the builder balked at putting the "specs and materials" for a $175,000 home in writing. Without knowing exactly *what* you're buying, you're almost assured of a disappointment. In the worst case, you might be a victim of a major rip-off when that $175,000 home turns out to be riddled with cheap materials and poor workmanship.

Market conditions will affect your ability to negotiate. Most contracts are negotiable. You can delete clauses you object to and add to the contract in an addendum. However, you're ability to do this is tied to whether the market is "hot" or "cold."

In cold markets, builders are begging for work. Hence, they may agree to a penalty clause that fines them for each day the home's construction runs late. They also may remove or modify clauses that limit your rights—such as the right to inspect the home prior to closing. In their desperation, builders may reveal to you the exact specs and materials used—and perhaps negotiate on upgrading these at minimal cost.

Hot markets are another story. In areas that are booming, builders can get very arrogant. It's a take-it-or-leave it world and they're the gods of new home construction. "If you don't like it, go live in an apartment," is the basic attitude. Sure, some builders will be willing to make a few concessions, but most might tell you to take a hike when you want contract changes.

Of course, in the real world, most communities are neither extremely hot nor cold when it comes to new construction. In a luke warm market, you'll find some builders willing to make concessions while others are intransigent. Your (or your attorney's or buyer's broker's) ability to negotiate will greatly impact the outcome of the contract negotiations.

Builders have expert lawyers and take extensive classes all designed to limit your rights—and their liability for problems. One reason you need an experienced real estate attorney to review your contract is because the builder has one. In fact, many builders (especially the large production builders) have batteries of high-paid attorneys who stay up late at night to ruminate endlessly on finding new ways to limit your rights.

Builders also take seminars and read books designed to "limit their liability" (translation: strip you of your rights). For example, the National Association of Home Builders actually has a publication that advocates builders use contracts that "disclaim implied warranties in states where they are permissible." What's an implied warranty? As you'll discover later, this is court-mandated consumer protection for new homes which builders loathe. Some states allow you to sign away your rights for implied warranties and builders know it.

The result: contracts that are loaded with land mines that strictly limit the builder's liability for goofs or problems. Other clauses restrict your rights for redress. If you're not careful, the deck could be stacked against you even before the first shovel of dirt is thrown in the air.

As a side note, builders' sneaky and covert attempts to zap consumers with clever legal maneuvering belies the "trust factor." Many builders implore their customers to "trust" them and claim that they are acting on the customers' behalf. One builder we know actually wrote the trust factor into his contract, stating:

> *The contractor accepts the relationship of trust and confidence established between he and Owner by this agreement. He covenants with Owner to furnish his best skill and judgement in furthering the interest of Owner.*

Gee, that sounds nice. But this same builder on the next page strips the consumer of important rights like implied warranties and redress of grievances in a court of law. We'd be more apt to believe the trust propaganda if the builders stopped trying to limit implied warranty rights and stopped setting up bogus 10-year warranty companies to dupe consumers.

A Special Warning

We do not intend to give legal advice in this chapter, but instead to provide a general discussion of several contractual issues as they apply to new construction. You should always seek professional counsel before signing any legal document—especially one that obligates you to pay big bucks, such as a new home purchase.

As a side note, there is no federal law for real estate. Essentially, every state (its legislatures and courts) has established different real estate laws. This patchwork quilt of 50 state laws and requirements is another reason to have a real estate lawyer look over your contract. What's a consumer protection or requirement in one state may be completely absent in another.

Sources for Sample Contracts

1 *American Institute of Architects (AIA) form contracts.* The AIA has standard form contracts for both architects/consumers and builders/consumers that have become the standards for the industry. The AIA acted as a semi-neutral third party in developing these contracts, with input from both builders and consumers. Copies are available from any AIA document distributor, member architects, and the AIA headquarters in Washington, D.C., by calling 1-800-365-ARCH. Non-members may have copies as well.

Despite their fairness, three big things are *missing* from the AIA contracts we first previewed. Fortunately, the AIA has addressed these issues in updated versions of their contracts:

- *Payment schedule.* When and how does the builder get paid? Besides the initial deposit, what is the "draw" schedule (if you control the construction loan)? Is any money held back at closing (payable in another 30 days) to make sure everything is satisfactory?
- *Inspections.* This includes both informal and formal inspections. Informal inspections by the home buyer at any time should be any consumer's goal—a key should guarantee access. Formal inspections by a private inspector should be clearly spelled out at certain points (foundation/footings, framing/plumbing rough-in, finishing work). In the next chapter, we'll discuss these key inspection points in detail. Your contract should clearly specify these points, as well as a time period for the builder to correct any defects.
- *Completion and starting dates.* When will construction begin? When is the home to be finished? Will there be any penalty fee per day for tardiness? Any "bonus" payment if the home is completed early? Builders will want to qualify any start or finish date to account for major acts of God such as earthquakes, tornadoes, and other minor delays. Be sure the wording here is not

vague enough to let the builder declare a vacation in the Bahamas as an act of God requiring him to take time off. Any delay that's clearly the fault of the builder (which delays the finish date) should trigger the penalty clause—if you can negotiate one.

2 **The Builder's Guide to Contracts and Liability (Home Builder Press, 1-800-368-5242, $16).** Published by the National Association of Home Builders publishing arm, this 52-page book gives you an interesting insight into contracts—from the builder's perspective.

You learn all kinds of creative clauses that can be used to limit your rights. Note "Chapter 3: Environmental Liability in Real Estate Transactions," which provides a fascinating discussion of how builders can avoid liability for homes built on hazardous waste sites. Builders also learn how to avoid responsibility for new homes that are contaminated by high levels of radon gas.

Wading through all this as a consumer may be somewhat challenging since the legalese is thick and the jargon can get rather technical. Nonetheless, reading this book puts you on equal footing with builders in negotiations. You also may gain an insight into why certain provisions appear in your contract.

Key Clauses to a Good Contract

Remember, the basic ingredient of a good contract is that it's *written*. Also, any changes, letters or notices regarding the contract should be written. Verbal agreements are an invitation to trouble.

1 **Work Description**
Will the builder construct the entire home? Or will you do some of the work, such as painting, landscaping, etc.? You must clearly specify what each party (you and the builder) will do, including any authorization for the builder to purchase materials for the job.

We spoke with one home buyer who ran into a big dispute with his builder over this issue. The buyer and builder agreed verbally that the buyer would paint the exterior of the home—but both failed to write this down in the contract. As the project went on, the builder failed to do several other tasks, claiming that the buyer had agreed verbally to take care of them. Since there was no written contract, it was hard to figure out who agreed to do what.

2 **The Money Stuff**
How much will the home cost? What's the deposit? How (and when) will the builder be paid the balance? If there are draws off a construction loan, what is the procedure for payment? Is the deal contingent on financing? Must there be any proof or evidence that the buyer has obtained permanent financing?

Another area of concern may be change orders. Does the builder charge a fee to process a change order? How is such a charge calculated? Are there any allowances?

Most homes are built on a "fixed price contract." This means you pay X dollars for the home. The only exception to this could be soil conditions that increase excavation costs—some builders won't lock into a specific figure for this on custom homes.

The alternative to the fixed price contract is a cost-plus deal. Here you pay a certain fee or percentage above the costs for the builder's profit. In rural areas or difficult to build on sites, builders may tell you this is the only option since estimating costs for a fixed price contract is difficult. The problem with cost-plus is, what exactly are the costs? Are they just the materials and labor? What about rental charges on equipment needed for excavation? How about sales taxes or impact fees? Don't forget travel expenses—some builders try to tack this onto the "costs" category.

It's this difficulty in defining "costs" that makes fixed price contracts more attractive for home buyers. If the only option is cost-plus, you might want to have an architect or buyer's broker help you negotiate a fair definition of costs. If you aren't careful here, the builder could include everything under the sun as costs, driving your final price through the roof.

3 | *Difficult Sites*

As mentioned above, some builders like a provision to cover themselves in the case of difficult soils or site conditions. Especially for semi-custom or custom homes, this can be an expensive clause for the buyer.

Insist the builder give you a specific budget for excavation and back fill. (Back fill is explained in the next chapter.) For our home, this came to $2300. Now, if the soil under your home is nice and soft, the allowance should cover the costs of basic excavation and back fill. But...what if they hit bedrock? Rock-hard limestone? Clay? A high water table?

All these cases almost always mean higher excavation costs—and you're on the hook here. In our case, we ran into limestone and the excavation costs went through the roof (or the floor, more accurately). Final tab: $3500. Ouch. There went an extra $1200 we had planned to spend elsewhere. This points out a major rule in home buying: LEAVE AN EXTRA 10% FOR EMERGENCIES. If you're building a $150,000 home, make sure you budget an extra $15,000 for little surprises like this and other cost overruns (your desire for an extra window here, nicer tile there, etc.). Even if you don't need the entire $15,000, it's nice to know you're prepared in the worst case.

A good way to spot difficult soil conditions is to do a soils test before you buy the lot. Make the purchase of the lot contingent on a satisfactory soils test. If you're purchasing a yet-to-be-built tract or semi-custom home in an existing community, the builder may have already done a soils test on your lot. Insist on seeing the test results and consider consulting with a soils engineer or geologist to get an opinion about the ease/difficulty of building on this lot.

Make sure your contract defines just what a "differing site condition" is. You also should have a certain number of days to inspect and confirm the condition if one is discovered. If everyone agrees this is a problem, a specific method of extra compensation to the builder should be identified. While some builders like an extra percentage of the sales price, we think the best course is the actual bill from the excavation company. Any real, documented amount over the original excavation and backfill allowance would be paid by the buyer.

4 | *Contingencies and Other Fun Stuff*

Do you want to make your purchase of this new home contingent on selling an old one? Your contract should specifically define a time period to sell the old house, including a refund in case the contingency falls through.

Many builders insist on contingencies regarding financing—that is, you, the buyer, must get a commitment or qualification letter for a permanent mortgage. You may be required to diligently search for financing within a certain time period—30 to 90 days is typical. If you can't get the money, the deal is off. Whether you get all your deposit back or whether the builder should be reimbursed for any out-of-pocket costs should be negotiated in this passage.

Another good tip: ask the builder to pay for an "extended coverage" title policy that gives you mechanic's lien protection. In some states, title companies offer this extra coverage that protects you against the builder who doesn't pay his bills (and then the subs come back and file liens against your home for their unpaid invoices). The cost is a mere $50 to $150—a wise buy even if the builder won't pick up the tab.

5 | *Time, Time, Time.*

When will the construction start? When will the home be finished? These seem like simple points, but like everything else in the world of home building, it's not as easy as it looks.

The start of construction may be contingent on you getting financing, the plans being finished on a certain date, all the permits being pulled, surveys and other tests on the lot being completed, and so on. Your contract should state that assuming all the above are accomplished (and weather permitting), construction should start on month/day/year.

Instead of specifying a completion date, some builders like to use a more fuzzy method—estimating a total number of calendar days. Most production houses are slapped up in 80 to 120 days, while semi-custom and custom homes can drag on beyond four, five, and even six months for the most complex homes. Be careful of loopholes in this process—the contract could call for 90 "working days," which is a lot longer than real calendar days.

And what exactly defines the word "completion"? Is it when a certificate of occupancy or final inspection from the building department is given? Or when the buyer takes possession and moves in? Or is it some other point in time, such as final stamp of approval from your private inspector? We prefer the last two methods—too many corrupt building departments have been known to give out certificates of occupancy on defective or unfinished houses. In the worst cases, the government inspectors take bribes from builders and never inspect the homes they "pass." As a result, you should trust only someone working directly for you (an architect, engineer, private inspector) to give the final stamp of approval. If you don't, the builder (with a bogus certificate of occupancy) may declare the home "completed" despite serious flaws or omissions.

We should note that some states or municipalities issue an Improvement Location Certificate (ILC) on completed homes. This document shows all improvements, a foundation survey, where the home sits on the property and so on. Lenders and title companies may require this as "proof" that your home is completed.

In a perfect world, builders would never fudge start or completion dates. Conscientious builders would be honest with their appraisals of work length: "Gee, Mr. Smith, I'd like to start your home June 1, but another home is running late and it looks like it might be June 15 before construction begins."

Back to reality. Some less-than-honest builders intentionally mislead you as to a start date just to get you to sign a contract. Since all the wheels are in motion by this time, it's hard to turn back when the builder announces a "two-week delay" *after* he took your deposit. Most home buyers just grin and bear it.

Holding a builder to a completion date is another quagmire. Do you want to pressure the builder into crashing the schedule, causing sloppy workmanship as subs rush to finish? While a little deadline pressure is healthy, too much may cause more problems in the end. Forcing the builder to pay your out-of-pocket expenses (such as hotel bills) is probably enough incentive to get the home finished on time.

Here's the bitter reality: most builders give overly optimistic finish dates. They know it's really taking 120 days to build a home, but they promise 100 to get your business (knowing full well they'll probably miss the deadline). As a result, you should build extra time into your moving schedule. If your home is "promised" October 1, make sure you can lease that retnal on a month-to-month basis until November 1 just in case. If you're selling an existing home, it's better to put the closing off that extra month than to be surprised about a delay.

6 | *Defaults and Delays*

What if the builder fails to build the home in accordance with the plans and specifications? What if you, the buyer, refuse to buy the home? How about delays—what if the builder intentionally delays completing the home?

This section of the contract should define what constitutes a delay and a default (on your or the builder's part). The builder will want a broad interpretation of "delay" including such fuzzy language as the "failure of the architect to cooperate." Of course, the architect could be balking at the builder's request to use cheaper materials or deviate from the plans.

As a buyer, you want a more limited definition. While bad weather always delays construction, builders like to blame the weatherman for many problems. Sure, a driving rainstorm or sudden blizzard makes it difficult to pour a concrete foundation. However, just because it's 25 degrees outside doesn't mean framers can't frame a house. One builder we know ran two months late on a home because he was too lazy to shovel the snow out of a basement to complete the plumbing and heating rough-ins.

"Acts of God" is another fun heading. What exactly is that? Does a strike by workers count? How about the unavailability of materials? What if the wrong materials arrive (because the supplier goofed or the builder ordered the wrong stuff)—what about the delay in getting the *right* materials to the job site?

Once you arrive at the definitions of defaults and delays, the next step is to allow for "liquidated damages." If the builder goofs and delays the completion date, should he pay for your hotel costs? The extra rent you incur during that period? Travel costs? Storage fees for furniture? Frankly, the builder should pay these and any other reasonable expenses you incur because of the builder's default. An alternative to this method would be a penalty clause that docks the builder a certain amount of money per day that the home is late. On the other hand, you may include a bonus payment in the (unlikely) event the builder finishes the home early.

As you might expect, your ability to get the builder to agree to a penalty clause/expense clause reimbursement depends highly on the market. In slow times, builders may go for it. In hot markets, your chances are diminished.

7 | *Termination of the Contract*

What if the whole deal falls apart? What if the builder balks at fixing a problem your inspector identifies? Does the builder have any time to "cure" such a problem? What if you fail to pay the builder?

Clear wording should define both your and the builder's rights in the case of termination of the contract. Remedies should also be spelled out—and that's where the fur may begin to fly. It's generally fair that you should be required to reimburse the builder for all work done to date. But what about the profit? If the house is 33% completed and the builder "defaults," does the builder deserve one-third of his profit?

What if the builder is incompetent and makes several mistakes that will cost you $30,000 to fix? If the builder has already done $50,000 worth of work, what do you owe? If the builder owns the lot, do you get all of your deposit back? If you own the lot, how much should the builder get?

All these questions must be answered. We believe if you default on the deal, you should pay the builder's profit to date (in addition to any other out-of-pocket expenses the builder incurred). If the builder defaults and you own the lot, you do owe the builder for any actual costs incurred—but no profit. If damages occurred because of the builder's negligence or default, the amount of damage (as confirmed by estimates from another contractor, architect, or engineer) should be deducted from any amount owed for work done. If the builder owns the lot, you should be entitled to an entire return of your deposit.

Of course, we should warn you that just because your contract says this doesn't mean you won't have to fight an expensive legal battle to get any money from the builder if he defaults.

8 | Arbitration

More and more lately, builders have been slipping arbitration clauses into their contracts. If a dispute develops, the contract may call for binding arbitration, in which a third party sits down with both sides, hears the dispute, and makes a decision to solve the problem. Proponents of arbitration say it lowers legal costs and keeps minor disputes out of the clogged court system.

There is a darker side, however. Just listen to what the National Association of Home Builders says about arbitration in their guide to contracts for builders:

> "Arbitration provides a mechanism for resolving disputes without the publicity, and probably the cost of litigation. Arbitrators, generally experts who may be more likely than a jury to understand the technical aspects of a construction controversy, may provide a more impartial forum for a dispute than a courtroom. Additionally, the mere existence of an arbitration provision may deter potential lawsuits. Builders should suggest arbitration or mediation procedures early in a dispute, before a buyer begins to suffer 'mental anguish' that a jury might find compensable in a damage award."

Now you see some of the builder's ulterior motives in promoting arbitration. Negative publicity is one of a consumer's few tools in fighting a builder—a protracted legal battle in the public spotlight that points out shoddy practices by the builder may cause significant harm to his reputation. Even the thought of this may drive some builders to fix the problem or settle the case.

Furthermore, arbitrators sometimes aren't the "expert, neutral" parties that proponents claim. Some are former builders who are quite sympathetic to their peers and not so to the home buyer. Others are idiots with little knowledge about construction who may be swayed by the builder over the consumer. Personally, we'd rather have a jury of 12 good citizens decide a defective construction case than a tainted arbitrator. And frankly, there really is "mental anguish" when the home you spent so much money on collapses, cracks, or in some other way fails. Choosing a route that eliminates mental anguish awards is risky.

Nonetheless, you are bound to run into arbitration clauses in the paper chase for your new home. Here are a couple thoughts on the process:

- *A third-party arbitration* service such as the American Arbitration Association (AAA) should be specified in the contract. The AAA has special "construction industry arbitration rules" that it follows. Be forewarned: these can be rather expensive since you and the builder will have to pay both the AAA and the arbitrators of the dispute. Another group that does arbitration is the National Academy of Conciliators (NAC). Builders think the NAC is less expensive and faster than the AAA.

- *An alternative to picking a service* such as AAA or NAC is for each party to choose their own arbitrators. Those two arbitrators then choose a third arbitrator. Obviously, three arbitrators instead of one will cost more as well.

One thing you can say about arbitration: it isn't cheap. The American Arbitration Association (AAA) charges a variety of fees for their service. Initially there is a filing fee that depends on the amount of the claim (example: if your claim is between $50,000 and $250,000 the filing fee is $1000). Hearing fees are $200 per day for one arbitrator and $300 per day for a panel—the fee is split evenly by both parties. There is also a processing fee payable by each party of $150 to $200 for the first 180 days of the arbitration process. Room rental for the hearing may also be required. Compared to the cost of going to court, however, arbitration may not seem as expensive as it does at first glance.

Whether arbitration agreements are binding varies from state to state. You may want to seek legal counsel on whether arbitration is a smart move or a big mistake.

9 | Inspections

As you probably have noted in this book, we are big boosters of private inspections during the construction process. There are two types of inspections for new homes that should be guaranteed in the contract:

- *Informal inspections by you.* We believe you should have complete access to your new home at all times. While you should pledge not to interfere with workers or get in the way, this does not preclude your right to visit the home (especially after hours, when the work has stopped for the day). Guaranteeing this right in writing is smart, as well as making sure you are entitled to a key once the home is locked up at night.

- *Formal inspections by a private inspector.* Specific inspection points should be clearly spelled out in the contract. Sample times include foundation/footings, framing rough-in (plumbing, electrical, and mechanical), as well as finishing work prior to closing. Decide on these times with your inspector before drafting your contract.

The builder should be given a reasonable period of time to fix any problems found during the inspections. Prior to closing, a punch list of "minor repair items" also has be given to the builder. A period of 30 to 45 days to fix these items is standard.

Be forewarned: many builders deny any responsibility for fixing any problems that are not listed on the signed punch list. The exception may be "latent defects" (those not visible at the time of closing), which are covered in the builder's warranty. As a result of these provisions, you'll want to make darn sure the punch list inspection is thorough—now you can see why having a private inspector at this point is so important.

10 Mistakes in the Plans
Whether the plans are supplied by your architect/designer or by the builder, most builders will absolve themselves of any liability for mistakes in the blueprints.

If an architect draws the plans, expect the builder to make sure you're on the hook for any delays or costs caused by any defect in the plan. On the other hand, some designers put statements on their plans that they *cannot* be held liable for problems with the design. We wouldn't buy a home if the plans were stamped with this clause, nor would we hire a designer who wouldn't take responsibility for his work.

In a classic case of "having their cake and eating it, too," builders also like to absolve themselves for any goofs in their own plans—except for protection provided by the builder's limited warranty (which might be quite limited indeed).

As a side note, it's probably a good idea to have a copy of the plans if the builder is providing them (as is usually the case for tract or semi-custom homes). This provides you with ammunition in case the builder deviates from them without your permission—you can't tell what's missing if you don't have the plans. Get a copy of the plans *as approved by the building inspection department.* Why? Building departments routinely require builders to modify the plans to comply with local codes. You'll want to know what these changes are.

Another good tip: make copies of inspection comments (these are noted on the building permit, which is stored in a box on the construction site). Obtain copies of any letters or documentation on your home held by the city inspection department. One expert told us "it's amazing how many times these documents disappear" after problems with the home arise.

11 The Model Trap Revisited
Remember when we told you that those gleaming models aren't

all they're cracked up to be? Well, you begin to get the picture when you read the fine print in many production builders' contracts. The bottom line: what you see in the model ain't necessarily what you get.

Many builders rather arrogantly reserve the right to change certain items in the home. What are those certain items? Building dimensions, room sizes, appliance brands ... just about everything. The "decoration and style" of the home also may change.

Basically, some builders want you to sign away your life in these clauses. Sample passages: "Buyer acknowledges and agrees that he/she has not relied upon the accuracy of any representations made by the builder with respect to the square footage of the home." Translation: the builder may show you a 2000-square-foot model and then deliver you a 1900-square-foot home. And that's just tough.

Here's another whopper: "Builder reserves the right to make changes or substitutions of materials of equal or greater quality than those shown in the model or specified on the plans and specifications." Translation: a home version of the bait-and-switch scam. Note that any written approval or even verbal notice is NOT required—the switcheroo takes place and you just have to trust the builder.

Furthermore, how many consumers can tell whether a substituted material is of "equal or greater quality"? Unless you have intimate knowledge of building materials, you could be hoodwinked. We urge consumers to insist on written notice of any "substitution" or change in square footage—you should have time to confer with an expert (your private inspector, for example) and the right to reject any proposed substitution. The builder also should document, for example, that those different shingles are actually better than the ones he originally promised.

Now, we're not saying that your home is going to be an exact clone of the model, down to the last atom. Small changes (due to the characteristics of the lot, for example) are alright, provided you're given notice. However, the switch of an appliance brand or type of sink faucet is suspicious. The natural reflex of most builders is to make a substitution that's cheaper in order to make more profit. As a result, signing away your rights on this subject is dangerous.

12 *Environmental Liability*

All the recent warnings about radon and other environmental contaminants have builders' attorneys working overtime to draft contracts that protect their clients (that's the builder, not you).

Some builders have been bold enough to try to avoid liability for hazardous materials previously on the site (such as homes built over landfills, toxic dumps, and other fun locations). Whether builders can truly exempt themselves from this is a matter for the courts. However, it brings up one good point: doing an environmental search of your property (as described in the Chapter 4, "If Dirt Were Dollars") is your main line of defense.

Be sure to confer with your attorney regarding any environmental clause. He or she might want a modification in the wording to protect you in the case of an environmental problem.

13 Gag Rules

Here's an exciting new trend: some builders have "gag-rule" provisions in their contracts. If you're unhappy about the quality of your home, some contracts prohibit your right to hang signs or picket the builder. Can you believe this?

Obviously, the constitutionality of these provisions is seriously in doubt. Recently, the Pennsylvania State Supreme Court struck down a gag rule provision in a home purchase contract as a violation of the First Amendment.

These gag-rule contracts point up how touchy builders are about bad publicity. Instead of building quality homes and not cutting corners, it appears it's easier for powerful builders to intimidate their customers into signing contracts that eliminate the right to free speech.

If you come across this type of provision, we strongly urge you to ask the builder to remove it. Consult with your attorney regarding your state's latest court decisions about gag rules.

14 Cleaning

You might assume you're going to move into a clean home—but think twice. Many homeowners we interviewed were forced to move into filthy "new homes." All that construction activity leaves tons of dirt, dust and other fuzzy creatures everywhere. The carpet may be soiled with the mud from workers' shoes; the bathrooms may be covered with all kinds of dirt; the windows may be splattered with paint. You may want to specify that the home should be clean in your contract. Even specifying the extent of cleanliness you expect is fine. Most builders omit any mention of this in their contract and some use this omission as proof that all they were supposed to do was build a house—cleaning isn't included.

15 Specifications and Materials

Finally, the exact materials and specs should be included with your contract. If an architect generated the plans, you should already have this as part of the construction documents. However, if this is the builder's design (as it is with tract, semi-custom, and other production homes), you must ask for it.

Builders have told us that they have entire booklets filled with specifications and materials—and guess what? Most consumers don't ask for them! Incredible—it's like buying that new car and never seeing the window sticker. In the following box, we give you an idea of what "specs and materials" really cover.

Whew! You might be wondering at this point, am I crazy? Why am I building a new home? We realize this is a very thorough list and all these details may make your head spin. However, if you don't have the builder provide these specifications, how can you be sure what you're buying? So, you thought the master bathroom shower was suppose to have a shower door—but it isn't in the specs and now the builder is balking at putting one in. You get slapped with a $200 bill for the shower door. By getting all the details in writing, you prevent such little surprises from zapping you down the line.

Getting Specific: Finding Out What You're Really Buying From a Production Builder.

Back when you were shopping for a builder, we strongly suggested you get the builder's specifications and materials up front. But what does that cover? How can you tell when a builder gives you a good list or one that is missing a few items? Here's a quick primer to the world of specs and materials—the following items should be clearly spelled out on a spec list:

1. **Water and sewer.** Where's the water coming from (city tap or well)? If there's a well, who drills it and to what depth? What type of pump? For the sewer, is it a city tap or septic system? The specs for any septic system done by the builder should be clearly outlined.

2. **Excavations.** How deep is the hole? Which trees will be removed and how will they be marked? Will any unmarked trees remain? What steps will the builder take to protect trees near the construction site?

3. **Footings.** The exact type and dimensions of the footings should be identified. The weight of concrete expressed in pounds per square inch (PSI) should be specified.

4. **Foundation.** As with the footings, the thickness (expressed in weight or pounds in the mix) for the concrete should be specified. How will the foundation be built (concrete block or poured concrete)? For poured concrete, what type of forms will be used (metal or wood)? Will you or your architect be able to approve in advance any additives put in the concrete? Will any reinforcing steel rods be needed? (The need for steel re-bar depends on the soil. This points up the need for a soils test and, in many cases, a professionally designed foundation/footings by a certified engineer.)

5. **Waterproofing of the foundation.** What type of water- or damp-proofing will be used? How will it be applied?

6. **Perimeter drain.** This drain is usually a black pipe that snakes around the foundation and empties away from the house, down a slope. The exact type and installation of drain should be specified. Where and how will it be "daylighted" (or emptied)? This information is provided by a structural engineer.

7. **Back fill.** What type of back fill material will be used? How will it be put in? To what depth and how far will back fill extend from the foundation?

8. **Sills, girders, and columns.** The sills sit on top of the foundation and should be pressure-treated lumber. How will they be attached to the foundation? What type of columns and girders will be used? For the columns, will they each have a separate concrete footing?

9. **Joists.** What type, size, and installation will be used?

10. **Framing.** What type of floor sheathing will be used? How will it be glued and nailed to the joists? How will the walls be framed (the exact grade of lumber and installation)? What type of wood will be used for door and window headers and how will these be done? Exactly what type of wall sheathing will be used? Will the roof be made from prefab trusses or rafters? Make sure all these details are spelled out.

11. **Siding.** What type of siding will be used? How will it be installed? Confirm the quality of siding and make sure enough nails are used to secure it in place.

12. **Roofing.** The exact shingle type should be specified. What type of installation and flashing will be used to prevent leaking? What type and weight of felt will be used?

13. **Insulation.** The exact type and installation of insulation for the floor, walls, ceiling and roof should be specified.

14. **Chimney.** A specific plan should be identified for chimney construction, including any necessary footers, materials (bricks, concrete blocks, etc.), and heights above the roof line.

15. **Windows.** The exact brand, type, and color of frames should be specified. Will they be low-E (a more energy-efficient window)? Will they be flashed to prevent water damage? What about the screens?

16. **Attic/roof ventilation.** Another often overlooked item, adequate ventilation is important to prevent excessive ice/snow buildup in cold climates. A specific plan for ventilation and the location of vents should be identified.

17. **Exterior painting/finish.** What type of primer will be used? How many coats of paint? How will it be applied? Careful—many builders omit use of primer as a cost savings for them. This means you end up repainting your house in a short year or two. Confirm that the exterior painting will be done by an experienced painter with the appropriate tools—not some high school kid with a power sprayer.

18. **Exterior doors.** What type of doors do you get? The type of locks? The brand name, and size should be listed.

19. **Interior doors.** What type of wood? Finish? Type of wood jambs? What brand/type of door hardware is included?

20. **Inside walls/ceilings.** How thick will the drywall be and how will it be installed? What type of finish will the interior walls have? Will the ceilings be finished the same or different? Don't merely assume you're getting a certain type of wall finish (orange peel versus a smooth plaster).

21. **Trim.** The exact wood should be specified, as should the finish/stain. Installation at doors, windows, and other openings should be called out.

22. **Cabinets, countertops, vanities.** Do you get plastic laminate or Corian? Most buyers get a cabinet allowance, which must cover both the cabinets and installation. Be careful of the lowball allowance game here.

23. **Stairs.** A stair plan should clearly identify the type, materials, banisters and handrails. Any finish or stain for the last two items also should be noted.

24. **Flooring.** What are the allowances for carpet, vinyl, or hardwoods? Does this include installation? Sub-floors also should be mentioned.

25. **Plumbing.** Make sure allowances for faucets, sinks, toilets, and other stuff are identified. If a specific bathtub is included, make sure the brand and model number are spelled out. Fixtures (including brand and color) should be identified if no allowance is given. Don't forget about shower doors or sinks

continued on next page

continued from previous page

in the utility room (plus the location of the washer/dryer connections). Most other plumbing details (such as pipe locations, materials) are spelled out on the plans. Confirm any exterior water spigots—the number and location. What type of drain lines are used? Be aware that if plastic (PVC) lines are used on the second floor for toilets and these lines are not insulated, you will be able to hear the toilet flush throughout the home. A solution is to use cast iron drain lines or insulate the areas around the waste lines.

26. ***Bath hardware.*** We realize this sounds trivial, but what type of toilet paper holders are specified? Towel racks? Towel rings?

27. ***Interior paint.*** As with the exterior, confirm the brand and application method. Color options should be spelled out. How many coats?

28. ***Electrical.*** This includes many items. Starting with the outside, how many exterior outlets are there? Will the owner specify the location? What is the fixture allowance? Does this include doorbells, ceiling fans, exterior lights, or range hoods? How many outlets are there? What type of light switch is included? Most electrical outlets and switches should be noted on the plans—what flexibility do you have in changing this?

As a side note, some builders may intentionally offer you an abbreviated version of the spec list, but we suggest you insist on the whole enchilada. The only way you know whether the builder is going to do a quality home is to check such obscure stuff as the foundation footings and the perimeter drain. If these details are omitted, *assuming* the builder will use quality materials and proper installation methods is a big risk.

 ### Money Bomb #1: The pressure to move in.
"We signed a contract to move into a partially built spec home on January 1. Well, the lease on our rental expired December 31 and the new home wasn't ready. We were forced to close and move in early! Much of the work was unfinished and the house was a filthy mess!"

Obviously, one of the truths about new homes is that they *always* seem to take longer than expected to build. Some of this is dumb luck—weather delays may push back the finish date. In other cases, builders intentionally lie about the completion date or their own incompetence delays closing.

The pressure to move in can be a powerful weapon . . . for the builder. If you have to close early and the builder gets all his money, the incentive to finish your home in accordance with the plans and specs goes way down. We've seen cases in which builders have turned on the "move-in pressure," forcing homebuyers to make concessions or accept substandard work.

The obvious tip: don't put your back to the wall. Make sure you can lease that apartment/home another month if need be. If you've sold

29. **Heating and cooling.** What type of furnace or air conditioner is included? Confirm that adequate ventilation (i.e., the number of vents) for each room is specified.

30. **Telephone jacks.** How many lines are in the home? The number and location of phone jacks?

31. **Gutters/downspouts.** What color? Type (aluminum or other; seamless)? Where will the downspouts dump the water? As mentioned, water should be deposited at least five feet from the house—a better arrangement is to pipe the downspouts to a location away from the house. This prevents pooling and settling.

32. **Finish grade.** An often overlooked item, final grading smooths out the dirt near the home. A nice gradual slope away from the home is preferred. This can be done with heavy equipment and/or a rake. Any disturbed areas may be re-seeded. Additional topsoil may have to be brought in—this comes out of your excavation allowance.

33. **Other stuff.** Is there a security system? Central vacuum? Home automation system? Window treatments? Appliances? Landscaping? Retaining walls? Any and all other deals you make with the builder should be specified to the same level of detail as the above items.

a previous home, put the closing date off beyond the alleged finish date of the new home. If the new home is to be "finished" August 1, set the closing on the old home September 1. In the worst case, the builder finishes on time and you pay an extra mortgage payment on the old home. (You may try to move up the old home closing at the point you know you can safely move into the new house.)

Moving from another town is tricky. If you arrive in town with all your furniture, what can you do if (or when) the home runs late? It's probably a hotel stay for you and a storage facility for your stuff. And, of course, in all cases you should make sure your contract says your builder will reimburse all these costs.

Money Bomb #2: The low-ball allowance game.
"We were given a carpet allowance of $15 per square yard. This seemed alright—until we actually priced carpet and found out anything decent that we liked costs at least $20 per square yard installed! Help!"

As you noticed in our discussion of contracts, you may get several "allowances" on your new home's construction. Everything from the excavation to the light fixtures may have a figure attached.

The obvious scam is the low-ball allowance—the builder knows darn well you can't buy an entire house full of light fixtures for $500. How do you know you're getting low-balled? Do your homework—ask an architect, an inspector, previous home buyers, anyone. Visit home centers and take notes on prices.

The worst case is to agree to an allowance first, and then discover later it's far from adequate. This money bomb can set you back hundreds if not thousands of dollars on your new home purchase—another good reason to leave a "buffer" figure of at least 10% in your target budget, as mentioned above.

While these money bombs are common in contracts, the most prevalent problem is the lack of any agreement at all. In the research for this book, we were shocked to find consumers whose entire contract to buy or build a new home was merely a generic real estate "buy and sell" agreement—no plans, specifications, materials . . . nothing but the home's address and price. We also found custom builders who gave out skimpy details about the new home—far from adequate protection for the consumer's need.

In the case of production-type homes, many builders have "specs and materials" lists that gather dust in a file cabinet because no one asks for them. Granted, many builders don't tell consumers about this information, nor do they include it in the slick brochures they hand out. It's there if you ask, but many builders figure what you don't know (or ask for) can't hurt *them*.

On the extreme fringe are builders who intentionally hesitate to tell you exactly what you're buying. "That's not how we do business," one builder told a home buyer who inquired about the specifications and materials for a $200,000 new home. "You have to trust us." Yeah, right.

The Wild World of Home Warranties

Warranties have always been the bug-a-boo of consumer protection. From the beginning of time, consumers have been endlessly pitched that a super-duper warranty will protect them. This car is better than that one because of the warranty; don't buy that toaster—the warranty is worse than that from a competitor. All the while, the salesperson gushes mountains of praise for this iron-clad, to-the-end-of-the-earth warranty protection.

Flash forward to when the item breaks. Then you discover the warranty is loaded with fine print that says, basically, it doesn't cover you. So, you haven't maintained that widget properly—not bathing it in hot acid every six weeks? Sorry, folks, your warranty is void.

And, of course, new home warranties aren't any different. The same rules apply. Except, as you might expect, home builders don't do anything halfway. When they create a warranty system, they go to elaborate lengths to make sure it defrauds as many consumers as possible. If it doesn't end up in a congressional investigation, hey, it wasn't worth it.

Such is the case with these fancy "10-year homeowner protection plans" that builders are pushing with such abandon today. In our opinion, these are the biggest frauds perpetrated on home buyers. And don't just take our word—so many consumers complained about these warranties that the Congress held formal hearings on the matter. The government's 455-page report is a shocking indictment of the questionable practices of the companies that sell and service these home warranties.

Before we get to the dirt, however, we'd like to point out three truths about all home warranties. Almost all builders provide one—whether it's a limited one-year warranty from the builder or one of the above-mentioned 10-year warranties from a third-party warranty company. Keep these in mind as you travel on your new home buying journey:

The Three Ugly Truths about New Home Warranties

1 **Warranties are worthless.** Surprising? But you have a document that says the builder will fix any problems during the next X years? The first lesson all home buyers must learn is that a warranty is only as good as the builder who's standing behind it. If the builder is honest and cares about his reputation and product, your warranty has value.

But what if something breaks and the builder doesn't care? What if he ignores your calls and letters that plead for help? Forget all the fancy wording and wonderful promises in your warranty. To enforce the warranty, you've got an expensive court battle looming: attorneys who charge big hourly fees, experts called in to verify the problem at hefty costs—the bottom line: you lose. We've spoken to many home buyers who spent $20,000, $30,000, and even $50,000 fighting a builder in court. And the amount of time involved and emotional torment are even worse.

2 **Builders load their warranties with fine print.** Even if you have a reputable builder who is willing to do warranty repairs, many warranty deals are loaded with so much fine-print that they're rendered useless.

One builder's "limited" warranty listed 23 exclusions that went on for 10 pages. The most common fine-print problem: builders who ask you to sign away your rights to any "implied warranty." As you'll see later in this chapter, this is a whopper.

3 **The best "warranty" to ensure a quality new home has nothing to do with the formal, written warranty.** That written warranty by the builder is nice, but what you should really count on is the "consumer warranty." That's the peace of mind you get if you follow the paper-scissors-rock strategy outlined in this book.

Start by quizzing the builder's references about warranty experiences. Did the builder respond quickly to warranty repair requests? Ensure you get good "paper" from the builder that includes thorough plans, specifications and materials. Hire a private inspector (engineer, architect or construction manager) to be a "scissors" for you—poking and prodding to make sure the home is built as promised. Finally, control the "gold," paying the builder the profit *after* he's fulfilled all the promises.

A good tip is to ask the builder for a list of *all* the homes he has built in the past five years. You should be able to contact any of these buyers, if you wish. This prevents the builder from giving you a list of just the most trouble-free homes. Whether you're building a $75,000 two-bedroom home or a $600,000 luxury estate, going the "smart" consumer route will be more insurance than any so-called warranty you get from the builder.

Now, back to the story about the bogus warranties that builders are suckering home buyers with. First, let's provide a little background about this mess.

You might think that homes built 40 or 50 years ago were better quality than the homes built today. And you may be right, except for one point. Until 1957, there was no warranty protection for home buyers. If you bought any home (new or used) and the builder offered no warranty, the home was "as is." Find a problem that was covered up by the builder? Tough. The buyer was stuck. Shady builders were able to wave their hands in the air and speak the only Latin words they know: caveat emptor—let the buyer beware.

The switch to consumer protection did not come from Congress or state legislatures. The powerful builder lobby throughout history has effectively blocked any legislation that protects consumers. But what about the courts? Judges, in most states, are not elected, nor influenced by the builders' lobby.

Therefore, the first rays of hope came from the courts. In 1957, a court in Ohio held that if no written warranty exists, builders must give an "implied" warranty that the home is of good quality. This was taken a step further by Colorado, where the state supreme court became the first court in the U.S. to say an implied warranty for a new home means it is suitable for habitation, built in a workmanlike manner and meets all building codes. Formally, this became known as the "implied warranties of habitability and good workmanship."

This was a bombshell. Builders could no longer slap up a defective house, sell it without a warranty, and expect to get off scotfree. While it sounds like a simple principle, builders were held legally responsible for making sure the home was built with good workmanship, met all building codes, and was "habitable."

States across the country rushed to adopt the Colorado decision. As of this writing, most states recognize implied warranties with new homes. Georgia is the only exception—there is no implied warranty protection there. Nonetheless, the courts in most states have ruled that new homes are covered under implied warranties.

The court's reasoning for this action was quite simple—how could home buyers tell whether a home was defective? If the walls are all sealed up, could you really tell that the wiring or plumbing is defective? How many home buyers are experienced enough to determine the quality of construction? The courts reasoned it was the *builder's responsibility to not sell a "lemon" house.*

As you can imagine, builders by this time were squealing like stuck pigs. To add insult to injury, many courts held that builders must honor an "implied warranty" on homes for *10 years.* "Ten years!

That's outrageous!" the builders screamed. After several months of cursing, the home builders decided to get even.

The first tactic was to try to put disclaimers into contracts saying a new home was sold without any implied warranties. Of course, this was usually in the fine print, readable only with a magnifying glass. Naturally, the courts frowned on this. In Texas, a court ruled that any disclaimer for an implied warranty must be "accomplished by clear and unambiguous language, which is narrowly worded and specific." Basically, it has to be in all capital letters and buyers must be made aware of it (usually done by having the buyer initial the clause).

Not all states went along, however. Several ruled that such disclaimers were illegal. Other states followed Texas' lead and required adequate notice. Since the issue is decided on a case-by-case basis in each state, you probably need to ask your attorney about the current status of implied warranties and disclaimers in your state.

By this time, however, the genie of consumer protection was out of the bottle. Builders feared that many states would actually adopt laws that required all new homes to be sold with written warranties. Yipes! (Actually, the builders were right—many states did just that. These include Connecticut, Maryland, New Jersey, Virginia and West Virginia.)

So the builders went back to the laboratory and cooked up a monster. In a burst of ingenuity, they decided to "regulate" themselves. If they set up their own warranty system and pretended to police themselves, builders figures they could head off the impending flood of regulation.

Hence, on a bright, sunny morning in October 1973, the Homeowner's Warranty Company (HOW) was born. The proud parent was the National Association of Home Builders (NAHB). HOW was first a subsidiary of the NAHB, but was later spun off in 1981 as a separate company. (Actually, HOW and the NAHB still share strong family ties. One of the NAHB executive officers always serves on the HOW board of directors.)

To show their belief in the free enterprise system, the NAHB also encouraged other companies to get in to the builder warranty business. Hence, Home Buyer's Warranty Insurance company (HBW) based in Denver, Colorado, and other companies sprung up as "competitors" to HOW.

"A builder-owned company designed by builders for builders."

That's how HOW describes itself in a brochure pitching builders to sign up. And it's an apt description. But just what is the mission of all these warranty companies? Basically, it is to provide insurance to protect builders from lawsuits over defective construction, in our opinion. As HOW puts it in its builder brochure, the warranty is "designed to help you (the builder) avoid costly and time-consuming court battles. HOW protects your good name and reputation."

How is this done? Basically, HOW and the other companies offer "2-10 insured warranties." The builder takes care of any problems outlined in the limited warranty (faulty workmanship and structural defects) for the first two years. Then, as HOW says, "for the next eight years—when major problems can often occur—HOW insures you (the builder) against the cost of repairing specified major structural defects. We take care of these repairs for you (the builder)!" (As a side note, if the builder skips town in the first two years, HOW claims it is responsible for the "builder's performance.")

You'll note the warranty period is 10 years—by sheer coincidence, the same period many courts have assigned for implied warranties. By now, you may be thinking that HOW should be renamed BW, for builder's warranty, since the protection really applies to them, not the home buyer. Given the true nature of these warranties, how could the builders ever convince home buyers they should pay (in the form of higher home prices) for this builder protection plan?

Slick marketing is the answer. The builders tried to market HOW as *consumer protection*. This was truly a deceptive marketing milestone in American business history. Here are some of the things HOW specifically promises *consumers* in their literature:

A *Quality checks on builders.* HOW promises to be selective about the builders allowed to offer their warranty. "HOW evaluates (builders) in three fundamental areas: construction competence, financial stability, customer service. Even after a builder has been accepted, HOW has a staff of trained construction investigators throughout the country who selectively monitor new home construction for acceptable construction practices." The message: if you see the HOW logo, the builder is reputable, has been checked out, and is monitored for quality.

B *Written, approved quality standards.* "The (HOW) warranty is *in writing*, not simply a vague verbal promise to 'take care of everything for a while.' You'll note, for example, that the warranty incorporates Approved Standards, developed by HOW, which outline minimum performance standards and tolerances to which the home must be built and maintained." Sounds tough, right?

C *"Unique, no-cost dispute settlement."* "If you and your builder disagree on any issue of coverage under the Builder's Limited Warranty, HOW arranges, *at no cost to you*, for an independent dispute settler to review the facts with both of you and render a decision on the responsibility for repairs." Wow, that sounds neat. But just how independent is the dispute settler?

If you thought the above stuff was attractive, you're not alone. HOW and other warranty programs have been very successful. HOW alone has sold more than 2 million warranty policies. 12,000 builders participate in the HOW program. Amazingly, more than one out of every four new homes sold is "covered" under a HOW warranty. When you add in the other home warranty companies, government experts estimate 75% to 80% of all new homes are sold with some type of warranty.

Everything was going fine for the warranty companies, until a trickle of complaints from consumers turned into a flood in 1991. The man consumers turned to in Washington was Henry B. Gonzalez, chairman of the Congressional Committee on Banking, Finance and Urban Affairs. The builders had met their match.

Truth Squad

All of those aforementioned benefits sound wonderful—except the congressional investigation found most of them to be false. Witness after witness testified to Congress in October 1991 about the reality of homeowner protection plans. Here's what the committee heard.

A **Builder quality checks?** Don't bet on it. A report by a Virginia insurance regulator revealed that HOW's "Level 1 builder program [a HOW-member builder who has been in business for a short time] does *not* require screening for customer service reliability. This appears to be misleading and contradictory as the advertisements state the builders are screened for [this]."

Furthermore, according to congressional testimony, HOW had only 12 inspectors nationwide in the mid-1980s. These inspectors were supposed to inspect 1.4 million homes a year built by HOW's 11,500 builders. A San Antonio, Texas, consumer who successfully sued HOW for failing to fix his home discovered that no HOW inspector had ever visited his home—or any other home the builder built once he had been accepted into the HOW program.

B **Written, approved quality standards?** The fine print in these homeowner warranties defines a structural defect as "actual physical damage to a load-bearing element of the home which makes the home unsafe, unsanitary or unlivable." Translation: Unless your home is falling down, you're not covered.

That's what consumer after consumer complained about at the hearing. When they discovered a major problem, the warranty company refused to cover it unless the home had collapsed or was "unlivable." As you might expect, many defective homes didn't quite meet the standard—and many claims were denied.

The Virginia state regulator called HOW's advertisements "misleading." While HOW promises to cover major structural defects for 10 years, the reality is that only those defects that make the home "unlivable" really qualify. Just because you've got a giant crack in your foundation doesn't mean the house is unsafe or you can't live there, right?

Consumer advocates charge that the warranty companies only settle large claims when it appears the consumer will hire an attorney. Small claims, they allege, are allowed to wallow in a bureaucratic limbo. The warranty company balks at settling and tries every delaying tactic imaginable.

C *Unique, no-cost dispute settlement?* Well, unique is a good description. However, HOW's promises of an "independent dispute settler" are open to debate.

The Virginia regulator disagreed with HOW's claims here as well. It turns out the dispute settler is actually paid by HOW—regulators questioned how independent this person really is.

HOW and other warranty companies promise the dispute settlers will be experienced in the construction industry (retired contractors, architects, and the like). However, one New Jersey couple found out their expert dispute settler was a landscaping salesperson with little building experience.

In at least one case, the whole issue of no-cost dispute settlement was revealed as a sham. Take the Seville Place Condominiums in Florida, for example. This famous case involved defective condo construction so egregious that it made national headlines. Of course, the condos were covered by a HOW warranty. After a HOW inspection denied any structural defects (HOW claimed the problems were all "design flaws"), *HOW actually filed a lawsuit against the condo owners.*

No "expedited dispute settlement" was offered to the San Antonio, Texas, homeowner either. A jury found HOW guilty of violating the Texas Deceptive Trade Practices law. "The jury ruled that HOW had engaged in fraudulent practices . . . by misrepresenting the degree of protection provided by their warranty."

So what was the warranty companies' defense in the face of this onslaught of evidence? Would you believe the warranty companies (HOW included) didn't even show up for the hearing? That's right, HOW and the other companies refused to testify.

According to a source on the committee, congressional staffers met with the warranty companies before and after the hearings to discuss the charges. The companies basically told the staffers there was no problem and they planned no corrective action. Rather arrogant, huh?

In the industry's defense, the National Association of Home Builders testified that everything was just fine. The president of the NAHB said no further regulation of home building is required because there are already "a number of checks and balances in place." He claimed that local building codes are "strictly enforced" (please!) that, "most states already require a one-year warranty" (but what about the later years when serious defects can become known?) and that "legal channels are always open" to home buyers (but at what cost?).

Builders raised the specter of higher home prices to "justify" why this disgusting situation should not be remedied. "Unnecessary restrictions or requirements on warranties will merely create increases in the price of housing, resulting in a product that will be less affordable and less available to the buyer who needs it most." Translation: We shouldn't be held to the same standards as other industries. Builders wouldn't be able to rake in the big profits from building shoddy homes and then running from their responsibilities for fixing defects.

Well, Congress didn't take this lying down. Or at least Henry B.

Gonzalez didn't. The committee proposed forbidding the government from insuring mortgages on houses covered under these warranty programs. Since over one-fourth of HOW's business comes from FHA- and VA-financed mortgages, this action stung.

Unfortunately, the builders' lobby went into overdrive. It seemed every builder in the country called Congress and, under pressure, a compromise was reached. Congress ordered the Department of Housing and Urban Affairs to do a one-year study about eliminating the use of these warranties. That study is still pending.

Why These Warranties are Dangerous

Most warranties for other products are rather benign—if you get a lousy one, you have a few headaches, but no major problems. However, these "homeowner protection plans" offered by builders are dangerous for several reasons.

1 *Skipped inspections.* Believe it or not, the warranties let the builder skip inspections on some houses! For new homes financed by FHA or VA loans, there are usually three inspections by government inspectors. Obviously, since the government is insuring your mortgage, they want to make sure the new home meets certain standards.

However, if a builder buys a HOW or other "2-10" warranty for the home, two of those three inspections are WAIVED. Can you believe it? The government inspector just comes at the end of the project—after the walls have been sealed up. The bizarre reasoning is that the government doesn't need to look closely at such homes since HOW and the other warranty companies allegedly have done such a good job of screening builders and construction.

Builders love this since they save time and money—two fewer inspections are a major windfall for them. In fact, that's one of the big selling pitches the warranty companies use to sign up builders.

While you should never rely on any government inspector (from the FHA or the local building department) to ensure you're getting a quality home, the fact that these warranty companies (and, hence, the builders) have negotiated such a sweet deal with the government is rather shocking. While it is more expedient for the builder and the government, we're at a loss to explain any potential benefit to consumers.

2 *A false sense of security.* HOW and the other warranty companies advertise heavily in new home magazines. Over and over, they try to convince you that the best quality choice is a home that's covered by these warranties.

The propaganda war has now reached new heights. In a publication about Chicago housing, a builder pointed out that HOW "is the only insured warranty program endorsed by the National Association of Home Builders and the Home Builders Association of Greater Chicago." Gee, we wonder why the NAHB endorses HOW.

Ads also plug brochures that list HOW builders. "By using the

HOW brochure, the prospective home buyer already knows he's got a quality home backed by 10 years of protection." Please.

All this lulls the home buyer into a false sense of security. Why hire a private inspector if HOW is already monitoring the builder for quality? Why even check out the builder—hasn't HOW already done this for you?

3 *Waiving "implied warranty" protection.* What all these builder-sponsored warranty companies have done is gutted the implied warranty protection granted to consumers by the courts, plain and simple.

Instead of builders building quality homes and taking responsibility for structural defects that show up down the road, the builders have created a bureaucratic monster to swallow consumer complaints. It's a black hole where claims go in and they never come out.

All of this gives some shady builders a perfect excuse to pass the buck. "Oh, there's a major problem with your house in year three, Mr. Smith? Well, you'll have to talk to the warranty company about it. You filed a claim and the company is refusing to fix this $10,000 crack because your home is not falling down? Gee, that's too bad, but there's nothing we can do."

Our recommendation: Tell the builder to forget the "2-10" warranties insured by third-party companies. Ask the builder to take the fee he would pay to enroll your home and instead reduce the sales price. This is not to say that you shouldn't insist on a written warranty on your home. A basic warranty for one or two years by a quality, reputable builder is more than adequate. If a major structural problem develops in seven years and the builder refuses to fix it, the courts in your state may allow you to recover damages under an implied warranty.

Source: "Implied and Statutory Warranties in the Sale of Real Estate: The Demise of Caveat Emptor," William D. Grand, Real Estate Law Journal, *1986.*

 Call for updates! By calling our special hotline, you'll hear the latest news on building a new home! 1-900-988-7295 (See the back page for price information.)

Go!
Building the Home
and
Other Traumatic
Experiences

College of the Ouachitas

9

Key Inspection Points, Part One:

The Skeleton House

It would be nice and infinitely simpler if there was some giant "New House Machine" that plopped out a complete new home in one swoop. Just push a lever and plop! new home.

In reality, building a new home is comprised of hundreds of small tasks. Some can only be done in succession, while others are accomplished concurrently. While we don't expect you to become experts in new home construction techniques, it is generally helpful to understand the different phases your new home will go through.

In this and the next chapter, we outline most of the major steps. Special attention is given to suggested "inspection points," critical phases when you should have a professional inspector or architect make sure everything is on track. We also throw in money bombs that unlucky home buyers have encountered on this journey. In addition, you'll note eco-friendly alternatives to traditional building products and materials. These "green" alternatives are sprinkled through the next two chapters. Here we go!

Permits and Approval

Before you can begin building a house, your builder must apply for permits and approval from the local building department. In some cases, the builder will also need approval from the zoning department, the health department (if you plan to use a septic system), a local environmental authority, and even a homeowners association (HOA). Some HOAs have architectural control committees that will review your plans to make sure they meet any community covenants covering height restrictions, style, color, position on the lot, and whatever other insane rules they can dream up. After your plans are ready to go, the permit and approval stage can eat up a month or two in your schedule.

 Money Bomb: Bogus engineer approval.
"My builder told me I didn't need to hire an independent engineer—he had one he worked with who would make sure the foundation was sound. Apparently, this engineer just rubber-stamped the builder's plan. This was no problem until giant cracks appeared in my home's foundation. Another engineer we consulted said the builder's plan was woefully inadequate. Help!"

Some areas allow builders or developers to hire their own engineer to certify structural soundness of the plans. The city/county building department approves the plans by taking the word of the engineer for the structural soundness. The problem stems from corrupt or inept engineers who will put their stamp on any plan as a favor to the builder. Florida had this system until a flood of complaints about defective construction and design surfaced from home buyers who purchased homes that were "certified" by corrupt engineers.

Solution: The point is, just because the builder found an engineer to say your home's plans are sound is no guarantee—you must hire your own inspector to ensure proper design and construction.

Foundations

We realize it's a cliche, but a home really is only as good as its foundation. Get a lousy foundation and forget all the money you spent on nice carpeting or fancy furnishings. Your home's value may go to zero. Zip. Nada.

Given this fact, it's important to understand just what makes a good foundation. First, note that there are three different types of foundations: slabs, crawl-spaces and full basements. Basically, a slab-on-grade foundation is a flat concrete floor poured directly on the soil with no crawl space or basement. A crawl-space foundation is just as it sounds: There is a space between the foundation floor and the first floor of the house just big enough to crawl around in. Basements can extend under the entire first floor of the house or just part of it. Ceilings in basements range from seven feet to nine feet high.

Slabs are the most common foundation type—about 40% of all homes were built on slabs, according to the 1990 U.S. census. Full or partial basements came in a close second, with 38%. Only 21% of all homes had crawl-space foundations. However, as you might imagine, this varies dramatically by region. Basements are rare in Texas, crawl spaces are most popular in the Carolinas and so on. One architect we interviewed told us that basements are common in colder regions because the climate requires the foundations be dug below frost line. If frost line is four feet down, it isn't much farther to dig a full basement.

Foundations can be made from concrete blocks or poured concrete. Regardless of the method, footings are required underneath the concrete walls or blocks to support the weight of the walls. Most foundations also require the installation of piers or columns made of brick, concrete blocks or steel beams to hold up the main support beam of the house.

During our research for this book, we read a number of books written by the National Association of Home Builders (NAHB) for builders. One book we read, *Production Checklist for Builders and Superintendents*, made this astonishing statement:

> *"It is not uncommon for a foundation to be laid out and poured on the wrong lot, or placed too close to the property line. Occasionally, the front elevation is built facing the rear property line, or the building footprint is reversed. The wrong or unapproved plan can even be applied to the right lot. Sometimes the house just does not fit on the lot."*

Note that this book says "It is not uncommon" for such major screw-ups to occur—just one more reason to have an inspector on your side. (By the way, the book does point out that "Such mistakes cannot be justified. Not only are they costly, but also very embarrassing." No kidding.)

Key Inspection Point:
Expect your inspector or architect to inspect the site at several points in the foundation process. First, after the hole for the foundation and footings has been dug, an inspector can check for proper depth and layout. After the walls and footings go up, another inspection might be done to make sure everything is correct.

Tip: Get the "ticket" from the concrete subcontractor to ensure the correct mix of concrete was poured. If an insufficient amount of concrete is delivered to the job site, the builder may water down the concrete—a dangerous situation since it greatly reduces the strength. Another issue is the outside temperature when the concrete is poured. If it's too cold, chemicals may have to be added to the mix. If it's too hot, the concrete may cure too quickly and sometimes crack.

Step-by-Step: Constructing the Foundation

Step 1: Stake out the foundation. Basically, staking the foundation allows you to see exactly where the house will sit on your lot—if you don't like it, theoretically you can move it at this point. However, if you want to move it, check to see if your homeowners association (if you have one) has to be notified. Staking

also helps identify which trees need to be removed and tells the excavator where to dig. Some builders mark trees that will need to be cut down while others mark the ones that will stay.

Step 2: Site preparation. At this stage, your builder will have the site cleared of trees and graded so trucks and heavy equipment can access the site. Beware of tree cutters who are not professionals. In the case of our home, the builder offered to let some amateurs cut and remove the trees from our lot (in return, they got to keep the wood). That was fine, except the tree removal crew almost took out their own truck with a falling tree during the process. This "wrecking crew" also damaged several other trees we wanted to keep.

Some homeowners choose to save a little money on site preparation by removing trees themselves. However, a chainsaw and "do-it-yourselfers" are not necessarily a good mix. Frankly, we recommend you bring in a pro. If you do it yourself, there's a lot more to it than just chopping down the trees. Stump and branch removal can be challenging. Best leave this to someone with the right equipment and courage.

Occasionally, the utility trenches are also dug at this time. If you're not on city water, a well is another item that may be dug at this point.

Tip: Make sure the well-drilling contractor is a Certified Pump Installer or Certified Well-Driller. Even better, see whether they're members of the National Well Water Association. The best well diggers are the ones who've been in business the longest period of time. You can't survive long in this business if you can't find water. Instruct the well digger to stop when he hit, an appropriate amount of water, instead of digging to a depth specified in a contract. This will save you money in case you hit water sooner than expected. One issue to consider is whether to dig the well deeper in order to provide more storage capacity. Discuss this with the well driller.

Step 3: Excavation. Here's where dirt starts to fly, literally. Excavators bring in the heavy equipment and dig the hole slightly larger than the area marked by the stakes. Excavation is not a precision science—some over-excavation or damage to nearby trees may occur.

Step 4: Footings. Footings are what the foundation walls sit on. They form the bottom edge of the walls and, as such, should extend out beyond the walls on both sides to spread out the house's weight.

Typically, most builders use concrete to create the footings. A trench is dug around the exterior of the foundation and then filled with concrete. Again, it is vital that the footings extend at least three inches beyond the edge of the foundation walls on either side.

Footings also may be poured as the base for piers or columns that will be used to support the upper floors. Again, the footings must extend beyond the piers or columns they are intended to support.

Footings are also used for masonry fireplaces. If you will be including a brick or stone chimney, be sure footings are poured properly. In one case we investigated, the builder did not pour proper footings for a large fireplace. What happened? In one short year, the chimney began separating from the house and was in danger of collapsing.

Step 5: Foundation and waterproofing. Foundations can be made of either poured concrete or concrete blocks. If it is common in your part of the country to use concrete blocks, be sure your builder will be using steel reinforcing bars extending through the blocks. Concrete should fill each block and they should be bonded together with mortar. The exception are two-story homes with no basement and minimal foundation walls. In this case, the blocks often are not required to be filled solid with concrete.

As for poured foundations, the process begins with the setting of temporary "forms" into which the concrete will be poured. The forms are either wood or metal. Once the concrete dries, the forms are removed. Depending on the soil condition, steel reinforcing bars are sometimes used in poured foundations.

After the walls of the foundation are poured or built, the outside wall will be waterproofed with some black gunk called asphalt compound. If you live in a very wet part of the country, you may even get asphalt-treated felt or plastic to cover the foundation walls.

Also at this stage, the builder will install a French drain or perimeter drain around the outer foundation walls. The drainpipe is made from clay or perforated plastic—the goal is to divert water away from the foundation. Ideally, the French drain should be completely encased in gravel to allow water to enter the drain and to prevent the drain's holes from clogging.

Step 6: Septic system. If you are required to have a septic system, we hope you have a "perc test" completed before you even buy the lot. The perc test will help you determine what type and location of the septic system are appropriate.

Trenches will be dug to lay the pipes from the house. These connect to another trench into which the collection tank is laid. Yet another trench is dug from the tank to the septic field where the solid waste will eventually leach out.

Step 7: Back filling. Once the foundation is completed, the excavator will come back and "back fill" around it with the dirt left over from the excavation. If you have a basement, the window wells will be added before back filling. The back fill should be tamped down to prevent settling.

Eco-Friendly Alternative

Lite-Forms by Dow Chemical (712) 252-3704 are rigid foam insulation boards that form the walls of your foundation. Unlike standard forms that are removed after the concrete is poured, Lite-Forms stay in place and provide R-20 insulation. Twenty percent of the polystyrene that makes up the Lite-Form is recycled from fast-food containers. Even the ties that hold the forms together are made from recycled milk jugs and other plastics.

Money Bomb #1: No soils test.

"I had to pay an extra $3000 to have the foundation of my house excavated because the excavator hit limestone. What could I have done to either avoid this or at least be prepared for it?"

A soils test, plain and simple, would be the solution to a problem like this. Whether you have rocky, sandy or clay-filled soils, you can't tell just by looking. In many cases, you can't even tell by the kind of soil the neighboring house is sitting on. Insist on a soils test before you even buy the lot. If you're buying a spec house that is already under construction, ask to see a copy of the soils test.

In some areas of the country, "open-hole inspections" take the place of soils tests. This inspection occurs after the foundation is dug—an engineer checks the soil condition and recommends any foundation modifications.

Some builders intentionally "lose" the soils test or fail to do one altogether. That's because some homes are built on dangerously inadequate soil like loose fill dirt, landfill debris and worse—we've heard all the horror stories. Basically, if you don't have good soil, your house could "settle" to China. Cracked walls, disintegrating tile, destroyed concrete—you can avoid all of this by simply getting a copy of the soils test or open-hole inspection on any new home you're buying.

Money Bomb #2: Undercut footings or no footings at all.

"I've been in my house for about a year and we have begun noticing severe settling in my house's walls and foundation. We hired a private inspector to find out what was happening. After he excavated the foundation, he found that the footings under our piers were 'undercut' and causing the house to sink on one side. What happened?"

Here is a situation that can be devastating: undercut or no footings. Footings are the basis of the support for your house—if they're not installed properly, your home may become unlivable. Repairs are astronomically expensive.

In the situation above, the builder did not pour the footings to create straight-sided "square" blocks. Rather the footings were undercut—curving under or rounded. The result is a "ball-and-socket" effect—this may be nice for hips, but it's hell for houses. That's because the house can move, causing major damage in the process. If the piers or foundation walls are sitting on an undercut footing, you've got big trouble.

Solution: The only way to ensure that you don't have missing or undercut footings is to have a licensed structural engineer or experienced inspector inspect the forms for the footings. Also have him attend the actual pouring of the footings and inspect them again afterward.

Can you do this after the home is bought? No, unfortunately, you can't. That's because the foundation and footings are "back filled," which basically means they're covered with dirt. Only by excavating the foundation or footings could you tell—an impractical solution to say the least.

 ### Money Bomb #3: No mortar between the concrete blocks.

"When I visited the construction site of a friend's new home, we noticed that the concrete block piers had no mortar between the blocks. My friend was outraged because the builder had told him the piers were completed and they were ready to move on to the next stage. Is this a common problem?"

It may sound rather elementary, but we've seen several cases of builders who merely "dry stack" the concrete blocks in order to save time and money. As you might imagine, a wall of anything without mortar or glue isn't the picture of stability. Drystacking is an obvious code violation in most parts of the country.

Perhaps the most vivid example of this we saw was in a PBS documentary about North Carolina building practices. In the documentary, an independent inspector took the reporter out to a building site and proceeded to push over piers that were dry stacked, illustrating the poor building practices of that builder.

Solution: Once again, here is where the inspector comes in. The builder should not be allowed to proceed with the next phase of construction until your inspector determines that the job is done to code.

 ### Money Bomb #4: Incredible shrinking concrete.

"I can't believe I've only been in my house for six months and I'm already starting to see huge cracks in my foundation. The inspector I hired claimed the problem could have been caused by watered-down concrete. Is this true?"

Yes, your foundation could be suffering from extreme shrinkage due to too much water in the concrete. This may happen if the concrete company is unscrupulous, or your builder may have been trying to cut corners and eke out a little more profit. By adding water to the concrete, the builder can save money (since he has to buy less of it). Unfortunately, when you add water to concrete, you dilute its strength.

As a result, watered-down concrete may not even be strong enough to support the very walls of your house. (An exception: Additional water may be added to the concrete to make it easier to place and finish the foundation.) Another rip-off: Some builders add rocks and dirt to concrete to reduce the amount they need and hence lower their concrete bill.

Solution: When the concrete is delivered, insist on getting a ticket for every load of concrete the subcontractor pours. The ticket should spell out the kind of concrete used, the "cement sack mix," and the water ratio. The architect or engineer who designed your foundation should have specified the proper mix.

How can you stop a builder who's intent on watering down the concrete to save a buck? Frankly, you or your inspector must be on site when the concrete is poured to make sure no watering down occurs. Home buyers who've been a victim of this scam say they should have paid an inspector to be on the site the entire time concrete was poured. Whether you want to go to this extreme will depend on how prevalent this problem is in your area—ask an architect or inspector for some advice.

If you discover the builder has used watered-down concrete, what do you do? If the builder can rip it out and do it again the right way, this is the best solution. However, such drastic action may not be practical. At that point, you've got a serious problem. Consult with your attorney—the builder may be in default for such a breach of your contract.

Money Bomb #5: Shoddy waterproofing.

"After a major rain storm, we noticed water damage in our basement. After we called in an expert to evaluate the problem, he determined that the builder failed to waterproof the foundation!"

What causes most foundation leak problems? Surprisingly, it's usually surface water from the roof or downspouts that are not properly drained away from the house. In a few rare cases, an underground spring or rising water table can cause the damage.

Either way, the problem is exasperated by shoddy waterproofing by your builder. In arid climates, most builders just use an asphalt compound to waterproof the exterior foundation walls. Felt or plastic treated with asphalt is more common in wetter climates.

Builders in a hurry may skip this important step—who can tell, anyway? After the back fill is brought in, you can't tell how much waterproofing you have or don't have. The foundation walls are all buried with dirt.

Solution: The only way to ensure you've got adequate waterproofing is to physically inspect the application of these materials before the back fill is done.

Money Bomb #6: Untreated wood used for supports.

"I thought the wood support columns used in my basement were only temporary until my builder could set up steel beams. However, he now tells me the untreated wood columns are permanent. Is this a problem?"

You bet it is! Untreated wood should NEVER be used in a foundation for the support columns. The lumber for sills that sit atop your foundation walls should be pressure treated as well. Some states don't require this—a big mistake in our opinion.

Untreated wood is subject to deterioration, susceptible to termite damage, and is a major fire hazard. You certainly don't want your entire house to be dependent upon a foundation of untreated wood.

Solution: Obviously, if you have a house designed by a competent architect and/or engineer, the plans will call for the proper foundation supports and treated wood sills. This is your insurance against a builder who "wings it" in the field and uses inferior materials. Your private inspector should be right on top of this and not approve untreated wood columns as permanent supports. (We should note that some builders use untreated wood columns in a basement for temporary support, before permanent steel columns are put into place.)The bottom line: Never accept a home with such an inadequate foundation.

Framing

Once the foundation is in, it's framing time! In a short time, you'll see the walls, floors and roof go up. Windows will be framed. Your new home will be a maze of two-by-fours and wood sheathing. At this point, the electrical wires, plumbing pipes, and mechanical systems (duct work, furnace, air conditioner) are installed or "roughed in", as the jargon goes.

Key Inspection Point

When you have an architect inspecting your house, expect him or her to visit the site at least twice during framing, if not more often. A private inspector will visit the site at least once during the framing.

The first framing inspection should confirm that correctly sized girders (which support the home) are used. Proper installation of critical structural elements (joists, beams, girders and so on) also is checked. An inspector may also note any warped or defective studs that may need to be replaced.

Another framing inspection may occur to check the electrical, plumbing and mechanical systems—more on this later.

Step-by-Step: Framing

Step 1: Floors. When framing the floor of your house, the builder should attach wood sills to the top of the foundation. This can be done with an insulating foam adhesive—in areas such as California, anchor bolts set in concrete are used. (This helps prevent damage during an earthquake.)

Joists are then attached to the sills. Joists are sometimes prefabricated or can be made onsite.

We recommend a quality prefabricated joist like the Silent Floor, made by Trus Joist Co. (800) 628-3997. Normal joists may be split or uneven; hence when a nail is driven into the joist to secure the sub-floor, the nail can begin to work its way out. This causes squeaky floors. Silent Floor joists are engineered to resist warping and shrinking; nails can't work their way out, eliminating the squeaks.

We have Silent Floors in our home and have been pleased. Some builders swear by them, while others try to get by with cheaper joists to save a buck. You can tell whether a home has Silent Floors since the name is stamped prominently on the joist.

After the joists are in, the subfloor is next. This is glued and nailed to the joists. In some parts of the U.S., gluing of the subfloor is not required. We suggest you insist on it and pay extra if need be.

The subfloor is usually sheets of plywood or "chip board" (wood chips formed into sheets with glue). To be honest, plywood sheets are much more expensive than chip board and aren't necessary to build a good house in our opinion. Save your money here and use chip board.

Step 2: Walls. Walls framed using 2x6 wood studs are the best. (2x6 means that the stud is about 2" wide and 6" long—the result are walls that are 6" thick). The larger-size stud allows for more insulation and, hopefully, lowers heating and cooling bills. Some builders use 2x4s to save money. In this case, insist on blown-in ground paper insulation, which has a higher insulation value than rolls of fiber glass.

On tract and some semi-custom homes, the walls are fabricated in sections on the ground then "raised" to their positions along the ground floor. On custom homes, walls are built in place. Either way, this is the fastest part of building the house—some framers can frame a 3000-square-foot home in only a couple weeks. You'll probably be amazed at how fast your house is taking shape—but don't get out the moving boxes yet. The time-consuming finishing work is just around the corner.

By the way, if you or your inspector notices warped or uneven studs, insist on having them replaced with more sound pieces. Warped studs can cause "drywall popping," in which your walls separate from the studs—not a pleasant experience.

Another note of caution: Your builder should be spacing the studs 16 inches apart (called "16 on center" or 16 O.C. in builder-speak). If the studs are farther apart (say, 24 on center), the exterior siding material may pop loose. The siding materials need to be nailed to studs that are closer together for better support. Ask an inspector, architect or other design professional for specific advice on your home.

Step 3: Roof framing. Two methods are used for framing the roof on a house. One is to manufacture the rafters, ridge board and collar beams on site. A ridge board is the board that makes the top point of the roof. Rafters are the side boards that form the "A" in a peaked roof. The collar beams are cross pieces that connect to the rafters.

The second (and more popular) method of framing a roof is to use prefabricated trusses. These wood structures look like "A's," of various sizes and are connected by metal brackets. The truss manufacturer makes the trusses and then delivers them to the site. Prefab trusses are usually put in place by a crane or by crazy framers who have a death wish.

Builders give the truss company a set of the house plans and the truss company's engineers determine what size to make the trusses. It can take as much as a month to get the trusses delivered; therefore your builder will need to order them early in the process.

Finishing: When building a spec house, many builders also finish off the roof at this time. They do this because the house looks more attractive to potential buyers with the roof complete. The process requires the installation of a treated felt base. Next, the shingles are applied, starting from the bottom of the roof line and moving upward. See the section on finishing for more details on roofing.

Step 4: Sheathing. The walls are typically sheathed on the outside with plywood, chip board, or "oriented strand" board, among other materials. The roof and floor are usually sheathed with plywood although chip board is also common.

Some builders also use a "house wrap" to help better insulate the home. Still others might add rigid foam insulation board. We recommend Tyvek house wrap made by Dupont. Tyvek is an energy-saving air barrier that is literally wrapped around a house during construction. Made from polyethylene fibers, Tyvek keeps outside air from penetrating the walls of your home.

A local Tyvek dealer did a "House Energy Analysis" for a custom home in Denver, Colorado. The bottom line: Tyvek saved the home buyers enough money to pay for the installation in just 1.7 years. Total savings in energy costs over eight years ran $2322. For more information on Tyvek or to find a local dealer, call (800) 44-TYVEK.

Eco-Friendly Alternatives

 The Silent Floor's Performance Plus TJI Joists by Trus Joist Corp., (800) 628-3997. This flooring system uses pieces of aspen trees instead of the rapidly disappearing fir wood. Also, the ends of the joists are laminated instead of solid wood. As the name implies, Silent Flooring systems aim to reduce squeaks.

Steel Framing is becoming a more feasible replacement for wood. Although it once was popular only in Texas and Florida, builders are giving steel framing another look as the price of lumber soars. Two-thirds of the steel is recycled from scrap, old bridges, etc. The only negative: In some cases, the steel members arrive unassembled and uncut. This tends to vex framing crews, who aren't known for their mental acuity. For more information about steel framing, contact the American Iron and Steel Institute (202) 452-7100.

Stormguard nails by Maze Nails, (815) 223-8290, are zinc-coated nails made from "remelted" steel. The company completely recovers all the chemicals used in nail making, lowering water pollution.

LO/MIT-1 by Solar Energy Corporation, (609) 883-7700, is a paint for the underside of roof decks. The reflective-surface coating forms a "radiant barrier," blocking heat from radiating into an attic. The result: Cooling bills are reduced by about 20%. The cost is reasonable, running 25¢ to 35¢ per square foot installed.

Money Bomb #1: Warped joists and trusses.

"When our house was built, the builder had the floor joists delivered to the site weeks before framing begin. Unfortunately, it rained for days during that period. The joists weren't covered and we suspect they were warped. When we confronted the builder he said he would have the joist company replace them. However, our floor now has numerous squeaks—we suspect the builder never replaced the joists."

Warped floor joists (and roof trusses) may cause serious problems in the future. Frankly, in our inspection of construction sites we have frequently found materials left exposed to the weather. Even worse are materials delivery men who seemingly throw the materials off the truck—expensive products are strewn across your site like match sticks. Improper stacking of wood packs also can cause damage.

Unfortunately, some builders don't return warped or weather-damaged wood products to the manufacturer for replacement and instead "make do" with what they have. The typical excuse: Such actions are too time-consuming.

Solution: Insist that wood products (especially trusses and joists) be covered with adequate plastic sheeting or tarps. And if they are just plopped any old place by the delivery truck, insist that they be stacked properly.

If your inspector notes that warped floor joists or trusses have been installed, have the builder send back the problem pieces and get them replaced. One manufacturer of floor joists, TJI (Silent Floors), told us they are happy to replace any damaged joists. Better to accept delay in the construction schedule than to install defective materials.

The best way to monitor this situation is to visit your home site every two to four days. While you can't be at the job site 24 hours a day, an occasional visit will probably ferret out any problems quickly. What if you're out of town and can't visit the site at all? If money is tight, have a friend drop by to give you eyewitness reports. Or consider spending the extra money to have your inspector drive by every few days.

Money Bomb #2: Substitution of lumber grades.

"I don't know that much about wood, but some of the framing studs look like poor quality to me. The builder told me he was going to use top-grade lumber for my house. How will I know if he is?"

Lumber is stamped with various grades—trying to decipher these stamps is a science in itself. That's because lumber from different companies is graded in different ways. Often the salespeople at lumber yards aren't even aware of what all the stamps mean.

While grade is important, condition is critical. Lumber with the least number of knotholes is obviously preferred. Also, the best boards will not be warped or split.

How often do builders substitute cheaper grades of lumber? It's a common problem in some areas, several architects have told us. Perhaps this is so since such a switch is hard to detect.

Solution: Leave it to a professional (inspector or architect) who's familiar with lumber grades and qualities to discover this money-bomb. If your builder promises you high quality oak molding, your inspector better be familiar with the differences between oak and birch, so you don't get shnookered. Some good lumber yards will be able to give you advice, but don't rely solely on them to help determine the grades of wood used in your house. Also, a well-specified blueprint that clearly calls for certain grades and types of lumber is smart.

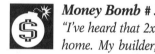

Money Bomb # 3: Four- or six-inch-deep walls.
"I've heard that 2x6s are the best studs to use when framing a home. My builder, however, suggested that 2x4s would save us money. What's the difference?"

The best builders usually use 2x6s when framing a house. Some builders use 2x4s to help cut costs. As mentioned above, having more depth for insulation will increase the R-value in your walls and ceilings, saving you money in the long run on heating and cooling bills.

However, the new cellulose blown-in insulation may be an exception. Supposedly, cellulose provides better insulation in shallow walls—hence builders use this in some houses framed with 2x4 construction.

Solution: Get it in the contract—we recommend 2x6 construction. If the "wrong" studs are delivered to your job site, insist the builder send them back.

Money Bomb #4: No "floating walls" in a finished basement.
"Two years after moving into our new home, we discovered cracks in our dining room wall. The builder did a cosmetic fix, but the problem recurred. We called in an engineer, who discovered the problem was in our finished basement—the builder didn't use floating walls. What's this all about?"

Concrete basement floors are not the world's most stable creatures—they may rise or fall slightly because of settling or other subsoil problems. Hence if you want to finish the basement, the builder should use "floating walls." Floating walls allow for slight movement in the basement floor. Without floating walls, the wall studs are directly attached to the basement's ceiling—if the floor moves, the entire wall moves, which might crack the upstairs walls. Since "floating walls" are an invisible structural component (you can't see them after the drywall is put up in the basement), many builders omit them to save money. You may end up paying later for this tactic.

Solution: Make sure floating walls are specified in your plans. An inspector should verify their installation on site as well.

Rough-in: Plumbing, Electrical, Furnace, Air Conditioner, Insulation

As the framing progresses, the next step is the "roughing-in" of all the mechanical, electrical and plumbing systems. Insulation is added in the final phase of the framing.

Key Inspection Point:

As you might expect, this phase is critical. Just before the walls are sealed up with drywall, an inspection should confirm the proper installation of plumbing, electrical wiring, duct work, and mechanical (heating and cooling) systems. Proper drainage of plumbing is verified as well. An optional inspection after the insulation is added is also a possibility.

This inspection point is crucial—you can't look at the home's wiring after the walls are up. No one thinks about their plumbing . . . until it fails. If you have a large or complex home, it may pay to have several framing inspections to ensure these "invisible" items are correctly installed.

Step-by-Step: The Rough-in

Step 1: Plumbing. During this stage, the pipes that lead from the main water and sewer lines are connected to the house. A plumber will install the hot and cold water pipes, and the waste pipes from the toilets. If the plumber is also the heating/cooling subcontractor (as is often the case), this system and all duct work will be installed as well. Once the rough-in of the plumbing pipes is completed, the basement concrete floor (if you have one) can be poured.

Step 2: Electrical. The electrical subcontractor will run electrical wires throughout the house to each light switch and outlet, as well as to all the light fixtures. You may go through the house with the electrician in advance to decide on the exact position of each switch—if you have an architect who supplied detailed drawings, this won't be necessary.

The electrician will also install phone lines and jacks—you should confirm these are put at the correct locations. Now is also an excellent time to have the electrician run speaker wires throughout the house for a future stereo or Surround Sound system.

Step 3: *Heating and air conditioning*. There are several heating options which are often put in by the plumber. If you plan to use forced air, the plumber will install ducts throughout the house to allow the warm air to blow into each room. The main furnace for the house is centrally located, usually in the basement or crawl space. Heat pumps are another option; these provide both heating and air conditioning, but they only operate on electricity, the most expensive energy option in many cold climates.

Tip: Don't have the furnace installed in the middle of your basement if you plan to finish it off at any time. Otherwise, you will have to locate rooms around the furnace instead of having a large, open space.

One of the best methods of heating a house is hot-water "radiant" heat. In this system, pipes from a central boiler circulate hot water to baseboards or radiators throughout the house.

Step 4: *Insulation*. You have innumerable choices of insulation types and brands. For example, most people are familiar with the rolls of pink fiberglass insulation. There are also blown fiberglass options and blown cellulose (which is made from recycled paper). One architect we interviewed doesn't like to use the blown cellulose because it settles unevenly and some people have an allergy to the Boron used in the product as fire treatment.

Talk insulation with anyone and you're likely to hear the expression "R-value" trotted out. Basically, an R-value is how resistant a material is to air infiltration (or heat flow). The higher the R-value, the better.

Depending on where you live, recommended R-values for the ceiling range from R-19 to R-49. Wall R-values range from R-12 to R-19 (most of them are R-19), while floor R-values range from R-11 to R-25. See the following chart for the R-values recommended in your area. You can also call Owens-Corning at (800) 447-3759, give them your zip code and they will tell you the appropriate R-values for your area.

Some people go for even more insulating power by using foam board. Most often used in basements and on cathedral ceilings, foam board is used with regular insulation for added R-value.

When your builder's subcontractor installs the insulation, be sure it is cut to fit snugly around pipes, trusses, ducts and studs. Any gaps will lead to future air leaks and higher utility bills. If the insulation in your house will be blown in, there is less of a problem; however, make sure there are no thin spots in the ceilings or walls.

Step 5: *Other details*. At this time, builders usually install windows, tubs and shower bases and any other items that can't be installed once the drywall goes in.

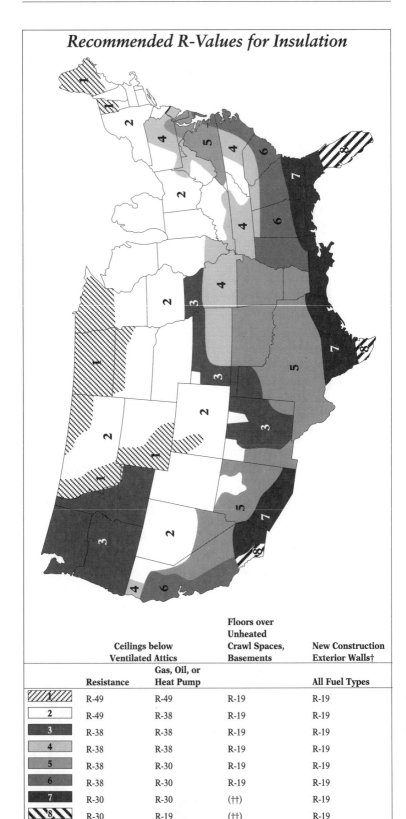

Recommended R-Values for Insulation

		Ceilings below Ventilated Attics	Floors over Unheated Crawl Spaces, Basements	New Construction Exterior Walls†
	Resistance	Gas, Oil, or Heat Pump		All Fuel Types
1	R-49	R-49	R-19	R-19
2	R-49	R-38	R-19	R-19
3	R-38	R-38	R-19	R-19
4	R-38	R-38	R-19	R-19
5	R-38	R-30	R-19	R-19
6	R-38	R-30	R-19	R-19
7	R-30	R-30	(††)	R-19
8	R-30	R-19	(††)	R-19

† The D.O.E. recommends R-19 for new construction exterior walls.
†† In these hot climates, additional insulation in the floor does not provide any cooling benefits.

Eco-Friendly Alternatives
Amofoam Insulation by Amoco Foam Products. All those fast-food containers are put to good use in Amofoam insulation, which is made from more than 50% recycled polystyrene. Call (800) 752-9821, and ask for consumer service.

Insul-Cot by Cotton Unlimited, Inc., is insulation made from recycled cotton. The product has an R-value similar to fiberglass "batts" (or rolls of the pink stuff). While it can be ordered directly from the company, it's still in the experimental stage and isn't generally available on the market. (806) 495-3501.

Nature Guard insulation by Louisiana Pacific, (503) 221-0800, is made from 100% recycled newspaper. The company claims it costs less than fiberglass insulation and offers a 38 R-value (among the highest available). If you blow this insulation into your attic and walls, the amount of recycled newsprint is what one individual would use in 100 years. For more general information on recycled newsprint insulation, you can also contact the Cellulose Insulation Manufacturer's Association (CIMA) at (513) 222-1024. (As a side note, CIMA claims that cellulose is better than fiberglass insulation at blocking air infiltration. As you might expect, the fiberglass folks hotly dispute this.)

The Earth Furnace by Earth Systems, (800) GO EARTH or (800) 688-0348, uses the energy stored in the ground to heat and cool a home. Loops of copper pipe are filled with Freon that is circulated in the ground outside the home.

Copper piping is also earth-friendly to a certain degree. According to the Copper Development Association, about 65% of the copper used in new homes is recycled from used scrap. In addition to plumbing, copper can be used in the home's wiring and roof flashing.

 Money Bomb #1: Trashed out vents and pipes.
"We moved into our new home during the winter and immediately turned on the heat. We noticed that some vents in the house seemed to blow little or no air at all. What happened?"

"In our new house, the main sewer line to our basement from the street continually backed up. It took expensive visits from three different plumbers before we discovered what the problem was—trash was stuffed down the sewer during construction!"

Construction sites aren't the cleanest places on Earth, to be sure. Empty caulk containers, packaging, and other debris is strewn around the house. Fast-food containers, soda cans, and other personal effects of the workers are also left behind.

Of course, workers are supposed to clean up after themselves during construction. Sometimes this entails throwing soda cans, fast-food wrappers, and cigarette butts down your heat vents or into your water/sewer pipes. Instead of getting disposed of properly (often there is a huge dumpster on the property that is ignored by crews), the trash goes down the nearest convenient hole.

Such debris can block hot air from making it through a vent, as in the first home buyer's case. The second story we cited, which actually happened to a neighbor of ours, was very expensive indeed. Once again the culprit was slovenly workers who disposed of trash down the homeowner's sewer pipes.

Solution: insist that all heating vents on the floors be covered during construction, until the floor coverings are installed. This will keep stray trash from falling down them and encourage the crews to use the real trash receptacles. If you have any doubts about trash in your vents, bring a shop vacuum to the site and try cleaning them yourself.

In the case of the sewer line, you may not be able to catch the trash. However, if you make your builder aware that he will be responsible for any future plumbing bills related to such trash, you may be able to ward off this problem. Having the house locked up as soon as possible once the walls are up will keep neighborhood vandals from contributing to this problem.

A quality builder will insist that the construction site isn't a pigsty. Careful supervision of the subcontractors will also head off most of these problems.

Money Bomb #2: No tub drain in the basement.

"Our basement has two problems: the roughed-in plumbing for a future bath doesn't have a tub drain and the furnace was installed too close to the future bath's plumbing. This means we either have to move the plumbing or the furnace. How could this happen?"

Several possibilities come to mind as the reason for this money bomb. Often, subs simply don't read the plans, forget what they're doing from one day to the next, and/or aren't supervised appropriately by the builder. In this case, the builder should cut out the concrete and put in the tub drain at his expense. The builder should also move either the furnace or the bathroom pipes—either way it's a big mess. In reality, the builder may balk at such extensive repairs and you may have an expensive legal battle looming.

Solution: Once all the pipes are roughed in, compare them to the electrical/plumbing schematic in your blueprints. Everything should be in the places specified in the plans. If not, you will have to insist that the problem is fixed before the basement floor is poured. Quick action here can prevent a costly fix later.

One couple we interviewed actually experienced the problem above and found themselves in quite a predicament. Unsupervised subs botched the location of the basement bathroom plumbing rough-in. Second, there was snow in the basement when the furnace installer arrived. Instead of shoveling the basement to find the correct location, the sub simply cleared a small space where he thought the furnace should go and proceeded with installation.

Note that the sub never looked at the plans to confirm that the furnace was in the right place—he later denied any responsibility for the mistake. The builder also failed to fix the problem, until the threat of legal action changed his mind. Even then, the builder didn't want to move the furnace. Instead he proposed chopping up the concrete basement floor to move the pipes. What a mess!

If you are buying a tract home or spec, check out the basement carefully before buying. If you plan to finish the basement, there should be plumbing pipes roughed-in for a tub or shower drain, a toilet, and a sink or two. Be sure they aren't located too close to the furnace equipment.

 ### *Money Bomb #3: Furnace disasters.*
"In my house, there aren't enough heat registers. One room is so cold we can't use it in the winter."

"Our furnace worked fine for a couple days and then conked out. This happened several times before the furnace supplier finally admitted it wasn't calibrated for our high-altitude location. We had to have it replaced."

"We had the local gas company come out to our house after it was built to do a study of its energy efficiency and they told us our furnace had a problem. The cold-air return was too small for the furnace to operate at peak efficiency. All that money for the high-efficiency furnace was wasted, thanks to sloppy installation."

The bottom line: it doesn't matter how energy efficient your furnace (or cooling unit) is. If it's installed improperly, you're sunk. Having too few heat registers, an improperly calibrated unit, or too small of a cold-air return can add up to higher heat bills and a very uncomfortable house.

Solution: The problem with too few heat registers (or cooling vents) is easily avoided during the design phase. Calculating the correct number of vents is best left in the hands of a professional. Make certain that your inspector counts the vents and notes their placement to make sure the builder follows the plans.

As for high altitudes or other extreme conditions, confirm you are getting an appropriate furnace. Check the invoice and paperwork to make sure you got what you ordered.

For force- air furnaces, the cold-air return must be the same size as the hot-air vent leaving the furnace. If not, your furnace will not heat your home efficiently. Have your inspector check the size of the return before you close on the house.

In addition, the cold-air return in the home should NOT be installed near a fireplace. If a fire is burning and the furnace kicks on, the fire will "back-draft" toward the cold-air return—not a pleasant experience. This is a common problem in some builder-designed homes.

Finally, have your inspector pay close attention to the duct work installation for the heating/ventilation and air conditioning system. A common problem with duct work is crimping that restricts air flow.

Money Bomb #4: Weakening the floor joists.

"When the electrician came in to string the electrical wires, he cut big notches in the floor joists to string the wires through them. Now we have a basement full of damaged joists. Is this a problem?"

In some cases, such damage to the joists can weaken their structural integrity. In plain English, this can be big trouble.

Every time you cut a hole in a joist, especially a large hole, you weaken the joist. The bigger the hole and the closer to the bottom of the joist, the greater the weakness.

Solution: Some pre-fab joist manufacturers (such as the Silent Floor by TJI) precut small holes in the joist for pipes, wires, and the like. If your builder doesn't use these pre-manufactured joists, insist that the subs drill small holes in the joists near the tops to ensure the integrity of these supports. Have your inspector check this item to ensure correct procedures are followed.

Money Bomb #5: Insulation quality reduced.

"I let my builder talk me into using 2x4 construction on my house, and then he shoved extra thick batts of insulation into the walls, claiming this would be better than regular insulation. I read the directions on the batts and found out they are supposed to be installed only in 2x6 walls. Do I have trouble here?"

Your builder is just trying to pull a fast one on you. You can't shove extra insulation into a too-small space and expect it to work well. In fact, any good insulation should allow for some air circulation. Squeezing too much into a small space effectively cuts out circulation, making your insulation less efficient and raising your heating and cooling bills accordingly. In areas with extreme climates and/or high utility costs, it may pay to have your inspector do an insulation inspection before the walls are sealed.

If you have any questions or comments on this chapter, please feel free to call the authors. See the "How to Reach Us" page at the back of this book!

10

Key Inspection Points: Finishing

S o, you thought most of the time-consuming stuff was over for your new house? The foundation is poured, the walls are up, the roof is sheathed—any day you'll be moving in, right? Hold the moving van, the fun has just begun. You've just entered the Finishing Zone.

While progress on framing the house was quite visible, you're now in for weeks, if not months, of finishing work that seems to move at a snail's pace. At the same time, the house is definitely crossing the line into becoming a home: the faucets are installed, light fixtures are added, and so on.

For simplicity's sake, we've divided this chapter into two parts: interior and exterior finishing. Outside finish work includes siding and roofing. Inside finishing includes drywall installation, painting, trim work, lighting fixtures, plumbing fixtures, cabinets, and a host of other items. In reality, some of this work is done concurrently—for example, your roof may be shingled at the same time the drywall is installed.

Here's an overview of the major milestones you'll pass:

Exterior Finishing

Key Inspection Points:
Finishing work is the icing on a cake. Now that you've made sure the home is structurally sound, the last thing you want is for the finishing work to be botched. As a result, it's prudent to have an inspector or architect out to inspect the finishing work. This can be done at several stages, culminating in the final walk-through where a "punch list" of problems to be corrected is created.

Specifically for exterior finishing work, inspectors are looking for proper installation of roofing materials, siding, and gutters/downspouts. Since these aspects typically come at the end of the building process, deadline pressure may cause the builder to make mistakes or cut corners—an inspector should be there to protect your rights on these critical and expensive finishing items.

Step-by-Step: Outside Finish Work

Step 1: Roof. Before the shingles are applied, a black felt sub-roof is first attached to the roof sheathing. Ideally, the shingles should be applied soon after—if not the felt may tear in the wind. Also, the felt sub-roof also doesn't completely protect the interior from rain or melting snow.

Many choices are available for roofing material—all of them should be fire rated. The best fire rating is A, followed by B, and then C. If you're looking at ratings on shingles, don't assume the rating means it is the best shingle—they're just a gauge of fire resistance. Our discussion of shingles covers seven major options, from least to most expensive.

Asphalt shingles (also known as composite or fiberglass shingles) are often the least expensive choice. Asphalt shingles have life expectancies ranging from 15 years to 25 years or more. If you don't plan to live in your house for 25 years, consider buying a 15- or 20-year shingle. Because of their low cost, asphalt or composite shingles are often used on starter or tract-style houses.

Some companies are now coming out with a thicker, three-dimensional asphalt shingle intended to look like cedar shakes. One company, Celotex (813) 873-1700, offers these shake asphalt shingles, which are guaranteed to last up to 40 years.

Metal roofs are more expensive than asphalt, but offer longer life spans. Although not common, metal roofs are seeing a resurgence in popularity. Whether they are galvanized steel or aluminum, one neat aspect to metal roofs is their colored finishes. We have a neighbor near us who has a dark red metal roof that really adds some panache to his house.

Buyers who want a more rustic look often choose *cedar* shingles or cedar shakes. Cedar shingles have a smooth appearance, while shakes have a rougher look; both weather to a gray color. Cedar roofing material is highly flammable and, in some areas, can raise your home insurance rates. Most cedar roofs last 10 to 12 years.

For a roof that will last 30 years or more (some manufacturers claim they'll last "a lifetime"), *concrete* roofing tiles are quite hip, especially with Mediterranean-style homes. Available in a variety of shapes and styles, concrete is an excellent option for folks who can't afford tile or slate—concrete is about half the cost. It also comes in a wide variety of colors including such exotic designer options as adobe, bronze, and alpine blue. Concrete (as well as tile and slate) requires a more substantial roof structure due to the materials' weight.

One of the most expensive options for roofing material is **clay tiles.** Seen mostly on Mediterranean-style homes (especially in California), tile is available in a variety of colors from classic red to brown and even blue. Except for the occasional broken tile, they have a relatively long life and a good fire rating.

Slate is mined mainly in Vermont, Maine, and other northeastern states. Because it is limited in supply, this is the most expensive roofing option. However, your slate roof will probably be around long after the house below it disintegrates! Some slate roofs have lasted several centuries. The colors available depend on the area the slate comes from— the most commons shades are maroon and black. There are three different grades of slate, with life spans ranging from 20 to 40 years for low grades to 75 to 100 years for the top grade. Be careful to buy slate that has been graded—poor-quality slate is often ungraded.

A note about flat roofs: There are several new "membrane roof systems" on the market today designed for flat roofs. We recommend consulting a roofing specialist about these new roofs, since correct installation is paramount. Plus, membrane systems are designed for different situations; therefore, a specialist will be better able to instruct you before you make a decision. If you have a low-pitch roof, you may consider using asphalt roofing rolls. Similar to shingles, they come in rolls and are simple to install.

Besides the shingles that go on a roof, you will need to have flashing installed. Flashing is metal strips installed under the shingles around the chimney, in the seams where different roof lines meet, and around skylights and vents. Flashing helps keep water from leaking inside your house by channeling the water into the gutters. Good flashing is a must—if you have a roof leak, the first suspect is usually inadequate (or missing) flashing.

Step 2: Siding. The options for siding are at least as varied as those for roofing materials. They include wood, vinyl or aluminum siding, cedar shingles, stucco, brick or stone veneer. Some homes combine styles, such as stucco accents on a cedar-sided home. Regardless of the type of siding you use, all openings (windows, doors, etc.) will need to be flashed to prevent water damage and air infiltration.

Wood. It pays to visit a local lumber yard or home center to see what options they offer for siding materials. Most have a display of various wood siding, including clapboard, weatherboard, drop siding, cedar shingles, etc. Plywood siding is also popular in many parts of the country—fiberboard is a close second.

Vinyl and aluminum. Vinyl siding manufacturers must have an inferiority complex—what else could explain why they stamp their product with a "wood grain" finish. It's an obvious fake and is a common sight on starter or tract homes. The irony is that real wood siding usually has a smooth finish and doesn't show a wood grain when painted! Also, when inexperienced installers put up vinyl siding, it can look extremely sloppy, especially where long pieces are connected.

Costs and Life Expectancy of Seven Roof Types

Product Type	UL Class	Installed Cost (per 100 square ft.)	Life Expectancy	Life-Cycle Cost
Asphalt Shingle (3-tab)	A	$145—165	15—20 yrs.	$8.85
Asphalt Shingle (heavy, laminated)	A	$175—225	30—40 yrs.	$5.71
Treated Wood Shakes	C	$350—450	15—20 yrs.	$22.06
Untreated Wood Shakes	n/a*	$250—300	9—12 yrs.	$25
Fibrous Cement Shake	A	$275—300	50 yrs.	$5.75
Concrete Tile	A	$270—300	50 yrs.	$5.70
Clay Tile	A	$290—400	50 yrs.	$6.10

* Untreated wood shakes are not fire-rated, but it's safe to say that they're a major fire hazard.

Source: Florida Forum Magazine, *July 1991.*

Vinyl siding does come in several grades—choose the thickest and you'll be happier. The best grades will also look much more natural. The biggest advantage of vinyl siding is that it doesn't have to be painted—ever. The color goes all the way through the vinyl and, except for some fading, will look as good as the day it was installed.

Aluminum siding is another option, although most people are using vinyl these days. Unlike vinyl, aluminum can be dented and scratched. No doubt the *Tin Men* image of siding salesmen as scam artists has contributed to aluminum's decline in popularity.

Stucco. Most commonly used in the West and Southwest, stucco can be either traditional concrete or a new, synthetic material. Traditional stucco requires expansion joints. Such joints help the concrete expand and contract without cracking, similar to the joints you see in concrete driveways and sidewalks.

Synthetic stucco doesn't require expansion joints. Nor does it have to be replaced as often as concrete stucco (it weathers better).

Either option of stucco can be tinted before being applied or painted after installation. The advantage of tinting is that you don't have to repaint—the color goes all the way through the stucco. And if you get tired of the tint, you can still paint over it.

Stucco seems less common in areas with excessive rain. Water damage to stucco is not pleasant to look at. We have seen stucco-sided houses that are streaked with black deposits from rainwater. The best way to avoid this is to make sure the drainage off your roof is adequate.

Brick and stone. Brick houses really just have a brick veneer, unless they were built prior to World War II. In other words, the brick is just a facade, like wood siding or stucco. Brick is very popular in the South, perhaps because it is less expensive there.

Brick requires a subcontractor familiar with masonry. This sub bricks the home's exterior, as well as any interior accents such as the fireplace. A less costly alternative to brick is a brick-faced plywood product, which "simulates" a brick veneer. Make sure that "weep holes" are installed in the veneer—this enables water trapped behind the brick to escape. A lack of weep holes may cause damage to the home's framing.

Stone is usually applied in the same manner as a brick veneer—by a masonry expert. Some composite stone options are less expensive than the real thing. However, the problem with such fake stone is that it looks, well, fake. Some buyers like to add a touch of brick, mixed with stucco or other siding. Be careful—the combination of siding elements should be designed by a professional architect. We've seen many "builder-designed" homes that mix and match siding in such a haphazard way it would make your head spin.

Step 3: Gutters and downspouts. Made of galvanized steel, aluminum, or vinyl, gutters and downspouts are typically cut to fit your home right at the job site. On our house, the gutter subcontractor must have had the IQ of a house plant—he cut the metal gutters in our neighbor's driveway, leaving sharp metal pieces behind. Needless to say, when our neighbor experienced a flat tire, we were far from the most popular people on the block.

Drainage is one of the most important parts of building a home—after all, if you end up with standing water you may have roof leaks or leaks into your foundation. Special attention needs to be given to make sure the design of the gutters and downspouts is correct—unfortunately, builders often botch this important step.

For example, our builder designed a main downspout to empty right next to the concrete front porch. Runoff from the roof washed away the dirt from under the porch and we had the fun experience of "severe settling." The result: part of the porch cracked and a set of concrete stairs separated from the home. While the builder made good at fixing the problem, it could have been prevented at the outset.

Here are some signs of well-planned drainage:

- Downspouts that empty at least 60 inches from the house—anything less could cause settling, water leakage into the home, or worse.

- Grading of the surrounding soil to drain water away from the house. Water only flows downhill—hence you must carefully design the drainage to keep it from damaging your home.
- Connect black plastic pipes to your downspouts to move water away from the home. These pipes can be buried underground, draining out 10 to 20 feet away from your house. Cover the end of the pipe with a wire mesh to prevent debris or small animals from blocking the pipe.

We eventually went with the black plastic pipe option and have solved our drainage problem. Unfortunately, most builders pay scant attention to this important issue.

Step 4: Exterior paint. Primer and top-coat paints should be applied to your house as soon as the siding goes on. Don't allow the builder to put off painting your house for longer than a week or two, or the ultra-violet rays of the sun may begin to damage the raw wood. If you live in a rainy climate, the paint should go on as soon as the weather is nice—don't wait!

Eco-Friendly Alternatives
Nailite Roofing Panels by GE Plastics, (800) 328-9018. How about plastic roofing? Designed as a substitute for conventional shingles, Nailite panels contain Norell, which is made by GE Plastics from used computer housings. The 20x40 panels cost about the same as cedar shakes, but they are lighter weight. The weight of Nailite panels is only one-third of asphalt singles and one fourth of cedar shakes.

FlexTech by Bomanite Corp., (800) 854-2094, is a non-slip surfacing material made from recycled rubber that is used for patios, pool decks and paths. The surface, which is made from rubber pellets, is installed over a solid (or concrete) base and can be textured or colored.

Timbrex by Mobil Chemical's Composite Products Division, (800) 972-5355, is a plastic wood that also contains recycled wood fibers. Timbrex resists water damage and is used in applications that normally require treated wood, such as deck planks and window trim.

Money Bomb #1: Improper installation voids warranty.
"Our house has a great-looking roof made of tile. The problem is that the roof is leaking like a sieve. The roof manufacturer refuses to fix the problem because they say the builder installed it improperly. Can they do this?"

Many manufacturers we spoke to told us they can't guarantee their products if the builder or subcontractor installed them improperly. (This goes for many products, not just roofing.) If the builder balks at fixing the problem, the frustration level can reach a boiling point. You may end up in a ping-pong game, where the roofing manufacturer blames the installation (that is, the builder) and the builder blames the product.

Solution: An experienced private inspector or architect should be able to determine whether the roof is installed correctly. This monitor will need to visit the site while the roof is going on. Insist that your inspector get up there and take a look. If your inspector isn't familiar with your roof system, most manufacturers are happy to provide literature that details the installation process.

What if you discover a defective roof too late (that is, after you move in)? Get to the bottom of the issue by discovering the root cause—you may have to call in an engineer, an inspector, or another roofing contractor to assign the blame. By presenting this "third-party" evaluation to the roofing supplier and builder, you may get some action. If you don't, a sharply worded letter from your lawyer may loosen up the logjam.

Money Bomb #2: *The overzealous painters.*

"Just after moving in to our new home, we noticed we couldn't get the garage door open without the help of the Incredible Hulk. So we called the subcontractor who installed the door. When he came out, we were informed that the house painter had painted over the vinyl strip at the top of the door, causing the door to stick. To make matters worse, the sub pointed out a tag on the garage door specifically directing painters not to paint the vinyl."

Yes, it does seem as though painters' answer to a job is to slop paint on any bare surface. In this case, the paint actually caused a malfunction with the garage door. In other instances, it may mean painting over electrical outlets, wood that should be stained instead, and more.

Solution: Obviously, you need a builder on site to supervise these problems. In the case above, no supervisor was present during the painting of this house. It also would be nice if the painting subcontractor could or would read warning tags.

Barring all these intelligent checks on gung-ho painters, your inspector should check for painting problems during the finishing inspection. Make sure the inspector notes any improper painting and insists that the builder correct it.

Money Bomb #3: *No primer means painting again in a couple years.*

"When my builder painted my house a couple years ago, I assumed the paint would last at least five years. But here I am, two years later, painting it again. What caused this?"

If your builder didn't use a primer coat on your house before painting it with top coat, the paint may not last very long. In fact, in the area where we live, most builders don't put on a primer coat—and many recently-built houses are beginning to show it. Builders here are simply trying to save a few bucks by not using primer. Their excuse is, "It wasn't in the contract."

Solution: Insist on having the paint subcontractor use at least one coat of primer before the final paint or stain is applied. Once the primer is applied, have the painter do the top coat as soon as possible. Contrary to some painters' opinions, the primer does not need to "cure" or sit around in the sun. In fact, the longer the primer is exposed to UV light, the less effective it becomes, according to experts we've consulted.

Interior Finishing

Interior finishing includes everything it takes to make your house livable: drywall, doors, windows, floor coverings, trim work, brick accents, etc. While we can't possibly detail every minute aspect of finish work, we will try to give you a good idea of the major components.

Key Inspection Points

The finishing inspection can be one major inspection, or a series of shorter visits to check quality. Important points to consider are the hanging of the drywall and setting of windows, as well as installation of the floor coverings and the trim work. If you have a brick or stone fireplace, you may want to have this inspected as well.

Step-by-Step: Finishing Work

Step 1: Windows. Windows come in every price range and size with every possible energy-saving option imaginable. We discuss the differences, advantages, and disadvantages of windows from leading manufacturers at the end of this book.

As for installing the windows, your builder's framing team will have framed out each window and door opening. We recommend requiring the framers to use a double thickness of "headers" (blocks of wood over the window/door opening) to protect against future warping.

Your inspector will be able to determine whether the windows have been anchored to the frame and are supported properly. All windows should be level (or "plumb") and most important, properly flashed. Flashing windows is similar to flashing a roof: galvanized metal strips or well-painted wood is used to guide water away from the window opening, down the side of the house.

We have actually seen the effects of having no flashing around the windows on a Florida home located near the coast. In a state like Florida, you can imagine that flashing would be even more critical. Unfortunately for this home buyer, the lack of flashing led to the rotting of the windows as well as damage to the interior of the house. Your inspector must inspect the flashing *before* the siding goes up on the outside of the house.

Step 2: Drywall. Once the insulation has been installed in your house, the drywall can go up. Referred to as gypboard, wall board or sheetrock, drywall is a sheet of gypsum sandwiched between two pieces of paper.

Wallboard should be installed using drywall screws, which hold the walls to the studs better. The other alternative is nails, which can pop out if the stud is warped or the drywall is improperly installed. Be sure the screws are inserted roughly every 12 inches to ensure the board is secure.

Once the drywall is installed, the seams are covered with a joint compound (known as "mud"). Next, the seams are taped with a special paper tape and then spread with more compound. Any "dimples" from where the drywall screws are inserted should also be leveled out with joint compound. If your walls are going to remain smooth (as is common in the Northeast), a good taping team will come back after the compound dries and reapply a second coat. Then, after this dries, the crew sands the surface smooth.

In many parts of the country, smooth walls have been replaced with textures. In my parents' house (built in the 1960s) the designs were elaborate, including scalloped ceilings. Today, the most common texture is called "orange peel."

Textures are used since they save time and money. Only one layer of joint compound is used, and then the texture is applied over it. Texture will hide poor taping and sheetrocking jobs. If you plan to have textured walls and ceilings, have your inspector check out the sheetrock job carefully *before* the walls are textured.

Step 3: Interior paint. Once the drywall is completed, the walls can be painted. Most paint and hardware stores are happy to give you tips and pointers about the pros and cons of certain paints.

However, if you have children or pets, consider using a semi-gloss or gloss paint inside your house. This makes it much easier to clean the walls should you have a drooling Rover or a budding Rembrandt.

Tip: Be sure to keep extra cans of paint around the house after it's completed, so you can do any touch-ups. If all the paint and trim stain have been used, get the names of each type from your builder, buy a can or two and keep them in a safe place. This goes for the outside paint or stain as well.

Step 4: Trim work. Trim work includes doors, mantels, window frames, floor trim—anything that requires a little wood to finish it off. Trim is used to cover the bare ends of drywall, the tops of fireplaces, and the frames around windows and doors. We also include doors in the trim work because the painting or staining of inside doors is done at the same time as the rest of the trim work.

Trim work should be stained before it is installed. Once stained, door jambs and frames should be installed first, and then the doors are installed. After the stained trim has been completely installed, the finish crew should go back through the house and fill in the nail holes with putty approximately the color of the stained or painted wood.

If you prefer painted trim, the wood should be painted after it has been installed (except for the doors). The nail holes should be filled before painting as well.

Trim work is a prime area for builder shenanigans. For example, on a house we examined, the builder was asked by a subcontractor where the redwood trim supplies were. Cheaper-quality cedar trim had apparently been delivered to the job site. The builder told the sub to put in the cheaper trim despite specific directions on the plans to use redwood.

If you expect solid oak, six-panel doors, don't settle for pine, hollow-core, flush doors. Specify the type of doors and trim (as well as the paint or stain) in your blueprints. Have the inspector verify this on the finishing inspection.

If you're building a custom home, all the trim work should be clearly called out on the specs and plans. If you're buying a tract or semi-custom home, make sure the builder clearly tells you the type of trim work you're getting *before* you commit.

Another point: if you expect your trim to be flush with the wall, you will have to inform the builder in advance. Often this problem is caused by sloppy drywall work, but it can be covered up at this stage with the infamous caulk gun (more on this later).

Step 5: *Floor coverings*. This stage includes the installation of carpet, tile, linoleum, and hardwood—finally, the house is beginning to look more like a home. Regardless of the finishing floor coverings you choose, you must insist on having an "underlayment" installed by the subcontractor. (The exception is hardwood, which can be nailed directly to the sub-floor.) Underlayments, usually made of plywood or mahogany, smooth out any bumps in the sub-floor. Varying thicknesses will help level the different floor surfaces in your home. A good underlayment costs about $1.50 per square foot installed.

***Hardwood floors*.** Most builders put in hardwood floors first because it's much simpler to fit other types of floor coverings to the wood, than the other way around. We watched a little of our wood floor being installed and it was quite impressive. The subcontractor moved at lightning speed as he pounded the boards into place.

At the ends of hardwoods, a cross-piece is used under a door or where the hardwood meets other types of flooring. Once installed, hardwoods are stained with several coats of a polyurethane stain. Polyurethane has made it possible for consumers to avoid time-consuming waxing that previous wood flooring required. Just a mild vinegar and water solution is needed to clean most hardwood floors.

***Vinyl*.** Used most often in laundry rooms or even in bathrooms and kitchens, vinyl is a cost-effective floor covering. Most vinyl is cheaper than tile, carpeting, or hardwoods. Vinyl runs about $6 to $20 per square yard—expensive "solid" vinyls can top $50.

Vinyl requires a smooth, strong underlayment—usually plywood. Once the underlayment is installed, the vinyl is adhered to the subfloor using a latex adhesive. The actual type of adhesive depends on the brand of vinyl used.

Carpeting. Whether berber or plush, carpeting can range widely in price. Our best advice: get carpeting with the highest nylon content (or wool content if it's berber). The more nylon, the better the carpet. It doesn't snag as easily and it resists traffic patterns better. If you plan to live in your house for many years, invest in long-lasting carpet.

Carpet is installed over an underlayment, just like vinyl. Padding (preferably 3/8-inch thick) is laid on top of the underlayment and the carpet is then installed on top. Some people use carpeting that already has padding attached to it—a cost-saving advantage.

Tile. Tile is often used as a floor covering in bathrooms, kitchens, and laundry rooms (not to mention as countertops, back splashes, and shower and tub enclosures). Large floor tiles may also be used in high traffic areas such as hallways. You will definitely need an underlayment below the tile. Often tile is set early in the process at the same time hardwood floors are laid.

Stone. Some folks with unlimited budgets choose to have flagstones set as floor covering. The cost, however, is prohibitive for most buyers. If a stone floor is appealing, consider having radiant heating installed under the stone to avoid cold floors in winter.

Step 6: Cabinets and countertops. Cabinets are usually thought of as part of the kitchen and the bathrooms. Cabinets can also be installed in your family room (a convenient hiding place for your TV), in the bedrooms, and in an office. Some people even want built-in cabinets in the laundry room and garage.

There are three basic types of cabinets: pre-fabricated, semi-custom and custom. Pre-fabricated cabinets such as those made by Merillat, Riviera, and Master Craft often are advertised in home magazines and on showroom floors in local lumber and home stores.

Pre-fabricated cabinets are available in a number of stock sizes. A cabinet representative measures your kitchen and bath areas to create a "schematic" of the cabinet design. If you can't fill the space up exactly, they may adjust cabinet sizes or the installer may fill in with a matching strip of wood to hide the gaps.

Some pre-fabricated cabinets are made of particle board covered with laminate and can look very cheap. Others are made of solid panels of hardwoods such as oak and are stained or painted to look quite attractive. Still other cabinets may have real wood doors with particle board and laminate "boxes." Shelves or doors may be a wood veneer over particle board. The basic rule of thumb: the price varies depending on how much real wood is used.

Semi-custom cabinets have more options for woods and styles than basic stock cabinets and as such are more expensive. They still come in stock sizes, however, and can be ordered rather more quickly than custom options.

Custom cabinets are noticeably more expensive because they are designed from scratch to fit your particular home. Often made in more exotic woods such as maple and cherry, custom cabinets are usually of much higher quality construction than pre-fabricated options.

So how much do cabinets cost in the real world? Well, for our home, we priced cabinets for an "average-size" kitchen (12 by 11 feet) with a center island. We also included cabinets for two bathrooms. Pre-fabricated cabinets were in the $2800 to $3300 range. Semi-custom would have run $4000 to $5000, while custom cabinets would top $6000 to $7000.

The best cabinets are those with interior construction as sturdy as exterior is beautiful. Four elements to look for in a good cabinet:

1 *"Dovetailed," solid wood drawers* that are not stapled or hot-glued.

2 *Shelves that don't bow* when weight is added (you might want to bring in a couple small barbells or other weights to test the sample cabinets). If the shelves in the showroom have a center support, ask whether this will be installed in your cabinets.

3 *Proper door alignment.*

4 *All-metal, hidden hinges.* The best cabinets have all-metal hinges that are hidden inside the door and are not visible when the door is shut.

After the kitchen flooring is installed, cabinet installation is usually done by an installer working for the cabinet manufacturer or their local representative. Occasionally, the builder or one of his workers will install your cabinets.

Countertops. Countertops may come in any variety of shape, forms, or style. The most common countertops (because they are the most cost effective) are *laminates*. Laminates are also popular because they come in so many colors and designs. The most famous manufacturer of laminates is Formica (others include Wilsonart, Nevamar, Pionite, and Micarta). There are approximately 300 different colors, textures, and designs in Formica's sample kit—if you can imagine it, its available. The cost of "color through" laminate ranges from $25 to $40 per lineal foot.

Of course, laminate countertops have some drawbacks. The disadvantages include scratching, lack of heat resistance, and seams that can be rather visible.

Ceramic tile is a step up in price and in elegance. The sub who installs any bath tile or floor tile will install your countertops as well. The least expensive option is the basic colored tile, either glazed or unglazed in solid colors such as black, white, mauve, etc. Some folks go hog wild with custom glazed and designed tile with scenes painted on it. Specially textured tiles are also in vogue. These options are considerably more expensive than the $2 to $20 per square foot price of plain tile. Tile also has a few disadvantages: the grout between the tiles can be a burden to clean. The noise from clanking dishes isn't fun either. However, tile is reasonably stain resistant and hot pots and pans can be set directly on it.

Solid surfacing materials are made by manufacturers such as Avonite, Corian (800-4-CORIAN) or Fountainhead (410-551-5000). Corian is a combination of acrylic and natural minerals, while the other brands include such ingredients as polyester or resin. Solid surfaces have color that goes all the way through (although the 20 color options are somewhat limited).

One advantage of solid surfacing materials: cuts and burns can be easily repaired by light sanding. Solid surfaces can be shaped into sinks, too—the result is an ultra-modern, seamless look.

Unfortunately, you will pay through the nose for solid surfacing materials—about 10 times the cost of laminates. In fact, the price ranges from $80 to $190 per lineal foot for the products. As a result, you tend to see Corian and its cousins in high-end luxury homes.

One product gaining popularity at the expense of solid surfacing materials is ***granite.*** Granite in many parts of the country is priced about the same as solid surfaces—$150 to $300 per lineal foot. In the move back to the "natural" look, many luxury buyers are choosing granite over the pre-fab solid surfacing stuff.

However, granite is very heavy, requiring more support from the cabinets. Also, it has no "give"—a glass dropped on granite will definitely break. If you can afford it, granite is an incredible option to consider. Colors are limited to nature (we've seen pinks, grays, blacks, and rusty reds), but the uniqueness of this product is fascinating.

One note: some buyers are interested in using ***marble*** as a countertop treatment. However, in a kitchen, the only place marble can be used is for a pastry board. The problem with this material elsewhere: marble absorbs grease permanently, leaving splotches. In baths, however, the problem can be held to a minimum. Marble is even more expensive than granite.

Depending on the type of countertop, you may have a tile expert do the installation, the builder's team or a countertop specialist.

Step 7: Lights. One of the last finishing jobs will be putting in the light fixtures. Surprisingly, many people don't realize they will have to supply the light bulbs for each fixture—an unexpectedly expensive proposition. We were appalled to discover that the light bulb tab for our home topped $200—an unpleasant surprise late in the ball game.

By this stage in the game, the electricity should be hooked up to the house. The electrician usually installs the light fixtures for you, but he needs those light bulbs to test each fixture. If ceiling fans are installed at this stage, make sure adequate supports have been installed to carry the load of the fans. Simply attaching the fan to the ceiling electrical junction box doesn't cut it—the fan could fall.

Step 8: Appliances. Some builders will have the appliances installed by a representative of the manufacturer, but others will do it themselves. The exception: a gas stove or dishwasher, which must be hooked up by a plumber or special licensed contractor. Your inspector should test each appliance once it's been installed—run the dishwasher for a full cycle, grind up some food in the garbage disposal, and so on. The finishing inspection is the ultimate tire-kicking exercise.

The range of choices among appliances is incredible in this day and age, and we simply don't have enough room in this book to discuss all the best options available. As you might expect, we found *Consumer Reports* magazines to be the best authority for the latest scoop on appliances. Many back issues of the magazine are available through your local library. The annual *Consumer Reports Buying Guide* book summarizes their reviews for items as well.

Step 9: Plumbing fixtures. Plumbing fixtures will also be installed at this stage. Your inspector will want to check that these fixtures work without leaking. Toilets should be flushed several times and faucets and shower heads should be run. Check to see whether the water from the hot water faucet gets hot—sometimes the hot and cold pipes get switched. Also, make sure there are no leaks under the sinks—letting the water run for a few minutes will help determine this.

 Eco-Friendly Alternatives
Image Carpets. Ever wonder what use recycled plastic soda bottles can be put to? Image Carpets are woven from yarn whose fibers are derived from melted plastic bottles. (706) 857-6481.

Prominence ceramic floor tiles by GTE, (717) 724-8350, are made from waste glass from the company's light bulb division. Another recycled-glass product is Traffic Tiles from Stoneware Tile—70% of the tile is ground glass from the waste of automobile glass manufacturing.

FibreBond wallboard by Louisiana Pacific, (503) 221-0800, is 30% recycled paper (the balance is gypsum). Standard wallboard (which is nailed to the studs to create a wall surface that is later painted and textured) is nearly all natural gypsum. The only negative: the FibreBond panels must be handled carefully to prevent cracking. This is made more difficult by the fact that a 4x8 FibreBbond board weighs 15 pounds heavier than standard wallboard.

Armstrong, (800) 233-3823, manufactures ceiling tiles and panels that are made in part from recycled newsprint. The wood fiber in the tiles is 22% recycled. The company also offers a new vinyl flooring that eliminates the need for a wood sub-floor. In addition to smoothing out lumps in the existing floor sheathing, the flooring also requires less adhesive than regular vinyl flooring.

Premium windows by Owens-Corning Fiberglass, (419) 248-8000, are an interesting innovation. The frames are actually fiberglass similar to snow skis or car bodies. The company claims the fiberglass doesn't warp or shrink; the glass is argon-filled "low-E" for insulation.

Water-saving faucets, toilets, shower heads, and dishwashers are available from many national manufacturers. Some communities are requiring their use in new construction. The best deal: areas that offer utility rebates for the installation of low-volume toilets and the like. Contact your local utility company to see whether they offer any incentives.

As for specifics, Delta Faucets, (317) 848-1812, offers an Embracer shower head that meets mandatory conservation codes. Speakman's Model SD 8068 Sensorflo faucet conserves up to 85% of normal water use by using touch-free controls. For a Speakman dealer near you, call (302) 764-9100.

How long does it take to pay back the higher costs of water-saving products? Well, a low-consumption toilet costs about $300, while a regular toilet is about $100. When you consider the water savings, it takes about four years for pay-back.

Be wary of low-cost 1.6 gallon toilets—some don't perform well, forcing you to flush twice.

The AEG Favorit 875 Dishwasher (800) 344-0043 is a European-made dishwasher that uses less energy and water than traditional appliances.

The Frigidaire FPES19T6 Refrigerator (800) 451-7007 has 19 cubic feet of storage space. The company says it exceeds federal efficiency standards by 25%.

Sterling Domestic Appliances (617) 255-9909 makes a cooktop (model GCT 361-4) that saves energy through a Switch Back System feature.

Money Bombs

 Money Bomb #1: Substituting cheaper finishing materials. *"In our specs we listed special faucets with water-control devices. However, when we visited the site and looked at the faucet boxes, we discovered that the wrong faucets were ordered. The builder thought we wouldn't notice the difference once they were installed."*

In the next chapter, we'll discuss a builder's disease called the "diminishing-profit syndrome." Basically, this drives builders to make substitutions toward the end of the project to boost their profits.

This could happen with molding, doors, windows, tubs, faucets, sinks, carpet—basically, any aspect of the finishing work. In our case, our builder decided not to install a shower door in our master bath to save himself the expense.

Solution: To protect yourself from diminishing-profit syndrome, get every detail in writing. Our problem with the shower door occurred because we assumed every master bath shower has a shower door. It took a lot of negotiating to solve this problem because the door was never specified in the spec list.

If you suspect your builder might try to pull a fast one with the type of product you've specified, ask to see the boxes and look carefully at each receipt. If you're supposed to get cherry molding, be sure the receipt from the lumber yard doesn't say "birch." Being on top of everything is the only way to keep the builder from substituting cheaper materials. Once again, the strategy is "trust but verify."

 Money Bomb #2: Builders in a hurry leave out important items. "To finish our house on time, our builder worked around the clock. After moving in, we noticed that no one had connected the motor for the whirlpool tub. However, we couldn't connect the tub ourselves because the builder didn't cut an access panel out to get to the motor. This is insane."

Whenever you have a system such as a whirlpool motor, a water heater, a furnace, etc., you'll need to be certain it's hooked up and working. Don't assume something is hooked up because it's there. The major culprit is, of course, the rush to finish the home by a certain date. While a little deadline pressure is helpful, some builders bite off more than they can chew. The resulting work is sloppy, incomplete or worse.

Solution: Your inspector should be able to test each mechanical system as soon as water and/or electricity is available. If you discover such a goof, most red-faced builders will fix the problem quickly.

 Money Bomb #3: Costly last-minute changes.
"When we first designed our home, we didn't want a whirlpool tub. However, we changed our mind midway through construction and asked the builder to get us a whirlpool. He told us there would be a substantial restocking fee for the already delivered tub as well as a change-order fee. Needless to say, we decided to stick with the original tub."

Some builders do a lousy job of informing consumers about change-order charges and restocking fees. When you decide to change one or more of the specs you chose earlier, the builder may have already ordered the item. When the builder sends it back, he may be charged a restocking fee—this is passed on to you.

Change order fees are another bugaboo. Many builders claim this charge is necessary to cover the administrative time and expense. If you want a different tub, it may only be $25 more. But the builder may spend all afternoon calling around town to get information on prices and availability.

Solution: Ask up front about any change-order fees. In fact, get a schedule from the builder of exactly what it costs for minor or major alterations. Also, ask about deadlines after which changes incur such a fee.

 Money Bomb #4: Overzealous carpet installers freezing you out. *"When we moved into our new home this summer, we were really excited about the place. But once winter hit, we noticed the house was rather cold. Finally, we figured out the problem—and it wasn't the furnace. It turns out the carpet installers never cut out holes for the heat vents!"*

Yes, it's hard to believe that some subs can be so incompetent, but it happens. And heating your home is a little difficult when the vents are covered.

Solution: Make a note of where all the heat vents are on your copy of the plans before the floor coverings go in. Then when the subcontractors are finished, go back through the house and match up vents with your plans. This will help you make certain the vents are clear.

Money Bomb #5: New-carpet fumes. *"Right after we moved into our house, my daughter began to suffer from severe headaches and respiratory problems. We thought it might be a problem with the air conditioning, but we soon learned it was the fumes from the new carpet. Have you heard about this?"*

In October 1992, Congress held hearings regarding the potential health hazard of new-carpet fumes. Consumers testified that they became sick when they moved into homes with new carpet installed. A CBS News report cited a lab that found evidence that mice exposed to new-carpet fumes experienced severe health problems—like convulsions. Meanwhile, the carpet industry denies there is any problem and the EPA says they'll study the problem—in 1993. If you're concerned, you may want to pay close attention to the debate by getting the latest information. Consumer advocates want new carpeting to carry a warning label. Stay tuned.

Money Bomb #6: No underlayment under your floor covering. *"I love my linoleum in the kitchen but there's a huge step up from the kitchen to the living room carpet. There are also lumps and bumps under the linoleum. What causes this?"*

You probably don't have the proper underlayment under your linoleum. Many floor-covering manufacturers won't honor their warranties if an underlayment isn't put down first. Call your installer and/or builder immediately and have this remedied.

Solution: When you draw up your spec list, be certain to include underlayment in the contract. In one case, a builder tried to get out of using underlayment because it wasn't in the contract. Once again, don't assume anything. And if you notice lumps and bumps (caused by drywall mud or sawdust) in the floor, or the floor is lower than an adjoining floor, get the builder to fix it.

Final Grading

Final grading occurs when the house is completed and the builder has cleaned up the site. Grading is absolutely necessary to make certain that water drains away from the house, thus avoiding leaky basements or standing water in the crawl space.

Think of your house as a bowl. The bowl is filled in with dirt after the foundation is poured (technically referred to as back filling). The goal is to slope the dirt away from the house to ensure that water drains away too. Integral to final grading is your drainage system: downspouts and drain pipes from your roof. Downspouts should direct water at least five feet away from your foundation. If your downspouts are lacking, consider having the black drainage pipe discussed earlier installed. Watch out: Many builders skimp on the final grading, causing you major headaches down the line.

Any landscaping will also occur during this stage. Some builders merely offer to reseed disturbed areas with a natural grass seed. Others offer a "landscaping allowance" for more extensive options.

 Call for updates! By calling our special hotline, you'll hear the latest news on building a new home! 1-900-988-7295 (See the back page for price information.)

11

When Things Go Wrong:

Money and Other Sources of Friction

O ne of the things that just amazes us about most "how-to" books is how darned optimistic they can be. When we read other books on building or buying a new home, we were amazed at how happy-go-lucky this process is supposed to be. Friction, arguments or even minor disagreements are never mentioned. Everything just moves swiftly along without any hitches, glitches or semi-automatic weapons fire.

Well, as the veterans of at least one home building experience, we'd like to throw cold water on this notion. In interviewing other home buyers across the country, we found a similar pattern: In the real world, building a new home is no joy ride.

Sure, some of this tension is generated between spouses who argue over where that window should be or what color the carpet is in the master bedroom. Yes, but the real fountain of frustration for new home buyers is that darned builder.

No matter how carefully you select your builder, negotiate the contract and plan the design, there are going to be moments when you will want to shoot your builder. And not with any small handgun. We're talking a rocketlauncher. Armed with poison-tipped, nuclear bombs. If the explosion doesn't kill him, then the poison will make it a slow, agonizing death.

Given this natural urge on the part of all home buyers, we'd like to give you some advice on the subject.

Top Three Reasons Why You Shouldn't Kill Your Builder

3 | *Murdering your builder is against the law in most states.*

2 | *It leaves a big mess on the new carpet.*

1 | *You actually need this person.* Seriously, this last reason is for real. After you move into your home, you'll need the builder to come back to fix those minor problems you discover. Some of these will be on the "punch list" you draw up prior to closing—other problems may develop later, like a leaking skylight. Maintaining a relationship with your builder so you're on still on speaking terms greatly increases the chances you'll get this stuff done.

This does not mean you should be walked all over like a cheap carpet. You must stand up for your rights. Like a parent with an unruly child, you may have to scold the builder occasionally and even discipline him for mistakes. Nonetheless, you still must have a working relationship, not letting any dispute degenerate into a collapse of the deal.

Sources of Friction

To understand why many homeowners feel like killing their builder, it's important to understand the root causes of much of the friction. Here are the top suspects.

- **Inept subs.** Remember, your builder is not really doing much of the work on your new home—most of it is done by subcontractors. Ideally, every sub would be an expert, competently accomplishing every task. In the real world, you'll get some good ones and some stinky ones. On our home, we gave the electrician an A-, while the plumber deserved a D. The reason: The plumber sent in a "second-string" crew to do our home. Without proper supervision, the crew botched the job—three of the six sinks in our home leaked. If you're building a home in a hot market, all the good subs are busy and your builder may opt for an un-tried sub to get your home finished on time. Or the good subs may quickly add crews to handle the increased the demand. The work of these second- or third-string crews often isn't up to snuff, which causes friction.

Solution: While the builder is not *directly* at fault for poor sub work, it is his responsibility to supervise the subs and to make sure any poor work is fixed. And fast. In nearly all cases, the builder picks the subcontractors and it's the builder's neck on the line. Let the builder play the bad guy with lousy subs—he should crack the whip to make sure the work is done right. You have to make it clear to the builder in no uncertain terms that you will not accept lousy subcontractor work and you expect him to make it right. Or else you'll find another builder who can better supervise or control his subcontractors.

■ *Builder/architect animosity.* While both of these people should work together on the same team, the reality is friction often develops between architects and builders. Some builders just have a bad attitude about architects—perhaps they're jealous of architects' white-collar salaries and design skills. Other builders think all architects are idiots who design pretty houses but don't know one thing about the actual construction. And they resent having someone looking over their shoulder.

During the actual construction, the builder and architect may come to loggerheads at a number of flash points. The bane of many a residential architect is builders who make "field changes" to their design without permission. Or builders who try to nitpick the smallest design mistake, charging the buyer multiple change orders for omissions on the plans. On the other hand, builders may be frustrated by an architect who specs a material that is hard to source.

Builder-architect disputes can get rather nasty. Sometimes the fighting escalates to the point where the builder insists that you fire the architect. Big mistake—remember, the architect is working for you, on your side. Some builders would love to see an architect eliminated—the lack of tough oversight enables the builder to substitute cheap materials, get away with substandard work, and more. In one case, we heard of a builder who sabotaged a new home project by delaying or slowing down the work, blaming the architect for unspecified "design" mistakes. By wearing down the buyer, the builder succeeded in getting the buyer to fire the architect. What happened next wasn't pretty: Totally unsupervised, the builder's defective construction was a disaster, costing $300,000 to repair.

Solution: Communication is probably the key to solving these problems. Calling a "summit meeting" of you, the architect and the builder at a neutral location (such as Iceland) might be helpful. You may have to act as a diplomatic mediator, attempting to reach a compromise to keep your home moving forward. Face-to-face meetings tend to defuse tensions, as opposed to phone conversations, where it is easier to be a "difficult" person. In the worst case, you may have to fire the builder and find another. When should you fire an architect? Only in cases of clear incompetence (you may want to get a second opinion from another design professional about this). Builders may whisper in your ear, "Fire the architect," but we urge you to think twice before you do this.

As a side note, keep a detailed record of the communication between all parties. That means sending all letters to the builder and the architect certified mail, return-receipt. Take photographs during construction as well. Require that the builder notify you of any code violations found by building inspectors during the construction—this keeps everyone on their toes.

- **Cost overruns.** It seems that even a sneeze can increase the price of your home. Cost overruns tend to fall into one of two categories: those you pay for directly and those you pay for indirectly. Direct cost overruns are items that exceed allowances—if your builder runs into rock while digging your foundation (for custom or semi-custom homes), you may have to come up with hundreds of extra bucks. A mistake in the blueprints could also cost you (although you may "discuss" this with your architect, who should cough up the money). In some cases, cost overruns are all your fault—when you change or upgrade something, you must pay . . . not only for the item itself but perhaps a "change-order" fee as well.

Another category is cost overruns that you pay for *indirectly.* For example, if the cost of lumber goes through the roof, the builder is the one who pays for this (out of the home's profit). That's because most builders do homes on a fixed-price basis—if costs go up, they eat it. Or do they? A builder may fall into the "shrinking-profit syndrome," described next.

Solution: If a home always costs more than anyone expects, it makes sense to plan for this in advance. First, budget an extra 5% to 10% for cost overruns. Yes, we realize that means coming up with another $15,000 on a $150,000 home (see whether you can increase your mortgage or dip into savings). Control mistakes in the plans by hiring an experienced residential architect. Beware of the low ball allowance game, a common source of cost overruns described earlier in this book. Do your research on windows, appliances, and other products before construction begins—this lessens the chance of you wanting to make a change midcourse. Recognize that you can easily be "100-dollared to death" when you may be tempted to switch out a towel rack or faucet "because it's just another $100."

- **Shrinking-profit syndrome.** Near the end of your home's construction, your builder may be become afflicted with a sickness we call the shrinking-profit syndrome. What's this? Most homes are purchased on a fixed-cost basis—if the builder's costs go up, the builder's profit shrinks.

Who's fault is this? Sometimes, it's no one's fault. Weather delays can push up costs. If a supplier ships the wrong materials, that delay can also cost money. Other times it is the builder's fault—if the builder incorrectly estimates the cost of certain items, it's his neck on the line for the difference. If the builder estimates the insulation will cost $6000 and it really runs $7200, the difference comes out of the builder's profit.

Or does it? As the profit shrinks, some unethical builders look for ways to make it back. They may cut corners on installation of vinyl flooring, such as skipping the use of a flooring underlayment (this saves some bucks). Or they may outright renege on a contract provision, refusing to pay for an item they had promised. For our home, the shrinking-profit syndrome led to the builder denying his responsibility to put in a $200 shower door in the master bath. Another home buyer we visited was socked with a $6000 bill for utility tap fees when the builder reneged on his written agreement to pay for them—he claimed his profit on their home was too small at that point.

This scam is particularly potent since it comes at the end of the construction—when the pressure to movein or close on a mortgage is great. Some shady builders know you're worn down emotionally or that your mortgag-rate lock is about to expire. Since you're vulnerable, strong-arm tactics are more successful.

Solution: Use a "bad cop" to get your way. Instead of confronting the builder directly (and destroying any remaining goodwill), have a surrogate bad cop tell the builder that the last-minute substitution/omission is not acceptable. The bad cop could be a private inspector, buyer's broker, construction manager or architect. If the builder still balks, withhold an appropriate amount of money at the closing from the builder's final profit check/disbursement. While this sounds drastic, the mere threat of such action may get results. Consult with an attorney if the situation deteriorates further—a letter from an attorney may also get the builder's attention.

In our case, our buyer's broker squared off with the builder over the shower door. After a heated discussion, we got our shower door.

- ■ *Time, time, time.* Delays are inevitable when you build a home. A sudden rain storm may prevent the gluing of the sub-floor to the foundation. Bitter cold may delay a plumber from finishing work in a damp basement. Even weather that's thousands of miles away can work against you—many home buyers found lumber in short supply (and at higher prices) after Hurricane Andrew decimated South Florida.

The most frustrating delays are builder generated. A builder's incompetence at scheduling crews can lead to long delays. Inability to find a quality framing crew or good roofing subcontractor is often due to a builder's inexperience or lack of contacts. If the labor supply is tight, a builder may shift a crew who are working on your house to another, more expensive house the builder is rushing to finish.

Solution: Monitor the construction carefully. Try to visit the job site two to three times a week. If little progress is being made, confront the builder. Try to get specific commitments as to when certain phases are to be completed—stay on the builder when he begins to slip a deadline.

Understanding why delays are occurring is important. Your builder may blame the weather, but you might question him as to why other builders in your area are still working. Getting to the bottom of the excuses will help you decide on a course of action. If you find the builder intentionally dragging his feet, action must be taken. Have your "bad cop" discuss the situation with the builder. If nothing happens, write a "gentle" letter that you expect work on your home to get going. If more delays occur and the situation appears hopeless, consult with your attorney about firing the builder.

Above all, don't paint yourself into a corner. Putting yourself under pressure to move in or close by a certain date is a prescription for trouble. Build extra time into your own schedule (one month is smart) to account for "normal" delays.

- *Take-the-money-and-run builders: A vanishing breed.* What if your builder disappears altogether? A builder who's having financial problems may collapse into bankruptcy. Even worse are builders who disappear altogether, fleeing the state with a trail of unhappy home buyers behind them.

Telltale signs of the vanishing builder are a significant slowing in the work on your home. Failure to return phone calls or messages is a red flag. Some builders don't disappear quickly, but fade slowly. Like the witch in The Wizard of Oz, they slowly melt into a pile of goo. It's critical for you, your private inspector or construction manager to monitor the construction. While it's not important to be there every hour of every day, checking the home every few days is important.

You can also take several other precautions. First, don't give the builder any money before the home is completed. Sure, some builders ask for deposits, but try to hold this down to a token amount of money ($500 or less). Any builder who asks for your entire down payment up front may be on shaky financial footing. One buyer we spoke with gave the builder a $10,000 deposit and lost it all when the builder went under.

If you put any money down, put it into an escrow account (a buyer's broker, title company or mortgage lender can help you with this). The money is not to be released from escrow until the home is completed to your satisfaction. Never write the builder a check directly.

Control the construction loan if you can. Don't disburse money to the builder directly; instead write checks to the subcontractors or suppliers for specific invoices presented on your home. Some construction lenders don't like this process. They'd prefer to give the money to the builder and hope he'll pay the subs. Shop for a lender that will do it your (and the safe) way. Insist that the lender stamp the back of each check with a "lien waiver" that the sub must sign when he endorses the check.

Pay the builder his profit only *after* the home is finished to your satisfaction.

Solution: What if you're careful and the builder disappears anyway? What if the builder suddenly declares bankruptcy? Immediately, you will want to contact your attorney—an experienced real estate attorney can help you navigate the choppy waters ahead. Among the potential problems areunpaid subcontractors who may file huge liens on your home.

The second step is to call an emergency meeting of your "building team": the lender, architect/designer, private inspector and others. Keeping the channels of communication open at a time of crisis

The Caulk Reflex

If anything goes wrong with your house, it's likely your builder's first reaction will be to grab a caulk gun. Got a leak on your roof? Water dripping on your stucco? Gutters leaking? Caulk is so often the builder's answer you'd think it was programmed into hall builders' genetic code.

That's why we call it the "caulk reflex." It's the miracle drug of builder fix-its. If builders had problems with their marriage, we'd expect them to first try squirting some caulk on their spouse.

All this reliance on caulk would be fine if it actually worked. But often it doesn't. Why? First, understand that caulk is just silicone or acrylic sealant. While metal-to-metal caulking is alright, many builders try to use it on wood roofs—a use that even caulk manufacturers say isn't going to work. That's because the caulk doesn't form a complete seal to wood, thereby enabling water to seep in.

In other cases it has nothing to do with caulk itself, but the way it's used. Just like glue, caulk can only stretch so far. Specifications are printed right on the tube—they say caulk won't work for joints over 1/2" wide. Some builders ignore this and squirt caulk into huge gaps. A thick strip of caulk often loses its elastic properties, causing the joint to fail when the materials it's adhered to shrink or expand. The result: It doesn't work.

One home buyer we interviewed came face to face with the ugly reality of the caulk reflex. Water was leaking off homeowners' garage roof and damaging the stucco facade on the front of their home. The reason? An architect called in by the buyer blamed it on faulty design—the roofline was draining right onto the stucco. Who designed the home? The builder (who had no architectural background), of course.

We have to hand it to the builder—at least he didn't abandon the home buyer. Every week, he would come by and caulk the leak. After a while, there were probably three tons of caulk glopped up there. And guess what? It still leaked. Damage to the stucco was mounting.

An architect told the buyer the only way to solve the problem was to re-construct the roof over the garage. This would more than a $1000. And, frankly, the builder probably realized this, but he preferred to buy $4 tubes of caulk, squirt it up there and pray it would work. After it was clear the caulk wasn't working, the builder balked at doing more than the quick fix. At last word, the buyer was hiring an attorney to try to pressure the builder into really fixing the leak.

Sadly, the caulk reflex is symptomatic of the "quick-fix" mentality of too many building professionals today. Whipping out a caulk gun is a simple way for lazy and cheap builders to avoid addressing the real problem—faulty design or poor workmanship.

Should you be leery of builders who suggest caulking any problem? Not necessarily; in some cases (like metal to metal), caulk may actually work. However, if the answer to each and every problem is caulk, you can begin to worry.

is important to keep anyone from panicking (including yourself). You and/or your architect will need to begin contacting other builders to finish the home. The lender may need reassurance that the deal isn't going south. As a side note, some states have setup recovery funds to compensate home buyers who were jilted by bankrupt builders.

Top 6 Excuses that Builders Give for Shoddy Work and Mistakes

We'd be the first to acknowledge that builders are only mere mortals. And, yes, they do make mistakes. Some are unintentional goofs, while others are intentional efforts to pass off shoddy work. What particularly galls us about builder mistakes, however, is the peculiar "excuses" they concoct to explain away the situation. Here are some of our favorites:

1 *"We're not cutting diamonds here."* This whopper is often used to explain away "minor" imperfections like poor trim work, painting or other finishing details. The implication is that you must accept little "imperfections." A good counter argument to this excuse is to remind the builder about all the sales talk at the start that played up his or her "professional craftsmanship." When builders hold themselves out as professionals, you should actually get a professional job—that means something better than a seven-year-old could do.

2 *"I'm doing you a favor by building your home."* This often goes with the reasoning that "you're getting a steal of a deal on this home," so shut up and accept the flaws. It's quite amazing that anyone in business could demand $100,000 or $200,000 for something and then give you an attitude that they're *doing a you a favor* by taking your money. The reality is that no one held a gun to the head of the builder during the negotiating process, forcing him to accept an ultra-low price. You agreed to pay X dollars and he agreed to build a certain home. There's not much to do in a case like this but remind the builder that you are the *customer*. It's your money, not his. It'll be your home, not his. If he doesn't get it, perhaps he'd like to just refund all the money and both of you can part company and go your separate ways.

3 *"But replacing it would require such a delay."* It would shock you to know how often the wrong materials arrive at your home. Sinks that are the wrong color, a tub that's the wrong style, carpet that's not yours . . . just about anything can go wrong. Instead of sending the stuff back and getting the correct items, builders often give you a line that such a replacement would take *so long*. And it might delay the home's construction by days or weeks. And you want to move in, don't you? Such pressure convinced one home buyer to accept the wrong roof trusses that showed up one day—the resulting redesign nixed several windows in the living room. The home is now much darker than the buyer expected. In other cases, buyers have had to accept wrong faucets, incorrect colors and other mistakes because the builder pressured them with the delay excuse. The fact is replacing these items will incur some delay, but it should be the builder who gets on the phone and insists that the supplier fixes it ASAP. It's probably better to wait until the correct stuff arrives than to regret this compromise down the road.

4 *"It must be the subcontractor's fault."* You see, builders never make mistakes . . . in their own minds. At least they never admit them. It's always someone else's fault—the architect drew defective plans, the subs screwed up the installation, or the supplier shipped the wrong materials. This excuse often degenerates into a ping-pong game of delay. When a skylight leaks, the roofer comes out and blames the skylight company. The skylight guys look it over and pronounce that the problem is with the flashing, the roofer's responsibility. The roofer comes back and looks at the flashing and says it is actually the seal on the skylights. Ping. Pong. Ping. You're like a ball that's bounced back and forth. The fact is, it is the builder's ultimate responsibility to make sure the skylight doesn't leak—even though he didn't personally flash the roof or install the skylight. The builder must whip the subs into shape and resolve the problem.

5 *"That's not the way we do it here."* Building is a highly region-alized business—sometimes regional custom and traditions are adhered to like some sort of gospel. Hence, if you move to a different part of the country, you may find that builders have some strange ideas about "sound construction techniques."

Frankly, in some parts of the country building practices are deplorable. When a builder tells you, "That's not how we do it here," a translation closer to reality is, "I don't care if you're from an area where homes are built with quality—here we do it fast and sloppy."

If you get into a dispute with a builder, get a second opinion from your private inspector or architect. These people are working for you and should have a good grounding in what's right and what's wrong. The building code may provide some help, but it's usually just a series of *minimum* standards. The dispute may be over an extra measure of quality the builder may be trying to avoid just to save a buck.

6 *"The Building Code is not in line with current building practices."* Here's a favorite excuse builders give when home buyers or private inspectors turn up a violation of building codes. The fact is that 99% of local and state building codes are very up-to-date—in fact, they are *too* up-to-date for many builders. The codes require builders to use sound construction techniques and often provide extra protection for consumers. In Florida, for example, hurricane clips that attach the roof to the walls are used to prevent storm winds from easily damaging homes. In California, anchor bolts that tie the walls to the foundation hopefully limit damage during earthquakes.

These strict building codes are the bane of shoddy builders, who find the requirements too much of a hassle. Some builders try to blame the code for their problems. "Current building practices" that ignore consumer protection and sound construction are certainly not in line with the building code—but it isn't the code's problem. It's the builder's.

The point of this chapter (and this entire book, for that matter) is not to make you paranoid. If you follow some of the smart consumer tactics we've outlined, you'll certainly lower your chances of falling victim to a shoddy builder.

Nonetheless, there are fights and disagreements in even the best of marriages between builder and consumer. And it is just like a marriage—a long-term commitment by both of you to work toward a common goal. You see or talk to the builder practically every day and that can be tiresome.

Overall, building a home is a series of highs and lows. At times, everyone will function like a well-oiled machine. Other times it seems that nothing is going right. Recognizing this reality and taking precautions against those unlikely worst case scenarios will better prepare you for your new home journey.

 If you have any questions or comments on this chapter, please feel free to call the authors. See the "How to Reach Us" page at the back of this book!

12

Home Bargains

We realize that throughout this book we've been good at spending your money—recommending you use professionals such as an inspector or architect, for example.

So, to be fair, we wanted to include a chapter on home bargains—creative ways to save money on your new home. First, we'll go over discount catalogs that can save you money on everything from lighting to plumbing fixtures. Next, we'll explore the discount stores such as Home Depot and Price/Cosco. Finally, you'll learn about several mail-order discount companies that offer additional discounts.

Discount Catalogs

The Renovators
(800) 659-2211, (413) 659-2241, fax (413) 659-3113

The Renovators is one of the neatest home catalogs we've run across. They offer everything from sinks and toilets to copper weather vanes.

For example, The Renovators' last catalog featured about ten different pedestal sinks ranging in price from $79 to $219. Of course, you'll need faucets for those sinks, so The Renovators has 46 faucet options starting at a mere $24. Kitchen sinks and faucets are also available, along with a small selection of toilets.

The Renovators carries a smattering of floor and wall tile, plus linoleum products. Marble tile is available for $69 per 10 tiles; ceramic, hexagonal tile is only $27.50 per 100 tiles; and adobe floor tiles are $22 per 9 pieces.

What most impressed us was The Renovators extensive lighting fixture selection, which takes up 14 pages. This includes track lighting, recessed lighting, outdoor fixtures, and traditional chandeliers and sconces. As an example, dome fixtures ranged from $26 to $59, while wall sconces were $69 to $275.

The Renovators catalog includes quite a few other items from cabinet knobs to architectural accents, and bathroom accessories to embossed wall coverings. Even weather vanes and cupolas can be ordered including an outstanding copper eagle weather vane for $125. All Renovators products have a one-year warranty—a definite plus.

Home Decorators Collection
(800) 245-2217, (314) 993-1516, fax (314) 993-0502

Home Decorators Collection sells a diverse number of offerings. From chairs and tables to Tiffany-style lamps, they seem to cover all the bases with products for the home.

We were most impressed by their lighting supplies. For example, we noted that Home Decorators has halogen bar lights available for $74 to $479, depending on the number of lights on the bar. Six different wall sconces ranged from $54 to $130. Cast aluminum outdoor lighting included post lights as well as wall options in bronze, black, white and verdigris. Prices: $89 to $269.

For the bath, Home Decorators carried only a limited number of pedestal sinks, priced from $99 to $269 for white (there's an extra cost for ivory or gray). A nice array of bath hardware includes all-white fixtures (the "Avanti Collection") such as a 24-inch towel bar for $36. Overall, the prices were good—quantity discounts are available.

The Container Store
(800) 733-3532, fax (214) 484-2560

Based in Texas, the Container Store also has locations in Atlanta and Washington, D.C. But the best part about the Container Store is that you don't have to visit one to shop there—several catalogs are available for mail-order shoppers.

Among the best is the Container Store's "Closet Planning Guide." If you're going to be sacrificing a little storage space in your new home or just want to use the space you've got more efficiently, the "elfa" line of closet components is quite impressive.

We priced a series of components (drawers, shelves, and countertops) for our closet at $250. This provided two six-foot shelves, six three-foot shelves, and a set of three drawers under a countertop. The shelves, by the way, can also be used to hang clothes.

For an office, The Container Store also has components to design your own desk area. Two desks with drawers, a filing cabinet and a set of open shelves was $300. Considering that one good desk can cost at least $250, this price is a great deal.

The Container Store's catalog also contains suggestions for laundry rooms, kids' rooms, and utility spaces. They have a step-by-step planner in the back of the catalog and suggestions for planning walk-in, bi-fold, or hall closets—even your kitchen pantry.

We highly recommend The Container Store for their cost-effective, space-efficient closet components. And if you like these, you may want to get their regular catalog with samples of the rest of the stores' offerings. While The Container Store is not a discount haven, the company's unique offerings are worthy of mention.

More Deals:
Discount Stores

The Home Centers

Those giant warehouses that are stuffed to the rafters with building supplies and products have apparently captured the minds and wallets of consumers. In 1992, building supply home centers racked up $73 billion in sales. Much of this growth has been at the expense of traditional hardware stores and lumber yards, whose higher prices and limited selection has been their death knell.

Home centers are great sources for lighting and plumbing fixtures—two items you may have to select yourself for your new home. Here's an overview of the major players.

Home Depot

The undisputed king of home centers is Home Depot (404) 433-8211. And a recent visit to a Home Depot in Austin, Texas, convinced us that they are deserving of the crown.

We were impressed with the massive selection of lighting, including nearly 30 crystal chandeliers that ranged from $60 to $200. Outdoor carriage lamps were only $30 to $40, while a six-light, chrome bar strip for a bathroom was $21. The giant array of ceiling fans was the most extensive we found in any home center—selections ranged from traditional to ultra-contemporary and included such famous names as Casablanca.

The Home Depot we visited had an interesting kitchen and bath center with several eye-catching displays. The cabinet selection included such names as Kraft Main and Mills Pride—the ultra-contemporary Vantage cabinets were show-stoppers.

Famous brand names dotted other sections of the store—the wide selection of Kohler products for the bath and kitchen was fantastic. As for other items, we noticed a built-in ironing board for $300 and pedestal sinks ranging from $100 to $200. If we had to complain about anything, it would have to be Home Depot's smallish selection of track lights. Their small lighting lab was a disappointment as well.

The service was among the most helpful we encountered in our visits to home centers. No fewer than seven employees asked whether we needed help as we wandered about the store. Despite the warehouse trappings, the friendly service was most welcome.

Builders Square

We visited a Builder's Square right after Home Depot—and the contrast was not flattering to Builder's Square (512) 616-8000.

First of all, the lighting selection is more limited. As you enter the front door, you encounter the ceiling fan area, which includes some lesser-known names such as Bay Breeze. A small number of chandeliers featured a six-branch brass fixture for $96. Many of the light fixtures were crammed into a small area that made comparisons difficult. On the upside, the selection of outdoor and carriage lights was a winner. One 24-inch Catalina carriage light ran $40.

As for the rest of the store, it's a pale imitation of Home Depot. The kitchen and bath center had just a few sample displays. Cabinetmakers included American Woodmark and Schrock. The lack of brand names was also a bummer—in the sink area, we only found products by plain vanilla American Standard. The faucet selection was somewhat more extensive, including samples by Peerless, Moen, Delta, and Price Pfister.

The service was marginal—only one employee asked whether we needed help on our visit. The lighting department was empty and other departments had just a skeleton staff.

In more positive news, Builders Square recently rolled out an expanded store in Florida. The first "Builders Square II" opened there and includes about 50% more space, which houses an Idea Center. This area includes more upscale displays of kitchen and bath layouts, featuring everything from tile to window dressings. The company plans to open several more Builders Square II's.

Home Base

We purchased some of the lighting for our home at Home Base (714) 441-0171, another giant home-center warehouse. Particularly impressive was the track lighting, including a four-foot track with three lights for just $28.92—an amazing price. Bar lights for bathrooms ranged from $10.79 for three lights to $41.95 for six.

We were wowed by the sconces—several really neat designs with lucite panels and halogen bulbs ran $20 to $90. Dome fixtures were also good deals at $45 for a 15-inch swirl fixture.

Other parts of the store paled in comparison to the lighting section. The plumbing fixtures were nice and included some good brand names such as Kohler. The lack of an "idea center" with displays of complete kitchens and bathrooms makes Home Base less user-friendly than its competitors. A few small displays of cabinets by such names as Merillat failed to impress.

The service was marginal. Except for a service counter staffed by employees who seemed preoccupied with answering the phone, there were few staffers out on the floor. You're basically on your own.

Of course, Home Depot, Builders Square and Home Base are just a few of the dozens of home center chains that blanket the country. Check your Yellow Pages under building supplies for the nearest home centers.

The Warehouse Clubs

Like home centers, the discount warehouses are nearly everywhere today. If you live in any major city, you've probably encountered the names Sam's and Price/Cosco. But what do these warehouse clubs offer new home buyers?

Most carry electronics, groceries, clothing, books—and yes, even some building supplies. Our favorite is Price/Cosco, which carries several lighting fixtures at rock-bottom prices. For example, we found quite a few outdoor carriage lamps for just $19 to $38. A 150-watt halogen floodlight with motion detector was just $25.

If track lighting is your goal, a 24-inch white track with two heads was a mere $9.49. Peerless faucets ran just $45 to $93. How about a gas grill? Price Club had a nice one for just $269.

We've visited many warehouse clubs and were most impressed by Price Club. The club's bright interiors with white walls imparted less of a warehouse feel than their competitors.

We should note that most clubs charge a membership fee of about $25. Considering the savings, this may be a wise investment.

Discount Lighting

Lamps Plus
(Retail stores)
(800) 285-5267

This 36-store chain based in California also has stores in Washington, Arizona, Nevada, and Colorado. We were impressed by their well-stocked showroom that featured several big name brands. Selections ranged from ultra-contemporary to traditional and even antique reproductions.

Best of all are the "factory-direct" prices—up to half off regular retail. For example, we found verdigris outdoor carriage lamps for $49.95—the same light at a regular lighting store topped $100. Periodic sales provide even better deals. Lamps Plus stores also have a small lighting lab, where you can experiment with different lighting fixtures. The service is good, although the store we visited got rather crowded on weekends.

Golden Valley Lighting
(Mail-order company)
(800) 735-3377 or (919) 882-7330

This North Carolina-based mail-order company offers discounts of up to 50% off retail. More than 200 manufacturers are available, including Casablanca, Waterford, and American Lantern. Golden Valley has indoor and outdoor lighting, lamps, track lighting, ceiling fans—you name it. Styles range from "colonial" to "Oriental" and just about everything in between.

Here's how it works: you shop local lighting stores, find the fixtures you want, and get the manufacturer's name, model number, color and finish. Then call Golden Valley for a price quote. A 50% deposit is required, with the balance due *prior* to shipment.

Allied Lighting
(Mail-order company)
(800) 241-6111

Allied Lighting carries famous brands such as Stiffel, Baldwin Brass, Rembrandt, and more. The process is much the same as Golden Valley—you shop your local stores and then call Allied for a price quote.

Allied's brochure features crystal chandeliers, period lighting, track lights, lamps, outdoor lights and more. The company claims its prices are up to 60% off retail. Based in Pennsylvania, Allied takes credit cards (MasterCard and VISA), certified checks, and money orders.

AJP Coppersmith & Co.
(Mail-order and factory showroom near Boston, MA)
(800) 545-1776, (617) 932-3700, fax (617) 932-3704

AJP Coppersmith specializes in period reproductions. Their 30-page color catalog is filled with colonial lanterns, chandeliers, and other Early American lighting fixtures.

Four finishes are available: antique copper, antique brass, verdigris and pewter. Prices are reasonable, considering the quality and craftsmanship—for example, a 28-inch Cape Cod outdoor lantern is $275 to $350. The Country Brass Collection features five styles of chandeliers that cost $258 to $465.

If you're looking for hand-crafted antique reproductions, AJP is one company to check out. They do take credit cards and offer a 15-day money-back guarantee if you're not satisfied. AJP also has a "factory showroom" open to the public in Woburn, Massachusetts (just outside Boston).

Other Discount Lighting Sources

- **King's Chandelier Co.** (P.O. Box 667, Eden, NC 27288) sells Czech, Venetian, and Strass chandeliers. A catalog is available for $3.50. Up to 50% savings off retail.

- **Luigi Crystal** (215) 338-2978, specializes in crystal lighting fixtures. A $1000 minimum order is required. Up to 50% savings.

- **Main Lamp/Lamp Warehouse** (800) 52-LITES sells a wide variety of lighting fixtures, ceiling fans, and track lighting. There is no brochure or catalog, but a price quote is available by phone. Prices are up to half off regular retail.

Discount Carpeting and Flooring

- **Bearden Bros. Carpet and Textiles Corporation** (800) 433-0074 or (404) 277-3265. Bearden Bros. specializes in carpet and padding, plus vinyl and wood flooring. Manufacturers include

Armstrong, Interloom and Burlington. Savings up to 80%, and a free brochure is available.

- **Johnson's Carpets, Inc.** (800) 235-1079. Johnson's claims to save consumers up to 80% off retail on carpeting and padding. A free brochure is available.
- **Warehouse Carpets, Inc.** (800) 526-2229. Warehouse Carpets sells vinyl flooring as well as carpet and padding. They carry famous brands including Mannington, Armstrong and Congoleum at up to 50% off retail.

Discount Plumbing:

- **CISCO** (316) 431-9290. CISCO carries famous brand faucets such as Moen and Delta, Insinkerator garbage disposals, whirlpool baths, and Elkay sinks. No brochure, but price quotes are given over the phone—with up to 40% savings.
- **LIBW** (800) 553-0663. American Standard, Kohler, and Jacuzzi are just a few of the brands available at 33% savings off retail. A catalog is available for $5.

Discount Roofing

- **New England Slate Co.** (802) 247-8809. New England Slate is unique among slate roofing companies: not only do they sell brand-new slate, but they also offer "recycled" slate recovered from old buildings on the East Coast. With savings of up to 50% and six different colors, they offer quite a deal.

Call for updates! By calling our special hotline, you'll hear the latest news on building a new home! 1-900-988-7295 (See the back page for price information.)

What Does It All Mean?

At this point, you may be wondering, "Am I crazy? Why don't I just rent an apartment somewhere and forget this home stuff?" Your head may be swimming with foreign terms such as *points* and *load-bearing walls*.

It might be a good time to take a deep breath and look at the "wide view." What exactly is the goal here? Okay, besides spending obscene amounts of money. Yes, you're getting a new home. And it's more than just wood, bricks, glass, steel, and a few thousand nails.

Think of the new home process as a roller-coaster ride. You start off by waiting in line for what seems like an eternity. Suddenly, you're at the front and step inside a car. Then there's the long, slow climb to the top of the hill—think of this as the design process.

Next you reach the top of the hill and begin the construction. Whoosh! You plunge downhill, screaming all the way. There are going to be incredible highs and depressing lows. When the shell of the home takes shape, you'll be elated. When the builder announces yet another delay and cost overrun due to his own mistakes, you'll be crushed.

As you zoom around the corner, the end is in sight. After all the twists and turns, you suddenly find yourself in your new home. And, the best part, it's *your* home. If you follow the advice in this book and hire an architect or professional designer, the home will fit you like a glove. The kitchen is exactly as you've always dreamed. The layout of the rooms is just what you want. Everything down to the colors and style fits *your* needs, not the builder's or another hom owner's.

So, we urge you to keep your eye on the prize. The key to getting a good home is being a smart consumer. While the process of building or buying a new home may be a rollercoaster ride, the paper-scissors-rock strategy will keep you firmly strapped in.

And, of course, if you do decide to build, we have one final piece of advice: Good luck and Godspeed.

A

Product Reviews
Windows, Plumbing, Roofing

★	Poor	★★★	Good
★★	Fair	★★★★	Excellent

Windows

Andersen ★★ $^1/_2$ These widely available windows are priced similar to Pella and other expensive brands. Several energy-efficient options are available, including argon-filled and "high-performance" sun glass windows. Andersen says the latter option is 58% more energy efficient than a regular double-pane window. As with other high-end windows, Andersen windows are double sealed. The one disadvantage to Andersen: the exterior of the windows is vinyl clad, not aluminum. The problem is that UV rays in intense sunlight climates will take their toll on the vinyl. (612) 439-5150.

Hurd ★★★★ Our pick as one of the best quality windows around is Hurd. What most impressed us about this brand is their "heat mirror" technology. Instead of a mere coating on the glass, heat mirror is a thin layer of invisible metal on Mylar film that is placed between the two panes of glass. The result is super energy efficiency—Hurd formulates different versions of the heat mirror for hot and cold climates. Heat mirror also blocks 99% of furniture-damaging UV rays—compare that to 60% to 70% for other brands' top-of-the-line low-E windows. The only disadvantage: Hurd's aluminum-clad windows are expensive—a 5x4 casement window is about $450. (800) 223-4873.

Kolbe & Kolbe ★★★ This Wisconsin-based window maker does quality if not somewhat pricey windows. On clad windows, the exterior is covered in an aluminum cladding—no vinyl here. Standard features include insulated low-E, argon-filled glass and double weatherstripping. We priced a 5x4 casement window at $395, while the slider was $228. (715) 842-5666.

Marvin ★★★ Minnesota-based Marvin touts itself as a "made-to-order" window maker. That probably explains why they are so expensive—we priced a 5x4 casement window at a whopping $721. What do you get for that price? Marvin offers six glass options (including low-E, argon-filled glass) and nine exterior finish options. Dual-sealed, insulating glass is standard. Both wood- and aluminum-clad windows are available. Marvin windows are long on razzle-dazzle—their line includes seamless corner windows and curved glass windows. Marvin's "sash pack" for replacing windows is very good. (800) 346-5128.

Peachtree ★★ ¹/₂ An architect we interviewed recommend this brand, which comes with a "non-stop" warranty: all Peachtree windows are guaranteed for as long as you own them. The Ariel line features window interiors and aluminum clad exteriors, with a choice of three baked-on enamel finishes. (404) 497-2147.

Pella ★★★★ The Cadillac of windows has everything you'd expect in a high-end product, including the high-end price tag. Pella windows come in three flavors: the Architect, Designer and Pro lines. The Architect series is the most expensive and features authentic reproductions of separate-pane glass. The Designer line is intriguing—Pella has designed these windows with a pleated shade *between* the panes of glass. Meanwhile, the Pro line is their "builder" (read: cheaper) series that has fewer options, different hardware and a slider style available. Sample prices: a 5x4 casement window in the Designer line is $440; in the Pro line, it's $375. The same window in a slider version would run $300.

Pella touts the energy efficiency of all its windows, having an R-value from 2.6 to 4.1. Key features include double-coated, low-E glass and double seals. Pella says you'd save 28% off your heating and cooling bills with their windows, compared to single-pane wood windows. Pella windows come with a 10-year warranty. (800) 524-3700.

General Money-Saving Tip

Go with stock sizes. Many window makers stock certain common sizes—these are generally much less than windows that have to be custom made. Don't design a fancy opening in your new house that requires a custom-size window—you'll pay through the nose.

Plumbing

American Standard ★★ We always seem to see American Standard's basic lines at those discount home centers and have rarely been impressed. However, their full-line catalog does offer some surprises. The Amarillis line allows you to mix and match spouts, handles, and finishes. We liked the Lexington Amarillis line with its starkly contemporary look. Some lines are a bit hokey—the Sottini Classic collection is a loser. The effect is supposed to be like antique jewelry but falls flat. We liked the Cermix Electronix line of kitchen faucets that has a digital monitor in the handle that displays water temperature. (800) 821-7700.

Delta ★★★ Fairly basic and rarely ostentatious, Delta is the bread-and-butter brand of faucets. Most of the line is chrome or brass, although colors are available as well. Prices are moderate: the popular Euro-Style line runs $117 to $200 for a bathroom faucet. The Award collection is even more affordable, although the styles are very basic. (317) 848-1812.

Dornbracht ★★ Looking on the wild side for faucets? Check out the German company Dornbracht, whose faucets are quite amazing. Our favorite is the "Edition Delphini" which are faucets shaped like dolphins. Finish options include chrome, gold-plate, silver nickel and "durabrass." Ultra-contemporary "Edition Point" has conical and cylindrical forms with neon accents. Meanwhile, the Jefferson line is more classical and antique looking. Prices? Are you sitting down? We priced Dornbracht bathroom faucets that ranged from $492 to $634. (404) 416-6224.

Grohe America ★★ ¹/₂ A very European line from Germany, Grohe includes sleek, ultra-contempary designs. Prices are in line with Kohler; for example, bathroom faucets were $175 to $350. Penny-pinchers will want to pass up the optional 23K gold finish. (708) 350-2600.

Kohler (800) 4-KOHLER. (414) 457-4441. The hottest brand going in plumbing fixtures is Wisconsin-based Kohler. We divide Kohler's offerings into three categories: slightly expensive, very expensive, and out-of-this-world expensive. In the slightly expensive category, the Coralais line (★★) is "entry-level" Kohler (read: basic and boring). We priced a simple two-handled chrome Coralais bath faucet for $65.

More exciting are Kohler's mid priced offerings, including the Flair and Taboret lines (★★★ ¹/₂). A two-handled bath faucet runs $180 to $255 in this category. Flair is more traditional, while the Taboret is very contemporary. These lines offer perhaps the best trade-off between price and style.

In the "if you won the lottery" category, Kohler offers several premium faucets (★★★) that can run up to several hundred dollars. Alturna is a blocky, contemporary look with optional inset semi-precious stones in the handles. Kohler describes the spacey Pillows line as "flat, sheered plains flowing into smooth rounded edges, forming tiering pillows that invite the touch." Wow. Some lines are losers, however. The Bravura is an industrial-looking faucet line with notched handles that look more like clock gears than faucets.

In the tub category, Kohler's whirlpool baths weigh in at a hefty $2000. Kohler's creativity shines in this category, with offerings that include tubs with a unique hinged door. The Whitecap steam package has a foot whirlpool and optional steam bath. Total damage: $3600.

Overall, Kohler is perhaps the most creative plumbing-fixture manufacturer out there. The quality is unsurpassed—the faucet's single-cartridge system makes repairs easier, for example. They've got a color and style for anyone's fancy—the only problem is that Kohler's sky-high prices make extensive use of their products beyond the means of most home buyers.

Price Pfister ★★¹/₂ You've probably seen the ads for this well-known brand. Priced similarly to Delta ($101 to $285 for a bath faucet), Price Pfister spices up their offerings with some unique styles. The all-white Flying Colors collection includes interchangeable solid brass rings. PF's basic line is quite affordable and available in many discount home centers. (818) 896-1141.

Swirl-Way Tubs ★★★ This Texas-based company makes several interesting tub styles. All Swirl-Ways are made from acrylic and the color goes all the way through (this prevents chips and scratches like those that can happen with porcelain tubs). Our personal favorite is the sculpted, two-person Andiamo tub. Just about every color is available (40 in all), as well as optional mood lights, massage jets, and more. Sample price: a Trevi corner tub with seat is $1145 (or $2219 with the whirlpool jets). (800) 999-1459.

Roofing

Suspect your builder is installing the roof incorrectly? Here are some sources that give tips on proper roof installation, as well as general information on various roofing options.

- ***Asphalt Roofing Manufacturers Association*** (301) 231-9050 has a homeowner's guide to quality asphalt roofing. The brochure "Good application makes a good roof better" is also an excellent primer on installation.
- ***Cedar Shake and Shingle Bureau*** (800) 843-3578 has a publication called "New Roof Construction" that includes drawings and other useful tips.

Other Roofing Sources

- ***Evergreen Slate Company*** (518) 642-2530 has very comprehensive information on slate roofs.
- ***FibreCem Corp.*** (800) 346-6147 is also a maker of cement shingles that resemble slate products.
- ***Ludowici-Celadon*** (614) 342-1995 is a clay roofing tile company with several brochures on tile roofs.
- ***Resource Conservation Technology*** (410) 366-1146 manufacturers rubber-membrane roofs.
- ***Supradur*** (800) 223-1948 is a cement shingle maker that has a 20-page packet that includes installation information.

Glossary

2x4 construction Exterior walls are approximately four inches deep (actually $1\frac{1}{2}$" by $3\frac{1}{2}$").

2x6 construction Exterior walls are approximately six inches deep (actually $1\frac{1}{2}$" by $5\frac{1}{2}$").

2-10 warranties A third-party insured warranty purchased by the builder from such companies as Home Owners Warranty Corporation and Home Buyer's Warranty. The builder is responsible for covered repairs during the first two years. The remaining eight years are covered by the third party insurer.

16 on center (16 O.C.) Width between wall studs. "Sixteen On Center" means the studs are 16 inches from the center of one stud to the center of another stud.

acreage The amount of land area a property has, expressed in acres. One acre equals 43,560 square feet.

adjustable rate mortgage (ARM) a mortgage whose interest rate is adjusted periodically. The times and amount of the adjustment are defined in the terms of the loan.

allowances Sums of money that are "rebated" back to you to purchase various items such as light fixtures. A $500 allowance would allow you to purchase up to $500 worth of fixtures. Additional fixtures would be paid out of your own pocket.

aluminum clad Usually found on wood windows, the exterior is sheathed with aluminum

anchor bolt Required in many areas with seismic activity, the bolt is set in the concrete foundation and connects to the walls of the home. The goal is to prevent the home from moving or swaying in an earthquake.

Annual Percentage Rate (APR) The yearly interest rate percentage of a loan after all fees and charges are factored in.

appraisal An independent opinion of the value of a piece of property. One method of appraising a property is "market value" in which recently sold, comparable properties are used to determine the value of your property.

arbitration Third party dispute resolution method in which an arbitrator sits down with both sides, listens to their arguments and renders a decision (this decision could be binding or non-binding). It is used in some disputes to try to avoid legal action. American Arbitration Association or National Association of Conciliators are examples of organizations that offer dispute resolution.

argon-filled glass Specialized window with argon gas inserted between two panes of glass. Argon is used as an insulator, making such windows more energy efficient.

back fill Dirt used to fill in around the foundation after the foundation walls are poured or constructed.

blueprints (design, plans) Detailed plan that is used to construct a home.

boilerplate contract Contract that is so standard that you merely "fill in the blanks."

builder-grade materials Typically the least expensive, lowest quality materials available.

building codes Series of state and local laws that set a minimum standard for building practices.

buyer's broker Real estate agent who works exclusively for the buyer. Negotiates on behalf of and owes loyalty to the buyer.

carriage lamps Outdoor lighting that resembles lights once used on horse-drawn carriages.

cash flow Revenue less expenses. Does not include tax related expenses such as depreciation.

caulk Silicone or acrylic sealant used for filling small cracks and holes.

change orders Written order to change an item in the home. May incur an additional charge for administrative time.

closing Final exchange of money for the title to the lot or the home or for a construction loan.

closing fees Fees charged by the title company and lender to process the closing documents.

collar beams Used in a traditional rafter system for a roof. Collar beams tie together the rafters.

columns Vertical supports for the home made of steel, concrete blocks and brick or treated wood.

commitment letter Letter issued by a lender that says you have qualified for a certain mortgage amount on a specific property.

construction documents These documents include the blueprints, specs and materials lists and other instructions on the building of a home.

construction loan Short-term loan to construct a house.

construction manager Individual who works for the home buyer to supervise day-to-day operations at the building site.

construction to permanent loan Loan that finances the construction and then rolls over into a permanent mortgage loan.

contingencies Conditions or events that must occur before the contract is binding.

conventional loan Mortgage that is financed and obtained from a private lender, not a government institution.

cooperating agent Agent who finds a buyer, but is working for and must negotiate the best price for the seller. Hence, the agent is "cooperating" with the seller.

covenants Specifically as found in subdivisions, covenants are restrictions and rules placed on homes and property uses.

crawl space Half-size basement about four feet or less in height.

credit report History of a loan applicant with regard to loan payments, credit worthiness and any bankruptcies.

cul-de-sac A street that dead-ends into a large circle.

curb appeal How attractive a home looks from the curb or street.

default Failure of a party to a contract to take some action as required.

depreciation Due to age or obsolescence, the decrease in a property's value over time.

designer Person who offers architectural services limited to drawing blueprints. Typically not licensed by states, designers cannot refer to themselves as architects.

dimension plans Very basic blueprints that give a rough layout of a home's rooms. Such plans are missing separate framing, electrical and plumbing/heating plans as well as specifications and materials.

dovetail joints Locking in a zig-zag pattern, this joint resembles the feathers of a dove. Much stronger than other joint options for cabinets.

downspouts Gutters that empty water off the roof to the ground.

draws Payments from the construction loan to satisfy subcontractors' and suppliers' bills.

drywall (gypboard, sheetrock) A sheet of gypsum sandwiched between two sheets of paper. Used to cover studs and create walls.

dual agent A real estate broker who claims to represent both the seller and the buyer in a real estate transaction. Some dual agents represent *neither* the seller nor the buyer—they simply provide general advice and help with the transaction. Also referred to as a "facilitator" or "mediator."

elevations Exterior view of a home design.

Errors and omissions insurance Special insurance for builders and architects to cover mistakes in the home design or construction.

excavation Removal of dirt and trees at a home site in preparation for the foundation.

exclusive agency This contract between builder and real estate agent gives the builder the right to sell directly to consumers without the agent receiving a commission.

exclusive right to sell This contract between builder and real estate agent mandates the agent receive a commission on the sale of property—even if the builder sells the home directly and the agent plays no role.

Fannie Mae The Federal National Mortgage Association, a private company that both buys and sells mortgages from lenders.

FHA loan Loan insured by the Federal Housing Administration, enabling buyers to get loans with low down payments.

field changes Alterations made to a home on the construction site not in accordance with the blueprints.

fill dirt Soil used to back fill foundations.

fixed-rate mortgage Mortgage whose rate is fixed for the term of the loan.

flashing Sheet-metal strips installed under the shingles, around the chimney, in seams where different roof lines meet, and around skylights, vents, windows, and doors. Flashing prevents water infiltration.

floating walls In the basement, these walls are engineered to allow movement in the basement floor without damage to the walls.

footings Structural element at the base of foundations, piers or columns used to support the home.

Freddie Mac Another private company that buys and sells mortgages from lenders.

free-market lots Any building site where you are free to choose any builder you wish.

gag rule Contract provision that prohibits your ability to hang signs outside your home complaining about the builder. Many gag rules also prohibit picketing the builder's offices or model homes as well.

general contractor Builder who is in charge of project and hires all subcontractors and materials' suppliers.

girders Cross-beams that support the floor joists.

good-faith estimate Lenders are required by law to provide an estimate of all closing costs and escrows within three days of your application.

green A product that is environmentally friendly.

hazard insurance Insurance that covers the home against damage by such hazards as fire, hail, wind and so on. The perils covered vary by policy.

headers Cross- beams above windows and doors.

heat mirror Thin layer of invisible metal on Mylar film placed between two panes of glass.

Home Owners Warranty (HOW) Third-party insurer that offers builders 2-10 warranty coverage. (*see* 2-10 warranties)

Homeowners associations   When subdivisions or communities are established, the developer may incorporate a series of "covenants, conditions and restrictions" on the lots. A homeowners association is usually set up to enforce the covenants.

house wrap   Energy-saving air barrier that is wrapped around a house during construction. Made from polyethylene fibers, house wrap keeps air from penetrating the walls.

impact fees   Taxes imposed by local communities on new homes to fund schools, parks, etc.

implied warranty of habitability   Established by the courts, this doctrine states that all new homes are assumed to be suitable for habitation, to be built in a workmanlike manner and to meet all building codes.

impounds   Amounts of money collected by a lender to pay for insurance and real estate taxes on your property.

joists   Small beams placed parallel on top of the sills. Supported by columns or piers, the joists in turn form the support for the sub-floor.

limited warranty   Any warranty that has specific exclusions and conditions.

listing agent   Agent who obtains the listing from the seller/ builder. This agent is working for and owes loyalty to the builder.

load-bearing wall   Structural element of a home that is carrying a substantial weight. Without it, the home would collapse.

lock   Agreement by a lender to give you a certain mortgage at a certain percentage rate providing you close within a specified number of days.

"low-doc" loan   Mortgage loan that requires little documentation of income and asset levels.

low-E   Window type that has "low emissivity," a measure of how much heat a window allows to escape or infiltrate.

managed-competition lots   Building site where you must choose from among a list of several approved builders.

mechanic's lien   Encumbrance placed against a property to satisfy any unpaid invoices to a subcontractor or supplier.

mortgage   Loan to purchase real property (vacant land or a house).

mortgage brokers   Companies that make mortgage loans but do not fund them from their own money.

Multiple Listing Service (MLS)   Catalog of all real estate that is listed by real estate agents in a certain area.

municipal housing inspector   Employed by a city or county, this person inspects construction sites to determine whether builders are adhering to local building codes.

negative slope driveway   Driveway that drops in elevation from the street to the garage.

no-competition lots   Building site that requires you to use a specified builder. The lot is usually owned by the builder.

"no-doc" loan   Mortgage loans that require no documentation of income. Granted only in cases of large down payments.

origination fee   Charged by lenders, this fee covers the cost of making a loan.

percolation (perc) test   Test to check the feasibility of a site for a septic system.

permanent loan   Typically a 30-year mortgage loan.

piers   *See* columns.

points   Fee associated with obtaining a mortgage. One point equals one percent of the mortgage amount.

pre-approval letter   Letter from a lender indicating that a buyer can qualify for a certain size mortgage at a specified rate.

primer   Paint undercoat used to prepare siding for top coat.

production home   Mass-produced homes built in a tract-type development by one builder. Very limited number of home styles.

punch list List of items that require repair or correction. Prepared before closing (usually at the "walk-through").

quit claim deed Giving over title to a property but not admitting or ensuring that the seller has any ownership rights.

R-value How resistant a material is to air infiltration.

rafters Support beams in a roof.

Realtor Real estate agent who is a member of the National Association of Realtors.

recording fees Charges at the time of closing to record legal documents with the county.

ridge board Top board of roof system that runs horizontally above the rafters.

rough-in Installation of various mechanical systems such as plumbing, electrical, heating, etc.

schematic designs Rough sketches of a home's floor plan and exterior.

seller carrybacks Financing arrangement in which the seller loans the purchaser money to purchase the property.

selling agent *See* listing agent.

semi-custom home Type of home where the buyer can make changes to the design, except for exterior and load-bearing walls.

septic system Waste removal process utilizing micro-organisms to break down wastes.

setback The minimum distance between a lot line and the location of structures or buildings.

sills Wood that sits atop the foundation walls (usually treated but not always).

slab-on-grade foundation Foundation that is built directly over dirt with no basement or crawl space.

soils test Test to determine subsoil conditions that impact on the foundation's design.

spec (speculation) home Home that is built on speculation—without a buyer at the start of construction.

specifications (specs) Brand names, types of materials, and installation methods to be used in a new home's construction.

stucco Exterior finish of a home made from wet plaster or concrete.

studs These are the 2x4s and 2x6s that make up the skeleton of your home.

sub-floor Plywood sheathing that sits atop the joists.

sub-agent *See* cooperating agent.

subcontractors (subs) Independent companies or workers who are hired by the general contractor to perform various construction tasks on the home.

survey Measurement to determine the exact boundary lines of a property.

tap fees Charges by utility companies to hook up new homes to their systems.

title Ownership of a piece of real property.

title company Company that issues title insurance and participates in the closing of property transactions.

tract home *See* production home.

trusses Prefabricated roof system.

Two-step loan (7/23, 5/25) Mortgage that has one rate for a beginning period (five or seven years) and then adjusts to another rate for the remaining years.

underlayment Layer of wood between sub-floor and floor covering.

VA loan Loan insured by the Veterans Admin. and usually available only to veterans.

vinyl-clad windows Wood windows that have a vinyl-sheathed exterior.

walk-out basement For houses on sloping lots, basements can sometimes be built with a door to walkout at ground level.

water witch Person who helps find a good location for a well. Interesting superstition many people swear by.

zero-lot-line homes Homes built right next to each other, with "zero clearance" between the structures. Also referred to as "cluster" or "patio" homes. Most have little or no yards.

zoning Laws that restrict the use of property to several defined applications.

Bibliography

Kiplinger's Buying & Selling a Home, 1991, the staff of *Changing Times* magazine, Kiplinger Books, Washington, D.C. $12.95. A good overall introduction to buying a home. Best section: house-hunting strategies. Worst tip: recommending Home Owner's Warranty Corporation (HOW).

And They Built a Crooked House, 1991, $12.95; ***Crumbling Dreams,*** 1993, $8; Ruth S. Martin, Lakeside Press, 5124 Mayfield Rd., #191, Cleveland, OH, 44124. Books can be ordered by calling toll-free 1-800-247-6553. A fascinating tale of a defective house and the exhaustive legal battle the author endured. ***Crumbling Dreams*** rehashes the first book and adds in tales of woe from other home buyers. Although a little rambling at times, both books are recommended reading for new home buyers.

How to Survive a Homeowner's Association, 1992, Willowdean W. Vance, distributed by Index Plus, 24331 Muirlands Blvd., Suite 4-148, Lake Forest, CA, 92630. $18.95. A choppy, hard-to-read guide that nonetheless provides some insights into crazy homeowner's associations.

The Big Fix-Up, 1992, Stephen M. Pollen and Mark Levine, Fireside Books, New York, NY. $11. A guide to remodeling that also provides excellent advice on building in general. Perhaps one of the best books on the shelf. Highly recommended.

The Walls Around Us, 1992, David Owen, Villard Books, New York, NY. $12. A funny and ingenious look at what makes a house tick. Author Owen uses his own Connecticut home as a blackboard, dispensing good advice on the "fear of lumber" and "the best paint in the world." Highly recommended.

Tom Philbin's Do-It-Yourself Bargain Book, 1992, Tom Philbin, Warner Books, New York, NY. $10. An incredible guide that gives money-saving advice on everything from power tools to building materials. Specific brands and prices are quoted. Highly recommended.

The Anatomy of a House, 1991, Fayal Greene, Doubleday, New York, NY. $9.95. Ever wonder about the difference between crown molding and a dentil? This slim book has more than 100 pages of illustrations of stonework, molding, shingles, and more. Helpful in the design process.

The Well-Built House, revised edition, 1992, Jim Locke, Houghton Mifflin, New York, NY. $10.95. Stuffed with good (if somewhat technical) information on the actual construction process, this book is a good read. The only negative is the skimpy advice on the design process and what can go wrong during construction.

Everything You Need to Know About Building the Custom Home, 1990, John Folds and Roy Hoopes, Taylor Publishing Co., Dallas, TX. Advice on how to be your own general contractor. While not overly-technical, the book's charts are somewhat ponderous.

Getting a Good House: Tips and Tricks for Evaluating New Construction, 1990, Bob Syvanen, Globe Pequot Press, Chester, CT. $12.95. An illustrated 135-page book that gives advice on chimneys, gutters, foundations and more. Best for very basic homes, the simplistic advice is somewhat helpful.

HOME BUILDER PRESS OF THE NATIONAL ASSOCIATION OF HOME BUILDERS (NAHB), Call 1-800-223-2665 to order. The NAHB produces several interesting books that are meant for builders—however, consumers might be interested to see what tips and tricks the builders are learning from the following titles:

The Builder's Guide to Contracts and Liability, 1989, Legal Department, Builder and Association Services of the NAHB. While avoiding much legalese, this book advises builders on how they can limit their liability by carefully wording their contracts. 1-800-223-2665.

Customer Service for Home Builders, 1990, Carol Smith and William Young. How things are supposed to be in a perfect world. 1-800-223-2665.

Dreams to Beams: A Guide to Building the Home You've Always Wanted, 1988, Jane Moss Snow. $9.95. A happy-go-lucky look at the process of building a home. Perhaps the most comprehensive book offered by the NAHB. 1-800-223-2665.

The Positive Walk-Through: Your Blueprint for Success, 1990, Carol Smith. A fascinating look into the techniques and tricks builders use to pacify consumers during the final walk-through. 1-800-223-2665.

Production Checklist for Builders and Superintendents, 1990, John J. Haasl and Peter Kuchinsky II. $16. A good overall checklist on the building process. Recommended. 1-800-223-2665.

Understanding House Construction, 1989, edited by Susan D. Bradford. $6.95. A very basic primer on the actual construction of a home. Lots of photos. 1-800-223-2665.

Warranty Service for Builders and Remodelers, 1991, Carol Smith. Topics include "how to manage customer's warranty expectations" and "surviving conflict with customers." 1-800-223-2665.

About the Authors

by ZuZu Fields

It was fairly obvious to me that I wasn't the first choice to write the "About the Authors" section. In fact, invitations were sent out to Bob Vila, Norm Abrams, Peter Jennings, Jay Leno, Oprah Winfrey, and 17 other important people. None replied.

So, you can imagine that they were rather panicked the day they came to me and asked me to write this. You've got to be pretty desperate to ask your dog to write your author biography. However, I had some time available in my schedule and, hey, 10 bucks is 10 bucks.

Let me start off with an amusing story about Alan and Denise. When the Fields, finished writing this book, they sent it off to some architect big-wigs in Washington, D.C., for comment. One of the architects wrote back that "the tone of the piece is sarcastic, derogatory, and at times, defamatory toward contractors. Basically, the book is yucky." And that was one of the nicer comments.

Most writers would take this critique as an insult. But not these writers. Alan was particularly gleeful at this review. I should explain that Alan has an exceptionally warped sense of humor. This could possibly be explained by the fact that he grew up in Dallas, Texas.

Now, Denise had a relatively normal upbringing in Loveland, Colorado, a town famous for valentines and floods. She appeared to be just fine until she went to college at the University of Colorado at Boulder. There she studied Elizabethan England. Unfortunately, Denise learned that the job market for Elizabethan scholars dried up in 1603.

About this time, Denise met Alan, who had successfully escaped Texas and was majoring in Marketing for Idiots at CU. Shortly after they met, as the story goes, they were walking the campus late one night. Suddenly, there was a bright light. A vision in the night spoke to them and said, "Go forth and be great consumer writers. Right wrongs, stop rip-offs, and prevent scams!"

Or, at least that's the official version. Actually, sources close to the couple (me) credit their decision to become writers with the fact that unemployment for new college grads was running at 115%.

At this point, you may be wondering how writers, who are generally dirt poor, could afford to pay for groceries, much less build a new home and write a book about it. Let me say it in one word: *Oprah*.

You see, one of the first books the Fields wrote was called *Bridal Bargains*, a consumer's guide to saving money on weddings. The book was doing fine (read: selling slowly) until one day in May 1991. A producer at *Oprah* called—they were planning to do a show called "Brides having a breakdown." If there is anything Alan and Denise know about, it's breakdowns. Before they knew it, they were whisked to Chicago. The show aired June 13, 1991. The "wedding watchdogs" were born. The book went on to be a best-seller and I noticed that the quality of my dog biscuits improved dramatically.

After *Oprah*, Alan and Denise decided to build a home. And that's how we got here today. Of course, despite their success, the Fields have still maintained somewhat twisted sensibilities. Who would name a dog, for example, after a Mexican restaurant in Dallas, Texas?

Index

256 *Y O U R   N E W   H O U S E*

Is this book a library loaner?

Have you checked this book out from a library?

Do you find this book indispensable— but the return date is approaching fast?

Now, you can get your very own, personal copy of

YOUR NEW HOUSE

Just

(Plus $3 shipping)

Call toll-free

to order

MasterCard, VISA, American Express and Discover accepted!

How to Reach Us

Have a question
about this book?

Want to make
a suggestion?

Discovered a great bargain
you'd like to share?

Contact the Authors,
Alan and Denise Fields

Call us
(303) 442-8792

Or write to:
Alan and Denise Fields
Windsor Peak Press
1223 Peakview Circle, Suite 9000
Boulder, CO 80302

Call for Updates

Call 1-900-988-7295 to get
the latest updates on **YOUR NEW HOUSE.**
By calling our special phone line
(which is updated quarterly), you'll stay
on top of any changes.

1-900-988-7295

You'll hear about:

- Hints and tips from recent home buyers
- New bargains that were recommended
  by readers
- Corrections and clarifications in our book
- The latest in new home trends and news
- And much more!

So, if you want the latest news on
YOUR NEW HOUSE, call 1-900-988-7295

All this for just 75¢ per minute! The average message is four to six minutes. Available 24 hours a day from any touch-tone phone, our Update Hotline will keep you current! *(This is a toll call that will be billed to your local phone bill or you'll receive a separate bill from MCI.)*